# OVERLOOKED

The New York Times

# OVERLOOKED

A Celebration of Remarkable, Underappreciated People
Who Broke the Rules and Changed the World

AMISHA PADNANI AND THE OBITUARIES DESK

TEN SPEED PRESS
California | New York

For the people in this book,
and for those who continue
to fight for a seat at the table

# CONTENTS

———

# INTRODUCTION

BY AMISHA PADNANI

I DIDN'T GROW UP wanting to be an obituaries editor. Who does? It would be an odd—some might even say creepy—ambition for a child. But as a journalist, I always enjoyed learning about life through the eyes of others, and I found myself turning to the obits page to learn about the remarkable people who shaped our world.

When I started working at *The New York Times* in 2011, I was curious to meet the team that put the section together. My chance came in 2016, when I joined the Obituaries team as an editor, and I soon learned just how challenging the job can be. Thousands of people die between one edition of the newspaper and the next. On the Obituaries desk, we hear about a scant few. Of those, we get to choose about three to spotlight. And so, each morning, my colleagues and I scan our list of names and ask, "Who is worthy?"

It's a tough question to answer. In some cases, the decision is obvious; newsprint is always reserved for those who have achieved the highest levels of fame—heads of state, chart-topping musicians, and Oscar-winning actors, for instance. But more often, the names on our list are not widely known, so we look for interesting people who have left their mark: the inventor of the wetsuit, a beach bum who simply wanted to surf in the winter; the owner of the world's only self-cleaning house; a professional prankster whose whimsical hoaxes fooled the world.

Still, as I sat in a room with my colleagues making these choices, I noticed a stark pattern: most of our obituaries were about men, mainly those of privilege. When I asked my team why this was, they said: "Obits are a rearview look at society. The people dying today are from a time when women and people of color weren't invited to the table to make a difference." While there was some truth to that answer, I still felt unsatisfied. As the daughter of Indian immigrants to the United States, I knew what it felt like to sometimes feel like an outsider—invisible even—and I longed to see myself, and a greater variety of people, reflected in our pages.

Where were the women, the people of color, and the LGBTQ and disabled communities who made history? What about the marginalized figures whose fierce advocacy changed the way society regarded them, whose curiosity and innovative spirit shaped the way we live, whose unique experiences left an indelible mark on the world? Soon, I found myself on a journey to find them, a journey that took me deep into *The New York Times*'s archives, from when the newspaper began publishing, on September 18, 1851.

I learned that the newspaper had failed to note the death of the pioneering athlete Major Taylor, who overcame racist brutal beatings and sabotage to become

> None of these people were
> "invited to the table" to make a difference,
> but they persevered and did it anyway.

the first Black world champion in cycling. Nor had it mentioned Bette Nesmith Graham, a single mom whose invention of Liquid Paper saved the careers of secretaries and kept students' notebooks tidy. I went as far back as 1858 to find that India's queen warrior, the rani of Jhansi, who fought to protect her kingdom from the British, was also left out of our pages.

But that wasn't all: the newspaper of record also did not write obituaries about Sylvia Plath, whose brilliant poetry and memorable prose gave voice to female anger and despair; Marsha P. Johnson, a central figure in a gay liberation movement energized by the 1969 police raid on the Stonewall Inn; or the trailblazing journalist Ida B. Wells, who started a campaign against lynching—even though all were notable in their lifetimes.

None of these people were "invited to the table" to make a difference, but they persevered and did it anyway. I went back to my team and asked, "What if we were to write their obituaries now?" My colleagues were excited by the idea.

And so, in 2018, I worked with dozens of talented editors and journalists to launch "Overlooked," a history series that seeks to go beyond the figures taught to us in classrooms—or celebrated by society's historically narrow lens—by telling the stories of extraordinary lives that have been hidden from view. This book expands upon the series to include a wide range of people who, across time and place and experience, staggered us with their bravery, expanded our understanding of the world by inventing and innovating, and broke constraints placed upon them in an unspoken mission to create a better future for others.

The strength these people exhibited in their lifetimes has propelled me to continue my research and has inspired my team to expand our criteria when we make decisions each day on the Obits desk. While we will never be able to publish obituaries about every single life, I hope this book expands our knowledge of whom we, as a society, value as worthy.

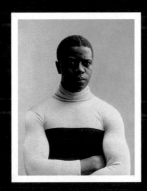

Clockwise, from top left: Rani of Jhansi, Ida B. Wells, Gil Cuadros,
Lisa Ben, Marsha P. Johnson, Major Taylor, Lee Godie, and Molly Nelson.

# Capturing
# Our Imagination

These fearless figures were willing to risk it all—
sometimes in the strangest of ways. Everyone you will
read about in this section set their sights on a personal
goal and tenaciously saw it through. Some weren't seeking fame but found it anyway, simply by following their
deepest beliefs. Others reveled in the spotlight, even
if their journeys didn't always end as they hoped. Each
grabbed our attention in ways worth remembering.

Annie Edson Taylor spent her final years posing for photographs for tourists at her souvenir stand.

Daredevil Who Tumbled Down Niagara into Fame

# Annie Edson Taylor

## 1838–1921

BY JESSE MCKINLEY

IMAGINE A BARREL four and a half feet tall, about as big as an antique icebox—or, perhaps more to the point, a small coffin. It's in a treacherous spot: bobbing and dunking in the Niagara River just above the cascading chaos of Niagara Falls.

Inside is a sexagenarian widow named Annie Edson Taylor, an underemployed charm school instructor who is about to add a new title, amateur daredevil, to her heretofore itinerant and largely unremarkable résumé.

Taylor, you see, is about to go over the falls.

In an era of Harry Houdini, Barnum & Bailey, and other death-defying showmen, Taylor, who was about sixty-two years old, became front-page famous when, in a moment of unequivocal courage and questionable decision-making, she crawled into a white-oak barrel of her own design on a late October afternoon in 1901.

She fell nearly 160 feet, hurtling toward the cauldron of rocks and raging water below, all in hope of landing in a far richer future.

Amazingly, she survived, becoming the first, and oldest, person to accomplish such a fearless, foolhardy feat. She is also the only woman to have done it alone.

Taylor openly admitted that she had made the trek to Niagara from her home in Bay City, Michigan, to "aid [her]self financially"—as well as to "succor two friends,"

who were also facing hard times—by catching a little of the glisten that accrued to such stunts.

The rapids below the falls had been the site of all sorts of daredevil attempts at the turn of the century. Stuntmen were gaining fame with feats in boats, on tightropes, or with sole reliance on the human body. In one famous attempt, the swimmer Captain Matthew Webb, the first known person to cross the English Channel without assistance, drowned in the Niagara rapids in 1883.

But no one had ever gone over the even more fearsome falls in a barrel. Taylor aimed to change that, and to capitalize on a crush of visitors in the area, drawn by the 1901 Pan-American Exposition in nearby Buffalo.

"The idea came to me like a flash of light: Go over Niagara Falls in a barrel," Taylor wrote in a slim 1902 souvenir memoir, *Over the Falls,* which she later sold for ten cents a copy at a stand near the site of her stunt.

The "Goddess of Water," as she was nicknamed, achieved instant celebrity status, complete with poetry penned in her honor.

One poem, printed in *The Lady Who Conquered Niagara,* a 1990 biography published by her descendants, had these lines:

**WOMAN GOES OVER NIAGARA IN A BARREL**

**She Is Alive, but Suffering Greatly from Shock.**

**Plunges from the Horseshoe Cataract—Thousands View the Attempt—"Don't Try It," She Advises Others.**

*Special to The New York Times.*

NIAGARA FALLS, N. Y., Oct. 24.—A widowed woman, Mrs. Anna Edson Taylor, safely passed over Niagara Falls in a barrel this afternoon. The trip from end to end was witnessed by several thousand people. The fact that Mrs. Taylor failed to go on Wednesday did not lessen the confidence of the public in her. Still everybody was agreed that it was a foolhardy trip.

As throngs of spectators watched, boatmen helped Taylor from the water after her stunt.

*This great heroine of our nation*
*has won both fortune and fame.*
*Now people all over creation*
*will praise this illustrious dame.*

While the sales of her memoir lifted her fortunes briefly, her fame and financial security were brief. She eventually fell into poverty and died in relative obscurity, on April 29, 1921. An obituary in the *Buffalo Express* said she had been swindled by "unscrupulous managers" during post-plunge publicity tours. As a final indignity, the miscreants even stole her barrel.

"She was persistently followed by ill luck," the newspaper reported.

Such a sullen end seemed incongruous for a woman who had spent much of her life searching for adventure.

Anna Edson was born on October 24, 1838, one of eleven children of Merrick and Lucretia (Waring) Edson, who ran a prosperous milling operation in the Finger Lakes region of New York and became farmers. The 1990 biography described Anna as a young woman with a dreamy disposition, uninterested in dolls—she preferred outdoor sports—and a lively imagination, "fueled by an insatiable thirst for adventure stories." Those dreams soon outgrew her surroundings.

If Taylor did not fit the mold of the dashing practitioner of derring-do, neither was she the image of the damsel in distress. After a brief marriage at eighteen—one she regretted, she said; her husband, David Taylor, was the older brother of a dear friend and died shortly after the wedding—she bounced from city to city, sometimes encountering perils. She survived a house fire in Chattanooga, Tennessee, and an earthquake in South Carolina, and a stagecoach in which she was riding in rural Texas was waylaid by robbers. When they put a gun to her head, she refused to give them her money, some $800 hidden in her dress.

"Blow away," she told them, as she recalled in her memoir. "I would as soon be without my brains as without money."

Taylor settled in Bay City, near Saginaw Bay, in about 1898, and there taught the waltz and table manners to children of the local gentry. But the income from her charm school dwindled as her students grew up, and she soon found herself searching for other opportunities to make money.

It was then that she read about the 1901 Pan-American Exposition and decided to do something that she had never done before.

She did not look the part of a daredevil: stout and graying, Taylor even lied about her age, telling reporters she was in her early forties.

She designed her vessel herself, sketching a diagram and making a prototype out of cardboard and string. A local company that made beer kegs constructed the barrel, and she selected each piece of wood. The finished product was uneven and oblong, less than three feet at its widest, and tapered at either end. It was secured by ten metal hoops and weighted with an anvil, to keep it upright along its watery course.

On the afternoon of the stunt, fresh air was pumped into the barrel before Taylor was sealed inside—enough for almost an hour, though her journey would take far less time. She was towed from the Canadian side of the Niagara River, where the waters ran deeper, toward the Horseshoe Falls, the biggest of the three falls at the site. After a brief goodbye to the boatmen who had pulled her toward the brink, Taylor was released and floated toward "the Mighty Cataract," as she later put it, protected only by pillows packed in around her.

"I felt as though I were being suffocated," she wrote, "but I determined to be brave."

The barrel swerved and swooped down the rapids toward the edge as the roar of the falls grew louder. After a brief spell of peculiar calm at the top, Taylor felt gravity take her.

"As I reached the brink the barrel did what I predicted it would do," she wrote, "paused for a moment, and then made the awful plunge."

Seconds later she hit the surface and sunk below it, the barrel spinning as it was tossed about before surfacing behind the veil of the falls. Water started to seep in, and the barrel bounced off the rocks before being shot, "like an arrow from a bow," back into the churn.

She was not adrift for long; as throngs of spectators watched from both the American and Canadian sides, she was quickly pulled from the water by a team of anxious boatmen, who tore the lid off the barrel and found her startled, seasick, bruised, with a cut on her head, and clutching a waterlogged pillow.

"Good God!" shouted one rescuer, a fellow daredevil named Carlisle Graham. "She's alive!"

Word of her success was shouted to spectators by megaphone, and a steamer, the *Maid of the Mist,* blew its horn in celebration. *The Boston Globe* said several days later that Taylor had accomplished a feat "never attempted except in the deliberate commission of suicide."

But as the years passed the plunge faded from memory, its details obscured. Some reports said it happened on October 21, but most others, including one in the *Times,* said it was on October 24, a more symbolic date—Taylor's birthday.

The feat has been replicated only a handful of times. For her part, Taylor returned to the falls in the 1910s to sell her memoir and try her hand at other moneymaking schemes, including working as a clairvoyant and offering "electric and magnetic" medical treatments. She also appeared in a silent-film reenactment of her 1901 stunt. But there was one thing she would never do again.

"I would rather face a cannon," she told the *Globe,* "than go over the falls again."

**JESSE MCKINLEY** is a Metro correspondent for *The New York Times,* after stints on Culture and National and life as a clerk. He has spent a surprising amount of time in Buffalo and its environs, both above and below the falls.

# Margaret Garner

## 1834–1858

BY REBECCA CARROLL

MARGARET GARNER, who was born as an enslaved girl, almost certainly did not plan to kill her child when she grew up and became an enslaved mother.

But she also couldn't yet know that the physical, emotional, and psychological violence of slavery, relentless and horrific, would one day conspire to force her maternal judgment in a moment already fraught with grave imperative.

In January 1856, when Garner, known as Peggy, was twenty-two and pregnant, she decided to flee the plantation where she was enslaved, in Boone County, Kentucky. She escaped with her husband and his parents, as well as their four children, and crossed over the frozen Ohio River to the safe house of Elijah Kite, Garner's cousin, a free Black man living in the free state of Ohio. Like hundreds of other enslaved Black men, women, and children, Garner and her family planned to use the Underground Railroad, which was then at its peak of operation, as the pathway to freedom.

Motherhood, across race, language, country, and culture, is understood to be complicated and powerful: a tsunami of gut and joy and fear and heartache. Garner found herself in that fleeting, lightless instant of a mother's incongruous love on a frigid night, when slave catchers surrounded her cousin's home and when she made the decision, in one soul-chilling moment, to slit the throat of her two-year-old daughter rather than return her to slavery.

Garner had already started on her three other children—she intended to kill them all, and then herself—when the federal marshals stormed the house to enforce the legal fact that she was not a mother or a wife, but the property of the man who owned her. She was immediately placed in prison.

Garner's story has been preserved in history as both sensational and singular. It writ large a question that had been unanswered in the homes and hearts of white people in pre–Civil War America: Was slavery a fate worse than death? Garner, with knife in hand, gave an answer that was impossible to ignore.

Scholars have written books examining the series of events that led up to that fateful night. For more than 150 years, poets and painters have mythologized her in their work. Most notably, Garner's case was the basis for Toni Morrison's 1987 Pulitzer Prize–winning novel, *Beloved*, which was made into a movie starring Oprah Winfrey and later became the inspiration for the 2005 opera *Margaret Garner*, composed by Richard Danielpour, with a libretto by Morrison and starring the renowned mezzo-soprano Denyce Graves as Garner.

THE MODERN MEDEA—THE STORY OF MARGARET GARNER.—Photographed by Brady, from a Painting by Thomas Noble.—[See Page 318.]

An engraving illustrating the story of Margaret Garner, from *Harper's Weekly* in 1867.

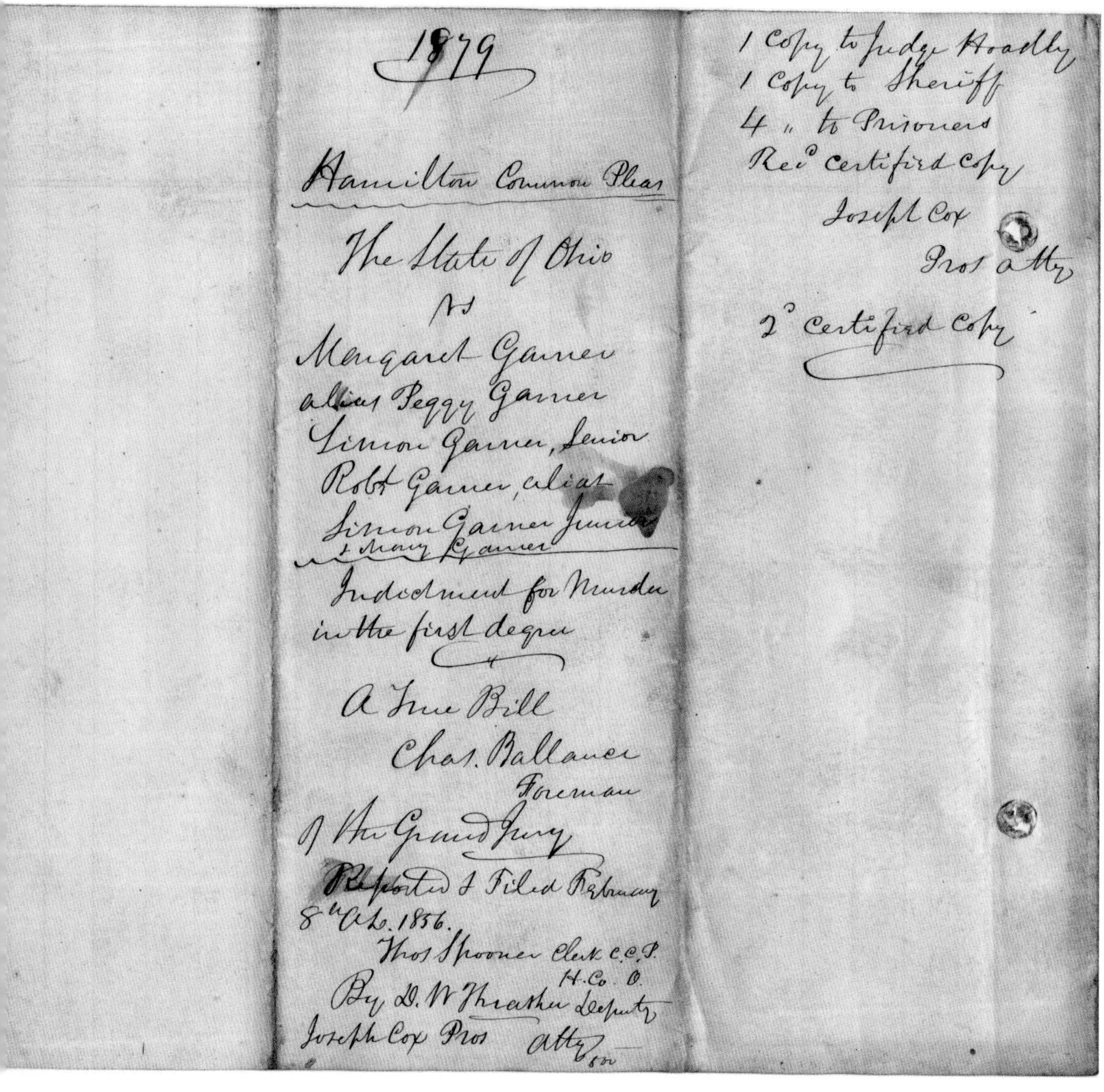

1879

Hamilton Common Pleas

The State of Ohio
vs
Margaret Garner
alias Peggy Garner
Simon Garner, Senior
Robt Garner, alias
Simon Garner Junior
& Mary Garner

Indictment for Murder
in the first degree

A True Bill
Chas. Ballance
Foreman
of the Grand Jury

Reported & Filed February
8" A.D. 1856.
Thos Spooner Clerk C.C.P.
H.Co. O.
By D. W. Thrasher Deputy
Joseph Cox Pros Atty

1 Copy to Judge Hoadly
1 Copy to Sheriff
4 " to Prisoners
Recd Certified Copy
Joseph Cox
Pros Atty

2° Certified Copy

An 1856 note by the prosecuting attorney describing Garner's indictment of first-degree murder.

# She continues to be measured not by infamy, but by the shadows of her fortitude.

Only in these fictionalized versions of Garner are we given an idea of who she might have been as a Black woman with an interior life, not just a runaway slave who committed a heinous crime.

She continues to be measured not by infamy, but by the shadows of her fortitude. Morrison told NPR in 2010 while talking about the opera *Margaret Garner,* "The interest is not the fact of slavery, the interest is what happens internally, emotionally, psychologically, when you are in fact enslaved and what you do in order to transcend that circumstance. That really is what *Margaret Garner* reveals."

Born on June 4, 1834, Garner was the product of the rape of her Black enslaved mother by a white slave master, and characterized as a "mulatto" at the time.

Garner worked as a house slave for her owner, Archibald K. Gaines, and his family. She was gifted to Gaines's wife, as was the case for many young light-skinned girls born into slavery. They were wet nurses and personal servants, faux friends and perverse doppelgängers. Historians speculate that at least two of Garner's four children, also characterized as mulatto, were fathered by Gaines.

A story syndicated in *The New York Times* in 1856 about Garner and her family said "cruel treatment on the part of their master" was most likely what drove them to attempt an escape.

Garner's case eventually went to trial. It lasted more than two weeks—one of the longest fugitive slave cases in history.

Newspaper coverage often described her physical appearance and noted that she gave her testimony while holding her youngest child. The *Cincinnati Gazette* reported, "The babe, with its little hands, was continually fondling her face but she rarely noticed it, and her general expression was one of extreme sadness. Only once, when it put its hand to its mouth, we observed her smile upon it, and playfully bite its little fingers with her lips."

The abolitionist and lawyer John Jolliffe asked that Garner be tried for murder, which would have set a civil rights precedent; instead, Garner was indicted on charges of damage of property.

Garner, her children, and her husband were all shipped to Louisiana and sold off to a brother of Gaines, their former slave master.

Garner never hurt any of her remaining children—one of whom drowned when the steamship transporting them to Louisiana crashed into another boat and threw her overboard.

She died in 1858 of typhoid fever.

———

**REBECCA CARROLL** is a writer, cultural critic, podcast host, and editor-at-large for the Meteor media collective. She has been called a "cultural icon" by Trevor Noah, and her 2021 memoir, *Surviving the White Gaze,* was described as "gorgeous and powerful" by *The New York Times.*

Houdini's Secret "Ghost-Buster"

# Rose Mackenberg

## 1892–1968

### BY GAVIN EDWARDS

SPIRITUALISM, THE RELIGIOUS MOVEMENT centered on the belief that the spirit survives earthly death and can communicate with the living, was at its peak in the early twentieth century; its most famous advocate was probably Arthur Conan Doyle, the creator of Sherlock Holmes.

With that movement came thousands of phony psychics claiming to be mediums who could connect people with their dead loved ones.

Harry Houdini, the renowned illusionist and escape artist, attended hundreds of séances, trying to communicate with his dead parents before deciding that many self-described seers were in fact con artists soaking the gullible.

He hinted at having occult powers of his own but ultimately declared that his stage act was "merely a matter of a sleight of hand," as Christopher Sandford related in his book *Masters of Mystery* (2011).

By 1924, however, Houdini wasn't content with renouncing any claim to having mystical abilities of his own. That year he published *A Magician Among the Spirits,* a book in which he debunked some of the effects that mediums produced, like wobbling tables and floating objects. "Whenever any of these alleged spiritual mediums tell you that they have supernatural aid," he told a reporter at the time, "you may safely set them down as frauds."

To expose fake psychics, Houdini employed a small army of undercover agents, calling them his "own secret service." Rose Mackenberg, a private eye, was his foremost operative.

By her count, Mackenberg investigated more than three hundred psychics and seers in the two years she worked for Houdini and many more after that. In a career that lasted decades and led her to testify before Congress, she proved to be quick-witted, adept with disguises, and unblinkingly skeptical. Speaking to a reporter for the Hearst newspapers in 1949, she boasted, "I smell a rat before I smell the incense."

In 1925, for example, Mackenberg visited Charles Gunsolas, a medium in Indianapolis who had described himself in an irate letter to Houdini as "one of the leaders of Spiritualism" in America.

Pretending to be a bereaved mother, Mackenberg told Gunsolas that her baby had died a few months earlier and that she wanted to check on the infant in the afterlife.

Gunsolas claimed to have contact with an eight-hundred-year-old Hindu guide in the spirit world as well as with his own "spirit-wife," as he called her, named Ella.

Rose Mackenberg in 1945. She attended hundreds of séances to expose fake psychics.

The many disguises Mackenberg wore to séances, as depicted in a 1929 newspaper article.

He told Mackenberg that for $25 he could teach her to access the afterlife by gazing into a bowl of water. He then said it would be easier for her to make contact with the Hindu guide if she took off her clothes. She declined.

She reported her findings to Houdini, who arrived in Indianapolis six weeks later to give a performance that Gunsolas attended. Houdini confronted him from the stage, telling the audience about Mackenberg's experiences. Gunsolas mumbled from his seat that he, too, abhorred fraud, and fled the theater to jeers and catcalls from the audience.

Mackenberg adopted a variety of disguises for the séances, she explained in a 1929 news article, among them the "rustic schoolteacher," the "credulous servant girl," and the "tipsy consultant." She used pseudonyms like "Allicia Bunck" (a play on "all is a bunk") and Frances Raud or F. Raud (for, of course, *fraud*). Often she claimed to be a grieving mother or a bereft widow.

"I never married," a wry Mackenberg told the *St. Louis Post-Dispatch* in 1937, "but I have received messages from 1,000 husbands and twice as many children in the world to come. Invariably they told me they were happy where they were, which was not entirely flattering to me."

She was frequently groped and propositioned by flim-flam men, but as Kenneth Silverman wrote in his book *Houdini!!!* (1996), she resisted Houdini's suggestion that she carry a gun.

In the line of duty, Mackenberg was ordained by so many Spiritualist churches (always for a fee) that her nickname in the Houdini organization was "the Rev."

Mackenberg's most newsworthy case came in 1926, when Congress was considering a bill to outlaw fortune-telling in Washington. Public hearings became chaotic as people made competing claims on the validity of divination. Houdini, a star witness, shared the results of his investigations into Spiritualism, calling mediums "mental degenerates" and cross-examining professional psychics himself.

Mackenberg, for her part, testified about her recent undercover experiences visiting Jane Coates, a notable

Washington medium. In an article included in a 2016 anthology about Mackenberg, compiled by Tony Wolf, she recalled, "It was my testimony, brief and pointed, that touched off the rockets and pinwheels and giant crackers of startled emotion when wrathful persons broke in with protestations and shouts of 'That's a lie!' and 'We never did such a thing!'"

Her bombshell: She said that Coates had confided to her that the proposed legislation would never be passed because her customers included four senators and because "table tipping séances are held at the White House with President Coolidge and his family." Coates denied the allegations, *The New York Times* reported at the time, noting, "Today's session was unusually disorderly and came near winding up in a free-for-all fist fight."

Rose Mackenberg was born on July 10, 1892, in Brooklyn to Lewis and Anna Mackenberg, immigrants from Russia. As a young woman she worked as a stenographer in a law office and as a private detective. When a banker asked her to look into a medium who had advised him to invest in a stock that proved worthless, she consulted Houdini, who was already famous for his crusade against psychic swindlers. He advised her on how to uncover the fraud and then recruited her to join him.

After Houdini died unexpectedly in 1926 at fifty-two, Mackenberg continued their work, taking on clients who had an interest in combating fraud, including police agencies, insurance companies, and Better Business Bureaus. She gave lectures on how to spot a phony psychic and revealed the theatrical tricks she had seen hundreds of fake mediums employ in darkened rooms (hidden harmonicas to produce ghostly noises, for example).

She also wrote numerous newspaper and magazine articles on the topic as well as an unpublished autobiography, "So You Want to Attend a Séance?" A 1949 Hearst syndicate article described her as "perhaps the only woman 'ghost-buster' in the world."

Despite a lifetime exposing charlatans, Mackenberg insisted that she wasn't a nonbeliever in Spiritualism and that she was willing to be convinced of the afterlife's existence. She had just never seen any proof of it, she said.

While Mackenberg never imagined an era in which purported psychics trolled social media for personal details about their marks, she continued ghost-busting long enough to spot trends in the Spiritualism trade. She said, for instance, that fakers proliferated when the United States was at war because they offered easy solace to an unsteady nation.

Before Mackenberg died, on April 10, 1968, at seventy-five, she lived for decades in an apartment at 310 West Twenty-Fourth Street in Manhattan. She kept it well lit because, after years of attending séances, as she told the Hearst syndicate in 1949, she'd gotten "tired of dark rooms."

——

**GAVIN EDWARDS** is the author of a dozen books, including *The Tao of Bill Murray*. His favorite ghosts are Casper, Banquo, and Charlie Brown's Halloween costume.

Sanmao, whose confident prose filled books of essays about her intrepid travels across three continents.

# "Wandering Writer" Who Found Her Voice in the Desert

# Sanmao

## 1943–1991

BY MICHAEL IVES & KATHERINE LI

IN THE EARLY 1970s, the Taiwanese writer Sanmao saw an article about the Sahara Desert in *National Geographic* magazine and told her friends that she wanted to travel there and cross it.

They assumed she was joking, but she would eventually go on that journey and write that the vast Sahara was her "dream lover."

"I looked around at the boundless sand across which the wind wailed, the sky high above, the landscape majestic and calm," she wrote in a seminal 1976 essay collection, *Stories of the Sahara,* of arriving for the first time at a windswept airport in the Western Saharan city of El Aaiún.

"It was dusk," she continued. "The setting sun stained the desert the red of fresh blood, a sorrowful beauty. The temperature felt like early winter. I'd expected a scorching sun, but instead found a swathe of poetic desolation."

It was one of many adventures she would have, and the books of essays and poetry she went on to write would endure among generations of young women in Taiwan and China who viewed her self-assured prose and intrepid excursions as glorious transgressions of local conservative social norms.

Sanmao died in 1991 after publishing more than a dozen books of essays and poetry, but she has not been forgotten. An account that publishes lines from her books on Weibo, a Twitter-like Chinese social media platform, has more than a million followers.

And an English translation of *Stories of the Sahara* was published by Bloomsbury in 2019. Mike Fu, the book's translator, said it was the first English translation of any of Sanmao's books.

"The fact that she's been able to endure this long in the Chinese literary imagination is something else," said Fu, the assistant dean for global initiatives at the Parsons School of Design in New York.

One reason may be that her writing style resonates with a current generation that is accustomed to self-promotion and oversharing on Twitter and Instagram.

"Although ubiquitous in the contemporary age of social media and commercialized feminism, Sanmao's unabashed self-aggrandizement and position of gung-ho empowerment was ahead of its time," Sharlene Teo, a Singaporean novelist who lives in Britain, wrote in the introduction of the English edition of *Stories of the Sahara.*

At the same time, Teo wrote, her soaring self-confidence is frequently undercut by descriptions of her isolation, melancholy, and "world weariness."

The essays, which were originally published contemporaneously in a Taiwanese newspaper, paint a portrait

"At a time when materialistic enjoyments were pretty limited in Taiwan, she yearned for something different, and showed younger girls that it's okay to be unique."

of the native Sahrawis, a nomadic people who have lived in the desert for generations. The Sahrawis fought a decades-long armed resistance against the countries—Spain until the mid-1970s and then Morocco—that administered the Western Sahara, a territory that stretches from Algeria and Mauritania in the east to the Atlantic coast in the west.

Sanmao became immersed in Sahrawi communities and sometimes trained a critical eye on some of their customs. She reacted in horror, for example, to a traditional wedding ceremony in which the goal was to take a young bride's virginity violently.

"That the ceremony had to conclude in such a way was deplorable and ridiculous," she wrote in an essay called "Child Bride." "I got up and strode out without saying goodbye to anyone."

Other essays document Sanmao's life as a bohemian expatriate. On her wedding day, for example, she treats her outfit as an afterthought as she throws on sandals and a hemp dress and pins a sprig of cilantro to her hat. Then she and her fiancé walk for nearly forty minutes through the desert to a courthouse for the ceremony.

"I didn't own a purse," she wrote, "so I had nothing to hold."

Her prose, which oscillates between memoir and fiction, has a laconic elegance that echoes the Beat poets. It can also be breezy, a remarkable quality at a time when her homeland, Taiwan, was under martial law in an era known as the White Terror, in which many opponents of the government were imprisoned or executed.

"She established a different and exotic place, a castle in the sand, for readers to enjoy," said Carole Ho, a professor of literature at the Chinese University of Hong Kong. "At a time when materialistic enjoyments were pretty limited in Taiwan, she yearned for something different, and showed younger girls that it's okay to be unique."

Sanmao, who wrote under a pen name and sometimes went by Echo Chan, was born Chen Ping on March 26, 1943, during World War II, into a well-educated Christian family in Chongqing, a city in southwest China. Her father, Chen Siqing, was a lawyer, and her mother, Miao Jinlan, was a homemaker.

After the war, the family moved east to Nanjing, and shortly before Communist revolutionary forces triumphed in 1949, they fled to Taiwan.

Sanmao was a restless student who spent much of her time reading Chinese and Western literature, including *Gone with the Wind* and *The Count of Monte Cristo*.

One day in school, she wrote an essay about wanting to be a garbage collector so that she could roam the streets and find discarded treasures. When her teacher called the idea nonsense and made her start again, she doubled down—by writing that she wanted to be a Popsicle vendor.

Sanmao in Latin America in 1981. A Taiwanese newspaper
sent her to the region on assignment.

Sanmao with her husband, José María Quero.

After studying philosophy at Taiwan's Chinese Culture University, Sanmao moved to Spain in 1967, later studied in Germany, and worked briefly in the law library of the University of Illinois.

She met her future husband, José María Quero, when she was twenty-four and he was sixteen and they lived in the same neighborhood.

"She had studied philosophy, languages, literature," Carmen Quero, José's sister, told the Spanish newspaper *El País* in 2016 about meeting her. "We were fascinated by her. He fell in love with her at first sight."

They married in 1974 and settled in Spain's Canary Islands, where Sanmao wrote the lyrics to "The Olive Tree," a song popularized by the Taiwanese singer Chyi Yu:

*Do not ask me where I'm from*
*My hometown is far away*
*Why do I wander around*
*Wandering afar, wandering*

In 1979, the year the song was released, María Quero, a scuba diver and underwater engineer, died in a diving accident. Sanmao returned heartbroken to Taiwan in 1981.

"She gave love and passion to everyone, but José took away an important part of her," Lucy Hsueh, a Taiwanese painter and one of her closest friends, said in a phone interview.

Sanmao spent part of the next decade teaching creative writing, becoming affectionately known as the "wandering writer." Among other places, she traveled in Central and South America on a six-month writing assignment from *United Daily News*, the Taiwanese newspaper that had published her essays from the Sahara.

Sanmao returned to her birthplace on the Chinese mainland in April 1989. The trip inspired her to write the screenplay for *Red Dust*, a 1990 film about a love affair in Japanese-occupied Shanghai.

Sanmao died in a Taiwanese hospital on January 4, 1991. She was forty-seven. The death was ruled a suicide and prompted an outpouring of grief in Taiwan.

Some speculated that her heartbreak over losing her husband had been too much to bear.

"Her extra twelve years after José passed away were for her parents," said Hsueh. "Perhaps she left us to attend a reunion she had long promised to attend."

Sanmao had once written of doing just that. "José, you promised to wait for me on the other side," she wrote in "The Immortal Bird," a 1981 essay about her own mortality. "As long as I have your word, I have something to look forward to."

Crown, Sanmao's longtime publisher, released her collected works in 2010. More recently, the Canary Islands and the Western Sahara have become popular destinations for Chinese tourists. Some Chinese websites offer directions to the Saharan church where Sanmao was married, and to a nearby hotel called the San Mao Sahara.

One of her last books, *My Treasures,* is a collection of eighty-six short essays that celebrate clothing, jewelry, hand-decorated bowls, and other objects that she purchased during her travels. In one essay, Sanmao pauses to analyze her own wardrobe and lands on a metaphor.

"The jeans I was wearing were bought in Shilin, my boots were from Spain, my bag was from Costa Rica, and my jacket was from Paris," she writes. "An international smorgasbord; and you could say they all united harmoniously and peacefully—and that's exactly me."

———

**MICHAEL IVES** is a general assignment reporter based in Seoul, South Korea. He used to teach *Stories of the Sahara* to journalism students in Hong Kong.

**KATHERINE LI** is a freelance journalist in California who previously worked in *The New York Times*'s Hong Kong bureau.

Emma Gatewood in New Hampshire in 1957 on her second hike along the Appalachian Trail.

# First Woman to Conquer the Appalachian Trail Alone

# Emma Gatewood

## 1887–1973

BY KATHARINE Q. SEELYE

WHAT THE PUBLIC KNEW about Emma Gatewood was already remarkable. She was the first woman to hike the entire Appalachian Trail by herself in one season. She was sixty-seven years old, a mother of eleven, a grandmother, and even a great-grandmother when she accomplished the feat in 1955. And she personified the concept of low-tech, ultralight hiking, spurning a tent and sleeping bag, carrying only a small sack, and relying on her trusty Keds.

But what the public did not know was equally remarkable. Grandma Gatewood, as she was called, had survived thirty years of severe beatings and sexual abuse by her husband. She often escaped from him by running into the woods, and she came to view the wilderness as protective and restorative.

During her trek on the Appalachian Trail, word of her passage spread from town to town along the route, just over 2,000 miles, from Georgia to Maine. Sightings of her were like catnip to local newspaper reporters, who took to the trail to interview her as she passed through.

One newspaper account found its way to her hometown in Ohio, which is how her children—by then grown and out on their own—learned where she had gone when she said she was going for a walk.

That Gatewood was alone and in her late sixties renewed interest in the trail, especially among women. If a woman of her age could hike it all the way in one season, many of them reasoned, they could, too. Her citation at the Appalachian Trail Museum concludes: "She inspired two distinct movements in long distance hiking, women thru-hikers and the ultra-lite movement."

By the time Gatewood died at eighty-five in 1973, apparently of a heart attack, she had hiked the length of the Appalachian Trail three times—the third time in sections—and was the first person, man or woman, to conquer it more than once.

Another woman, Mildred Norman Ryder, known as Peace Pilgrim, had hiked the entire trail in 1952, but she had done it in her mid-forties and with a companion. Earl Shaffer was the first person to hike the trail alone, which he did in 1948 at twenty-nine.

In 1959, Gatewood conquered the two thousand miles of the Oregon Trail, trekking from Independence, Missouri, to Portland. By this time, some newspapers called her "America's most celebrated pedestrian."

The story of Gatewood's battering at the hands of her husband did not emerge for more than a half century, when newspaper reporter Ben Montgomery wrote *Grandma Gatewood's Walk* in 2014.

Montgomery worked for the *Tampa Bay Times* in Florida, and Gatewood was his great-grandaunt. In his

Gatewood's 1957 entry in the logbook of the Carter Notch Hut in New Hampshire.

research for the book, her surviving children entrusted him with her journals, letters, and scrapbooks.

In that material he found stark references to what she had withheld from news interviewers: that her husband had nearly pummeled her to death several times. During one beating, she wrote, he broke a broom over her head. Her children told Montgomery that their father's sexual hunger had been insatiable and that he forced himself on their mother several times a day.

In 1937, she left him and moved in with relatives in California, leaving behind two daughters, ages nine and eleven, who were still at home. She was confident that her husband would not beat the girls, and she could not afford to take them with her. In a sorrowful letter to her daughters with no return address, she wrote, "I have suffered enough at his hands to last me for the next hundred years."

But unable to bear being away from them any longer, she returned after a few months. Back in Ohio her husband would not let her out of his sight. She later wrote that in 1938, he beat her "beyond recognition" ten times.

"For a lot of people the trail is a refuge," Brian B. King, a publisher of guidebooks and maps for the Appalachian Trail Conservancy, said in a telephone interview. "But seldom is it a refuge for something as bad as that."

Emma Rowena Caldwell was born on October 25, 1887, in Gallia County, Ohio. Her father, Hugh Caldwell, a farmer, had lost a leg after being wounded in the Civil War and turned to a life of drinking and gambling. Her mother, Evelyn (Trowbridge) Caldwell, raised the couple's fifteen children, who slept four to a bed in the family's log cabin.

At nineteen, Emma married Perry Clayton Gatewood, twenty-six, a teacher who later became a farmer. Almost immediately he put her to work building fences, burning tobacco beds, and mixing cement, in addition to her household chores. Three months after their wedding, he started to beat her, a practice he continued until, one day in 1939, he broke her teeth, cracked one of her ribs, and bloodied her face.

In that incident, Gatewood responded by throwing a sack of flour at him, prompting a law enforcement officer to arrest her, not him, and put her in jail. The next day, the mayor saw her battered face and took her to his own home, where she remained under his protection until she got back on her feet.

Gatewood filed for divorce, which was granted in 1941.

In 1949, she came across a *National Geographic* magazine article about the Appalachian Trail and became intrigued to learn in reading it that no woman had ever hiked it solo.

Gatewood's only real training for her historic trek was walking ten miles a day to build up her leg muscles. But in a sense, her entire life had prepared her.

Through endless farm chores, as a child and as an adult, she knew how to work herself to the bone. She found a haven in the woods—from her grinding chores and, later, from her abusive husband. Though her education ended in the eighth grade, she was resourceful and taught herself about wildlife and the medicinal properties of plants and which ones were edible.

Her first attempt at hiking the Appalachian Trail, in 1954, ended badly. Starting out in Maine, she quickly broke her glasses, got lost, and was rescued by rangers, who told her to go home.

The next year, she started in Georgia and successfully trekked north. In neither instance did she tell her children where she was going. Montgomery, the author, said she feared that they would try to stop her.

Gatewood sewed herself a small drawstring sack. In it, she carried as few items as possible, including a shower curtain to keep the rain off, a Swiss Army knife, a flashlight, Band-Aids, iodine, a pen, and a small notebook. Her larder consisted of Vienna sausages, raisins, peanuts, and bouillon cubes. She wore through seven pairs of canvas shoes, many of them Keds.

Gatewood had seen no need to lug a tent; she had planned to rely on the hospitality of strangers. And more often than might be expected, she was able to do just that, in part because of her growing fame. Still, she spent many nights on the cold ground, under picnic tables, and even on a porch swing.

She completed her first hike in 146 days, an average of about 14 miles a day. It was considered a remarkable pace, especially given her age, her limited gear, and the condition of the trail. She would often set out before sunrise and not stop until she was spent. The members of at least one Boy Scout troop and their leaders reported that they could not keep up with her.

As she closed in on Mount Katahdin, the northern terminus of the trail, in a rugged part of Maine, newspaper reporters extolled her achievement, and "much of America was pulling for her," Montgomery wrote.

People, he said, were "clipping newspaper articles at kitchen tables and watching her traipse across the evening news on television, wondering whether she'd survive, this woman, in so mean a place."

Little did they know what she had already survived.

———

KATHARINE Q. SEELYE is a former national correspondent and an obituary writer for *The New York Times*. She has climbed Mount Katahdin, but she started at its base, not from two thousand miles away in Georgia.

# Beyond the Obit: An Untold Story

———

## BY BEN MONTGOMERY

Before her death in 1973, Emma Gatewood wrote thousands of journal entries, letters, and poems. But I would not know that until getting to know her daughter, Lucy Gatewood Seeds. On one visit, she led me into a spare bedroom and pulled open the closet door to reveal several boxes stacked neatly on the floor. She had kept her mother's papers—a biographer's dream.

One particular autobiographical sketch struck me. Written for her descendants, it recounted the domestic abuse Gatewood suffered, highlighting a painful reality. For thirty years, this celebrated hiker had endured a hard-fisted, short-tempered man. She would escape from him by going on long walks in the woods, and when they split up, she just kept walking.

When reporters interviewed Gatewood about her trek along the Appalachian Trail in 1955, she told them she was a widow. Her ex-husband, alive and well, could have read the inaccuracy, which she repeated for decades.

Lucy and her siblings told me their own stories of seeing their father come undone, all fists and fury—painful memories they shared to highlight their mother's resilience. Her story was only true, they said, if told in full. Without understanding the violence at home, who could ever know the healing power of a good long walk?

BEN MONTGOMERY is great-grandnephew of Emma Gatewood and author of *Grandma Gatewood's Walk*.

The Motorcycle Queen of Miami

# Bessie Stringfield

## 1911–1993

BY NIKITA STEWART

SOMEWHERE BETWEEN MYTH, memory, and motorcycles, Bessie B. Stringfield was great.

In the 1950s, when women were relegated to housework, either in marriage or as domestics, Stringfield was married several times and worked as a maid yet revved and roared through Florida's palm-tree-lined streets on her Harley-Davidson, earning the unofficial title of "Motorcycle Queen of Miami."

She was posthumously inducted into the hall of fame of the American Motorcyclist Association in 2002, nearly a decade after her 1993 death. Hundreds of women motorcyclists made several cross-country treks in her honor. She has been memorialized in a comic book and mentioned in a documentary. Ann Ferrar, a friend and fellow biker, wrote a story about Stringfield in her 1996 book about women motorcyclists, *Hear Me Roar: Women, Motorcycles, and the Rapture of the Road*. Ferrar is also working on a biography about Stringfield.

A masterful storyteller, Stringfield amazed people with her accounts of being chased off the road as she traveled through the Jim Crow South; performing at carnivals and motorcycle events, some of which included a motordrome sometimes known as the "Wall of Death"; and serving as a civilian motorcycle dispatch rider for the US Army in the 1940s. Her childhood, in her telling, was

Dickensian: born in Jamaica to an interracial couple, left motherless at a young age, abandoned by her father on a Boston street, and adopted by a benevolent Irish Catholic woman who treated her so well that she gave her a motorcycle when she was sixteen years old.

Robert Scott Thomas was a little boy when Stringfield worked as a housekeeper for his family. He recalled thinking her stories were unbelievable but said, "I don't think she ever told me a lie. It was the dead-nuts right."

Thomas was named the beneficiary and the executor of her estate in her will; after all, she apparently had no survivors. Esther Bennett, Stringfield's niece, had a different version: "I don't know anything about Jamaican. She was never adopted."

"Her mother's name was Maggie Cherry," she added. "Her father was James White."

Old records show that they lived in Edenton, North Carolina, and said that they were both Black Americans.

She did not know how Bessie Beatrice White Stringfield, small-town Southerner, came to be Bessie B. Stringfield, big-city Jamaican.

Several websites, including Forgotten Newsmakers, BlackPast.org, and Timeline, say she was born Betsy Leonora Ellis in February 1911 in Kingston, Jamaica, to Maria Ellis and James Ferguson, with no explanation

Bessie Stringfield roared through Florida's palm-tree-lined streets on her Harley-Davidson.

Stringfield in the early 1940s. She amazed people with her tales of traveling on the road.

for how Betsy became Bessie. Her death certificate said she was born in March 1911 in Kingston to James Richard White and M. Cherry, a conclusion drawn by an attorney for her estate. According to a Social Security index, she was born in March 1912.

In tales that have been told about Stringfield, some true, some fabricated, she always came out on top by proving herself or by finding common ground: She won over a white Miami police officer by demonstrating her riding skills; she was followed through back roads by an angry white mob, yet she outran them; she once found a kind white gas station owner who allowed her to fill up her tank for free. There was also folklore passed from one generation of relatives to the next that Stringfield

30

had worked for the Federal Bureau of Investigation, and perhaps she had disappeared to protect them.

The stories were outrageous enough to ring true. Only Stringfield knew if they really were.

Ferrar had passed on some of the misinformation about Stringfield's early life at Stringfield's request. Asked recently about these untruths, Ferrar wrote in an email, "Bessie's running from her early past does not discount or in any way lessen her unusual achievements as an adult, and that is why Bessie continues to inspire new generations, and rightfully so."

"She asked me to tell her truth as her friend," Ferrar said in an interview.

Her lasting power was in her presence, especially in the eyes of children, during a period when seeing a Black woman commanding a Harley-Davidson was unprecedented.

Bennett and her brothers remembered how their aunt would whirl in and out of Baltimore, where they lived. Their mother was Mary Louise White Skinner, one of Stringfield's older sisters. They described their aunt as worldly and wily.

"I was knee-high to a duck. She would never tell nobody what her business was," said Robert Irvin Skinner, a nephew.

David Skinner, another nephew, said their mother would yell at Stringfield, "Get those boys off that bike!"

"She would stand up on that bike with one foot on the seat and one foot on the handlebars," he said, laughing, in a phone interview.

Bennett was once so rattled by a ride with Stringfield that she refused to get back on. "She jumped the track. I took a car back. She gave me car fare."

Motorcycle riding was unladylike according to societal norms in the early twentieth century, and the family elders did not approve, said Jackie Reid, the daughter of one of Stringfield's half sisters, who added that they were also worried about her safety.

There was an argument in the 1950s that the children were not privy to, and Stringfield did not visit again.

"The last they heard from her was she was in Florida," Reid said. "She was a wanderer."

Marriage records show Stringfield spent some time in Indiana. And 1945 census records show that she claimed Massachusetts as her birthplace, but she also said she had been born around 1918.

In the 1950s, she finally settled down in Miami, first working as a domestic and in nursing.

She befriended the families that employed her, making an outsized impression on Robert Scott Thomas and Tom Thomas, who were in elementary school in the early 1950s.

Their mother, delayed or forgetful, failed to pick them up from school one day, so Stringfield came to the rescue. "We found Bessie out there on her Harley and in her leather jacket," said Tom Thomas.

Both jumped on the motorcycle with her. "I was just a little kid so I was only wrapped around half of her," Robert Scott Thomas said. "I could feel the heat from the exhaust on my leg."

"All the kids were going crazy," he said.

Bea Hines, a columnist at *The Miami Herald*, wrote a profile of Stringfield in 1981. She made for a colorful interview, sharing her feats and her preference for men many years her junior. She claimed to have married six of them.

Hines also had a personal connection, remembering how Stringfield would lead a pack of motorcyclists, all men, in an annual parade. "I can remember being in awe of this beautiful Black woman with this big bushy hair under her helmet," she said.

———

**NIKITA STEWART** is editor of the Real Estate desk at *The New York Times*. She previously worked as a reporter and published *Troop 6000: The Girl Scout Troop That Began in a Shelter and Inspired the World* in 2020.

Balinese Dancer with "Divine Energy"

# Raka Rasmi

## 1939–2018

BY SETH MYDANS

SHE WAS A TINY twelve-year-old girl with wide, darting eyes and a big headdress, undulating across the stage in the graceful, highly stylized dance of Bali.

Her arms floated and twined, as if they had no bones or joints, as she dipped and rose to the urgent syncopated gongs of a gamelan orchestra.

It was 1952 in New York and the young dancer's name was Ni Gusti Ayu Raka Rasmi. She had never before left her home village, Peliatan, with its small, mud-walled houses surrounded by bright green rice fields.

Now she was the star of the Bali Dancers, a troupe that had traveled more than ten thousand miles into the alien worlds of the United States and Europe.

The troupe included two other female dancers about her age, Oka and Anom, and an accomplished young male dancer named Sampih.

"I was the smallest," Raka Rasmi exclaimed in an interview at her home in Peliatan in 2008, as she paged through an album of pictures from the trip. "I was the cutest!"

The dancers were accompanied by a forty-piece gamelan orchestra in which players used mallets to produce rapid, rhythmic, and hypnotic music on banks of percussion instruments.

Balinese dance, with roots in Hindu and traditional folk rituals, is central to the island's culture, performed in temples and courtyards for both religious and secular occasions.

It is characterized by slight, pivoting gestures of the head, the hands, the fingers, and especially the eyes, which are virtually performers of their own, round, intense, and expressive.

"When the music is dynamic you have to have a fierce look. You open your eyes wide. You can't smile," Raka Rasmi said. "When the music is soft and sweet, your eyes are also soft and sweet and you smile."

Brilliantly colored costumes and elaborate head-dresses add a ceremonial feel to the performances.

On the tour, Raka Rasmi performed a delicate new dance called the Oleg Tamulilingan, or the Bumblebee, in which a male and female dancer circle each other as if courting.

Audiences were ecstatic. The performances received as many as seven curtain calls.

In reviewing the show, *The Wall Street Journal* called the dances "an exotic elixir of sound, color and move-ment" led by "a 12-year-old virtuoso who brought down the house."

John Martin, writing in *The New York Times*, called Raka Rasmi "an utterly lovely wisp of a girl, as seri-ous as an owl until her smile breaks through." Her

dancing, he wrote, "was truly superb, technically and dramatically."

Ed Sullivan featured them on his Sunday-night variety show, *Toast of the Town,* just as twelve years later he would feature the Beatles on their concert tour of the United States.

The world tour would catapult Raka Rasmi into a lifelong career in dance. By the time of her death, at seventy-nine, on March 17, 2018, she would be known as one of the greatest Balinese dance teachers and performers of her generation.

In the years after the 1952 tour, Bali grew in popularity as a tourist destination and Balinese dance took its place as one of the world's distinctive dance forms.

"Ibu Raka was an excellent teacher and dancer, still performing till the day she died," said Rucina Ballinger, an American dance ethnologist who has spent decades in Bali teaching and dancing. (*Ibu* is a common honorific for an older woman.)

"As a teacher she was feisty and strong-willed," she added.

She embodied a quality the Balinese call *taksu,* which Ballinger described as "charisma, spiritual power, something that exceeds technical brilliance and is seen as a sort of divine energy."

Well into her seventies, Raka Rasmi continued to train students and to perform on special occasions, though she said her aging knees forced her to modify some of the moves.

She was training a student in front of a cracked mirror in her garden during the interview in 2008, her hands fluttering and twittering as she moved, as supple as a girl.

"It's difficult to be a good Balinese dancer," she said, and she demonstrated one of the exercises with her student.

"They pull your shoulders back until you choke to make the bones in your back narrow," she said, pressing a knee into her student's back and pulling on her shoulders, "like that."

Raka Rasmi raised herself on her toes and wiggled her feet to demonstrate a movement. "That's what the doctor told me not to do," she said.

Ni Gusti Ayu Raka Rasmi was born on March 10, 1939, to a family of farmers and raised with no electricity and no radio link to the outside world.

She first learned to dance when she was ten. She was playing near the rice fields where she helped her family by shooing away birds in the planting season and joining in the harvest.

"I was looking for grasshoppers when the teacher came by and said, 'Raka, come here, why don't you hang out with us, why don't you learn to dance,' and we danced around," she said.

At first her parents were against it, she said. "'Why are you putting on makeup and not helping on the farm?'" she recalled her father asking her. "Sometimes they didn't give me food."

But she said, "After I started bringing in money, they were happy. I was free then. They loved me again."

In 1952, John Coast, a retired British diplomat who had taken up residence in Bali, came to her village and proposed organizing an international tour for a troupe of dancers and musicians.

An executive of Columbia Artists Management, Frederick Schang, who would finance the American leg of the tour, came to see the dancers, and Raka Rasmi received her first rave review.

"The little darling—oh, the little darling!" Coast quoted Schang as exclaiming in his book *Dancing out of Bali* (1954). "Ni Gusti Raka—that's your star! She's great. She's so sweet I could eat her with a spoon. All the little darlings—the American public will go crazy about 'em."

In America, Raka Rasmi discovered snow and Coca-Cola and vanilla ice cream. She met Walt Disney on a visit to Disneyland. In London, she met the great ballerina Margot Fonteyn at Sadler's Wells. Later, she said, she shook hands with the actress Grace Kelly.

A high point of the trip, as she recalls it, was a visit to Hollywood, where together with the other two child dancers, she performed for Frank Sinatra, and he sang for them. "He was great!"

He invited them to his home, where she met Bob Hope

Raka Rasmi, left, performing in London in 1952. While there, she met the ballerina Margot Fonteyn.

and Bing Crosby, who had just completed the filming of a jokey movie about their homeland called *Road to Bali*.

The girls found the film hilarious, Coast wrote: "The movie had nothing of Bali in it, but everybody, and especially the little girls, loved the film. 'Itu Bob!' they exclaimed to one another helplessly—'That Bob!'"

In her photo album Raka Rasmi saved a picture of Bob Hope in a ski cap and Bing Crosby in a funny hat mimicking the gestures of Balinese dance, with three Balinese girls watching them and laughing.

Decades later, in 2008, she said she still practiced two or three times a week, in the morning and sometimes in the evening, to keep her body flexible, and to make her happy.

"If I couldn't dance I would cry, because I love dancing," she said. "I do it without music because I already have it in my head. I've memorized it. And even in bed, it's still there in my mind when I'm sleeping."

———

**SETH MYDANS** is a former foreign and national correspondent for *The New York Times* who met Raka Rasmi on a visit to Bali and was enchanted by her graceful movements as she practiced in her garden before a cracked mirror.

Katherine McHale Slaughterback in the 1930s with the rifle she used to fend off a snake attack.

Farmer Who Found Fame as "Rattlesnake Kate"

# Katherine McHale Slaughterback

## 1893–1969

BY AMISHA PADNANI

IT WAS A CRISP MORNING on October 28, 1925, when Katherine McHale Slaughterback, who was riding home on her horse, suddenly found herself under attack. About 140 rattlesnakes were slithering toward her and her three-year-old son.

What she did next would stir the imaginations of poets, songwriters, and reporters for decades to come: she single-handedly clobbered every snake to death, never getting bitten once.

It was a feat that sounded more like folklore than reality, and some historians believe Slaughterback's account could have been exaggerated. Slaughterback, after all, was no frontiersman of the Wild West. She was a simple farmer who toiled over her land in the rugged plains of Colorado. And she was a woman, albeit a hardened one, who raised animals rather than hunted them. But the attention brought her a sort of fame almost unimaginable today.

As the story goes, Slaughterback and her son were on their way home from collecting wounded ducks from a hunt that had taken place the day before at a nearby lake, when Slaughterback got down from her horse, Brownie, to open a gate in their path and heard the telltale rattle. She turned to find a snake coiled and ready to strike.

She picked up her .22 rifle and shot the snake, but two more appeared. She shot those, too, then saw dozens more heading her way, heads erect and tongues darting. She would later learn that the snakes were coming from a nearby den and that the "BANG!" from her gun had startled them. She was surrounded now, and there weren't enough bullets.

Fear struck her as she looked helplessly toward her son and her horse, only several yards away.

She spotted a sign that read "No Hunting Allowed," plucked its post from the soil, and, for two terrifying hours, spun and swirled about as she attacked the snakes.

"I killed five large rattlers without stopping but had made no headway," she later told a reporter, "for others kept coming in a hideous unending procession."

Snakes sprung toward her, she said, and she caught them in midair with the post, not more than three feet long, all the while screaming at her son to stay on the horse.

"I was drenched with perspiration and it ran down into my eyes and dropped from my hat brim," she recalled in an interview with the *Blade and Ledger* newspaper in 1931. "My face was swollen and my eyes were nearly swollen shut and I knew I could not last much longer."

Slaughterback wore a flapper-style dress consisting of
forty-seven snake skins to parties.

When the onslaught finally ended, she mustered what strength she had left, mounted her horse, and made her way home, "only to crumple on the ground." Her hands were covered in blisters and she "was under a doctor's care for several days," she said.

Once she recovered, she went back and collected "three washtubs" full of snake carcasses. By then, news had spread of her feat and articles were appearing in newspapers across the nation. Several people went to the scene to count the snakes. Some asked her for souvenirs, which she sold—a rattle for $2 or a cut of snakeskin for $1. One man told her of the benefits of snake oil and sent along instructions on how to extract it.

"Rattlesnake Kate," her admirers called her, a nickname that would stick for decades to come.

Katherine Ruth McHale was born on July 25, 1893, in a log cabin about nine miles east of Longmont, Colorado, one of three children of Francis Wallace McHale, a former priest, and Vesta Albina (Pease) McHale. Her mother died when she was three.

During World War II, Slaughterback worked as a Red Cross nurse, having trained at Saint Joseph Hospital in Denver, but farming occupied most of her life. She was resourceful and tough, living largely on her own and working her land, where she raised cows, chickens, goats, and pigs. She harvested corn, beans, and other crops that she would sell. She also took up taxidermy.

Slaughterback married and divorced several times but mostly raised her son as a single mother.

"She just didn't seem to get along all that well with being married to and having a man as the head of her household," the historian Peggy Ford Waldo told the podcast *Lost Highways* in 2020. "She was the head of her household. She was the mover and shaker in her own life. And she never wanted anybody to tell her what to do or not to do."

After she earned her rattlesnake fame, legions of fans flooded her mailbox with letters. She also gained the amorous interest of an older man, Charles D. Randolph, a poet from Iowa who called himself "Buckskin Bill."

In his first note, in September 1931, he asked her to send a photo of herself that he could use as inspiration for a poem. He would go on to write several about her, referring to her as his "pard of the plains." In one, he opined:

*Away out West, where coiling serpents watch and wait,*
*There lives the rattlesnake killer known far and wide as Rattle Snake Kate.*
*Away out West in the Silver State, where the vipers give you a thrill,*
*That's where you'll find Rattle Snake Kate, the pard of Buckskin Bill.*

Randolph's notes and poems were laced with heavy-handed desire. He writes that he was married twice, then he goes on to explain that he is looking for a wife who "looks just like" Slaughterback, saying, "She must be true to me, loving, passionate and honest, not rich—when I get one like that I'll go through 'Burning Hells of Fire and High Water for her.' "

Her letters were more matter-of-fact, describing her many chores and her struggles to make money amid droughts and the elements ("It has been awfully cold and blustery this past week"; "I had three leghorn roosters freeze their combs off and one froze to death"). She describes injuries, including spider bites, a kick from a pony, and burns from a fallen electrical wire.

But she also found solace in her relationship with Randolph. "Gee, I sure do like to hear from you," she wrote in one note, adding, "You must know I am a long way from a mail box, but I will try and let you know I am still looking for your letters."

Slaughterback invites him to visit a few times—"If you come out this way I would be glad to have you call on me a few days." And when she doesn't hear from him for a long time, she makes her worry known: "I am afraid you have put me out of your mind but I hope not as I know someday we surely will meet."

But though they exchanged letters for about forty years, there is no evidence that they ever did meet.

Slaughterback maintained her reputation as Rattlesnake Kate throughout her life. She began hunting rattlesnakes regularly and sent venom to scientists for research. She also fashioned clothing and accessories, including a flapper-style dress consisting of forty-seven snake skins that she would wear to parties, along with matching shoes, a belt, and a rattle necklace. In 1965, she estimated that her dress was worth $3,900 (about $34,000 in today's dollars).

Newspapers continued to write about her feat for decades. A children's book, *Kate Slaughterback: Legendary Rattlesnake Kate,* was published in 2013 by Lindsay McNatt.

And in 2019, the musician Neyla Pekarek released a solo album, *Rattlesnake.* She has performed in a replica of Slaughterback's dress. In one track, "The Attack," she sings: "Look to the front / Look to the sides / Don't forget your back else they'll have your hide."

Shortly after the album's release, Pekarek, a Colorado native, told NPR that she had learned about Slaughterback in college and was struck by her story.

"She lived very much outside of the box of what it meant to be feminine and what it meant to be a woman at that time," Pekarek said, "and I was really inspired by that."

Slaughterback died of an illness on October 6, 1969, at a hospital in Greeley, Colorado. She was seventy-six.

Two weeks before her death, she donated her dress to the Greeley History Museum in Northern Colorado. It remains on display there to this day.

———

**AMISHA PADNANI** is an editor on the Obituaries desk at *The New York Times* and the creator of the "Overlooked" series. She has been to Colorado, but she wouldn't know what to do if she encountered a snake.

"Rattle Snake Kate".

Slaughterback in 1925, with skins of some of the 140 snakes she single-handedly slaughtered.

Omero Catan in 1957, when he was the first paying customer on the Florida Turnpike.

Vacuum Salesman Known as "Mr. First"

# Omero Catan

## 1914–1996

---

### BY MARGALIT FOX

"THIS IS THE GREATEST achievement of my life," Omero C. Catan declared in 1937, on becoming the first toll-paying driver through the Lincoln Tunnel, the newly opened artery linking New York to New Jersey. "There will never be another like it."

In fact, there would be hundreds more: throughout most of the twentieth century, whenever a major public-works project arose in New York and beyond—an airport, a subway line, a bridge, a tunnel—Catan, a Brooklyn-born vacuum cleaner salesman, made it his mission to beat all comers into, onto, across, or through it.

Catan's dedication to dedications was not so much a hobby as a calling—one that by midcentury had earned him the sobriquet "Mr. First" in the national press.

He was the first person to ride the Madison Avenue bus when that route replaced the old trolley line in 1935 and the first to take to the ice at the newly opened Rockefeller Center skating rink the next year. He was the first motorist on the New Jersey Turnpike in 1951, the first paying customer to feed a New York City parking meter when the city installed them that year, and the first to cross Maryland's Chesapeake Bay Bridge in 1952.

In 1953, when subway tokens were introduced, Catan was the first to drop one into the turnstiles at the Forty-Second Street–and–Eighth Avenue station. He was the first motorist across the old Tappan Zee Bridge in 1955, the first to traverse (from the New Jersey side) the newly opened lower level of the George Washington Bridge in 1962, and the first to do a welter of other things.

Embarking on this vocation as a teenager and continuing into old age, he had bagged, by his own count, 537 firsts by the time the twentieth century had run its course.

A career as a professional firster, Catan made clear, was not for the faint of heart.

"You can't just get up early and be first in line," he explained in a 1945 interview, "because they won't let you park there indefinitely. You have to study the problem, map out all probable routes, grease a few palms."

Like a detective on a stakeout, Catan pursued his quarry with an exquisite combination of patience, perseverance, and preparation. For the Lincoln Tunnel assault, which entailed bivouacking in his car for thirty hours in the December cold to secure pride of place in the line on the New Jersey side, his supply list, the *New York Herald Tribune* reported, included these essentials:

"Six wool blankets; two pillows, extra soft; one picnic basket filled with sandwiches and fruit; one Thermos jug of coffee, hot; one camera for pictorial record of the honor; one checkerboard with checkers; one copy of

43

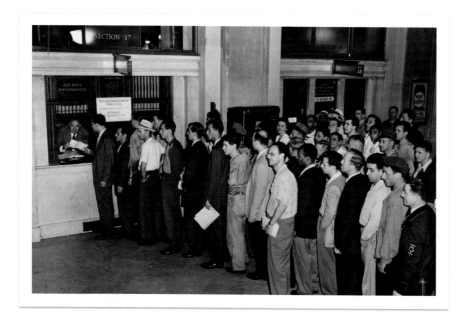

Catan was first in line to receive an application for a life insurance dividend in 1949.

'Kear's Encyclopedia on the Game of Draughts' (British word for checkers); two shaving outfits; one new 50-cent piece for paying toll."

To forestall sabotage by other would-be firsters, Catan often took along a confederate: sometimes a friend, sometimes—fatefully—his brother Michael Katen.

"You have to be on guard," Catan, discussing potential rivals, told the *Herald Tribune,* "or they will puncture your tires."

Amid the rigors of the Depression and wartime, Catan's exploits were rapturously celebrated by the newspapers.

"At a stroke we have left behind us the front page of wars and civil strife and revolution, of oppressions and massacres, of economic cyclones and earthquakes, of civilization shaken to its foundations," *The New York Times* declaimed purply of Catan's exploits in early 1945. "We are back once more in those sunlit, jocund days when the American people gave themselves over to champion 'firsters,' to champion gate-crashers, to champion flagpole sitters, marathon dancers."

Over time, though, in a drama of near-biblical resonance that was also covered avidly in the press, Catan

was forced to contend with an assault on his primacy by his own brother, Katen. Once an ally whom the newspapers had christened "Mr. Second"—he had helped his brother, for instance, during the great Lincoln Tunnel bivouac of 1937—Katen was, in later years, to hear his brother tell it, a pretender to the throne.

"There is only one Mr. First!" Catan, then retired to Florida, shouted in a 1995 interview with the *Miami New Times,* an alternative paper. "That's not my brother. That's not anybody else. That's me. I am Mr. First!"

Katen, however, beat his brother into the world. He entered it as Spartaco Catanzariti in Brooklyn on August 28, 1912. Omero Galileo Cesare Catanzariti followed on March 10, 1914, joining a large, lively, competitive Italian American family. (Their sister Mary, no slouch herself when it came to firsts, had made the inaugural transit-by-motorcycle of the Holland Tunnel and was almost certainly, *The New Yorker* reported in 1936, "the only person in the world who own[ed] a white car with red roses painted all over it.")

As young men, to forestall the anti-Italian bigotry that was keeping them from the job market, Spartaco and Omero Catanzariti Americanized their names. In what was perhaps a portent of their future rivalry, each chose to spell his new surname differently but both names were pronounced identically: KAY-ten.

Omero had begun racking up premieres as a teenager, inspired by the story of a family friend who had been among the first to walk across the Brooklyn Bridge after it opened in 1883. As an adult he held various jobs, including working as a salesman of Electrolux vacuum cleaners, a teller at the Corn Exchange Bank in Manhattan, and a catering manager with Harry M. Stevens, the ballpark food concessionaire.

The Lincoln Tunnel was at the heart of the rift between the brothers. In 1945, construction was completed on the tunnel's second tube, north of the one through which Catan had proudly driven eight years before.

When the north tube opened, Catan was overseas, serving as a private with a United States Army infantry outfit in England. He asked Katen to uphold the family honor by standing in for him as the tube's first paying customer, and on February 1, 1945, after a long, blanket-wrapped bivouac of his own, Katen did.

"I'll carry on," Katen gamely told *The New Yorker* that year. "It ain't much for him to ask."

He added, auguring the competition to come: "I was the first one over the Merritt Parkway when they opened it in 1938. I guess that gives me pro standing."

A mechanic for Trans World Airlines who later repaired jukeboxes, Katen went on to a string of impeccably planned firsts of his own, including making the inaugural drive across the Throgs Neck Bridge in 1961 and becoming the first paying customer on Miami's Metrorail in 1984.

But for Catan, his brother's renown rankled.

"Look here," he told the *Miami New Times*. "Michael claims that we were at over 600 openings. He knows that there have been only 537. Why would he lie like that? He's my brother, but he's the biggest goddamn liar in the world."

Before long, Catan said, he came to regard having given Katen his proxy that day in 1945 as "maybe the worst mistake [he] ever made."

Interviewed for the same article, Katen responded: "Even though he's number one—Mr. First—we're still tied together. That's the way it wound up now. We're one. We're not two any more. We're one. That's just the way it is."

But if Catan felt usurped as a professional firster, he had other passions to sustain him. Chief among them was shuffleboard, the subject of his 1967 book, *Secrets of Shuffleboard Strategy: Happiness Is Shuffleboard.*

He was so ardent an adherent of the game that he publicly offered to teach it to Pope John Paul II when His Holiness visited the United States in 1987.

"He can play in his gowns," Catan assured the *Miami Herald* that year. "I think he'll make a good player." (The pontiff's response is unrecorded.)

Both Catan and Katen were married men. (Catan's wife, Jeanne—with whom he took out the first marriage license issued in Manhattan in 1939—died in 2004.)

Though in retirement the brothers lived barely twenty minutes apart—Catan in Fort Lauderdale, Katen in Margate, Florida—they rarely spoke during the last decade and a half of Catan's life.

Curiously, neither brother received a news obituary in a major publication when he died—Catan in 1996, Katen in 2008. The absence underscores the ephemeral nature of fame and the peril of being first in pursuits where thousands are destined to follow.

But to Catan, the hordes that came after him did not matter: the making of posterity was his only object.

"This is something tangible," he said of his Lincoln Tunnel crossing. "My grandchildren will talk about this."

———

**MARGALIT FOX** is a former senior writer at *The New York Times.* Her latest nonfiction book, *The Confidence Men,* has been optioned, together with Fox's feature screenplay adaptation, by Thunder Road Films.

# Alice Anderson

## 1897–1926

BY BRIOHNY DOYLE

IN AUGUST 1918, a photograph in *The Australian Motorist* showed a newly licensed mechanic, Alice Anderson, in the driver's seat of a Dodge Tourer, elbow out, eyebrows raised, chin tilted defiantly, bobbed hair tucked into a chauffeur's cap. Her leather-gloved hand rested lightly on the wheel.

In an accompanying article, Anderson is described as "the proprietress, manageress and forewoman" of a new automotive garage that she intended to expand. The garage, which operated as a chauffeuse and automobile repair business, had a staff of all women, from mechanical engineers to professional drivers, "capable of doing the jobs any male member of the automobile industry would undertake."

"No man will have a chance on her payroll," the article continued, "but clients of both sexes will be taken care of." Anderson's all-women garage would be the first of its kind in Australia, and one of the first in the world.

About four years earlier, Anderson had received the keys to a new car for her eighteenth birthday. The enormous Hupmobile touring car—emblazoned with the family crest and the words "We Stoop Not"—was a gift from her father. It would remain in Anderson's possession as long as she could service the remaining debt.

Anderson couldn't yet drive, but she was driven. She handled administrative work at her father's transportation co-op, hounding the mechanics to learn all she could with the hope of convincing a garage to take her on as an apprentice. Soon she was driving not only the Hupmobile but also charabancs. It would have been a feat to maneuver these early, outsized buses on the dirt roads that cut jaggedly through the temperate forests of soaring mountain ash and dense ferns in the Yarra Ranges, fifty miles northeast of Melbourne.

Determined to develop her skills, Anderson began working a postal route along the notoriously treacherous blind curves and sudden drops of Black Spur Road. If the headlights failed, she held a flashlight to light the road. If she got bogged, she levered herself out of the mud with branches and whatever else was around.

"I got the opportunity to vacate the office stool for the wheel and I took it," she told *Woman's World* magazine in 1922. (By 1926, she was writing a regular motoring column for the publication.)

Anderson soon expanded her opportunities as a tour operator and chauffeuse, taking small groups out for scenic jaunts and chaperoning country girls on shopping and theater outings in the city. Occasionally, Anderson was called on to play the boyfriend for a picture or a ball dance. This was not so unusual—women danced together when men were away at war. They didn't tend

Alice Anderson in the early 1920s. Her tie pin was engraved, "Nothing ventured, nothing gained."

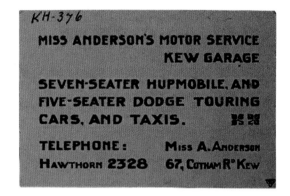

*One of the business cards Anderson used to promote her garage.*

to dress like men though. They didn't look like Anderson, who was known to wear slacks, a pressed shirt, and a neatly pinned tie.

Anderson completed her mechanic's apprenticeship and, in 1919, finally opened her expanded garage, moving it from a rental property to land she secured with a loan. The one-story building—including a workshop, a storeroom, and a small bedroom for herself—was a humbler utopia than she had initially imagined, replete with residential space for any garage girl who needed it.

At the opening party for the Kew Garage, women drivers and mechanics in breeches and ties served sandwiches and tea to guests including the famous opera singer Dame Nellie Melba, the future Australian prime minister Robert Menzies, and what was known as the "university crowd," a group of women and out lesbians who worked at the University of Melbourne and regularly patronized Anderson's businesses.

Here, Anderson trained twenty-nine women whom she called her "garage girls," gave driving and car maintenance lessons to area women, and offered Melbourne's first same-day comprehensive service, which she called "the once-over." At the Kew Garage, the cars were given girls' names, like Natalie and Phyllis, and the workers went by their surnames. The "once-over" was done using the "get down and get under," a wheeled trolley of

Anderson's invention, an apparent precursor to today's popular creeper. Photographs show Anderson and her staff in smart, boyish uniforms, crouched over engines while wielding tools or hand-machining spare parts at the lathe.

Alice Elizabeth Foley Anderson was born on June 8, 1897, in Melbourne, to Irish parents. Her father, James Thomas Anderson, who was known as J. T., was an engineer; her mother, Ellen Mary, was a homemaker. Alice was born five months before the very first automobile arrived in Melbourne from Chicago.

At first, her family had the makings of a middle-class immigrant success story. J.T.'s company landed the Australian patent on a concreting technique that would revolutionize roads and bridges, "literally laying the path for his daughter Alice's future success," the biographer Loretta Smith wrote in *A Spanner in the Works: The Extraordinary Story of Alice Anderson and Australia's First All-Girl Garage* (2019).

The family's aspirational trajectory took a sharp turn, however, when a dearth of luck and business sense put J. T. out of work. Seeking better prospects, he moved the family to Ireland, but when the best he could find was a part-time teaching job, they returned to Australia to live in their remaining asset, a remote bush property with few middle-class comforts.

There, Ellen Mary sewed Alice and her sisters bloomers to accommodate life in the bush and secured them an education.

Alice's few years of secondary school education were rounded out by the vicissitudes of family life. In Dublin, she had ridden a bicycle, which ignited her passion for speed and steel. In the bush, she took to shooting and horse riding. She grieved the fact that she could not enlist in the military, and grieved harder when her only brother drowned at twenty-one years old while fishing near his military barracks in South Head, Sydney.

Despite challenge and tragedy, Anderson remained brave and headstrong. She embodied a particular ideal of practical, active, courageous Australian femininity, "quite different from British and American women, which reflected the historical circumstances of colonial life and even the characteristics of the landscape itself," the historian Georgine Clarsen wrote in *Eat My Dust: Early Women Motorists* (2008).

Still, Anderson's mother disapproved of her career and worried about marriage prospects, though her daughter, who was now living in her garage, declared in a letter home that she wasn't interested. Not "until I get a man a durn sight better than me," she wrote. "Which is going to be hard to find." In the same letter, an unnamed foreigner's earnest proposal was described as "the scream of the garage."

At twenty-nine, Anderson became the first woman to drive from Melbourne to the desert settlement of Alice Springs, traversing more than 1,500 miles of outback terrain that still rattle today's motorists with bone-jangling corrugations. In 1926, most travelers took the more practical option: a camel. But Anderson, along with a companion, Jessie Webb, the first female lecturer of history at the University of Melbourne, embarked on the arduous journey in a fully sponsored Baby Austin. The car, at the time the smallest in the world, was donated as a marketing promotion by the Austin Motor Company. Anderson removed the doors to strap on supplies. She boiled acrid water for Billy Tea, and when they ran out of food, Anderson shot their dinner.

When she returned, Anderson planned to study for her pilot's license and organize a networking trip to a woman-run garage in Kensington, England, which was owned by Marion "Joe" Carstairs, a tattooed lesbian oil heiress who counted the *Peter Pan* novelist J. M. Barrie among her clients. Anderson had also advertised a road tour of the United States that was nearly sold out. But she never got to go.

Anderson is believed to have been cleaning her guns on September 17, 1926, when one of them went off, killing her. She was twenty-nine. Unsubstantiated rumors of suicide or a violent lover's quarrel circulated, but the courts ruled it an accident. A revolver, the *Geelong Advertiser* reported that year, "was not a safe thing for a lady to be playing with." At her funeral, fourteen garage girls in a two-line formation set her in the ground.

Whatever the circumstances of her tragic death, it's clear Anderson had more living to do. Her last column for *Woman's World*, published posthumously in the October edition, was a practical guide to the features a woman should look for in an automobile. Power was desirable, of course, but driving and mechanical skill could overcome a deficit. The writer, after all, had just driven the smallest car in the world across the Never Never.

Anderson's story was distorted and forgotten for decades, but today, Smith's biography puts it in order. An LGBTQ advocacy group has taken the name Alice's Garage, and Anderson's tie pin, engraved with the same Joan of Arc–inspired motto that was stamped on her business cards—"*Qui ne risque, rien n'a rien*," or "Nothing ventured, nothing gained"—is on permanent display at the National Motor Museum in Birdwood, South Australia.

———

**BRIOHNY DOYLE** is a lecturer at the University of Sydney and the author of *Echolalia*, *Adult Fantasy*, and *The Island Will Sink*. At eighteen, she drove around Australia in a battered blue van.

# Terri Rogers

## 1937–1999

BY JEANNE THORNTON

A WOMAN CLAD IN BLUE VELVET and wearing a tiara walks onstage and greets the audience. In her right hand is a microphone; in her left, a ventriloquist doll. Her voice is demure, her British accent posh.

She tells the crowd she lives in a small village with her family—and her cat.

The doll interrupts her: "It's dead."

"What's dead?" she asks.

"Your cat is dead," he says.

The woman flinches. "You mean to say you waited until we were in front of all these people to tell me my cat is dead?" She adds, "Couldn't you have broken it to me quietly?"

The doll repeats the news, this time lowering his voice to a whisper. "Your cat's dead."

The doll describes the cat's dismembered body as the woman listens, aghast, her eyes on his face, making it easy to forget that she's the one playing both parts.

The comedic bit, from 1974, was one of many that the ventriloquist Terri Rogers performed with her doll, Shorty Harris (Cockney slang for "short arse"), after rising to stardom with a breakout performance at the Theatre Royal Stratford East in 1968.

"Ventriloquism comes from lip control, puppetry and acting," the historian and ventriloquist Geoff Felix said in an email interview. "Many ventriloquists have two of these. Terri Rogers had all three."

In performances, Rogers's voice is rich and regal, her doll's a crass tenor, like Margaret Dumont and Groucho Marx living in the same throat.

"Would you like a roll on the drums?" Rogers asks Shorty in a 1981 performance. "Yeah," he replies, "but they'd probably collapse under the weight."

Rogers was born on May 4, 1937, in Ipswich, a port town in Suffolk, England. Her father was a factory worker. Growing up, she was a loner and a devotee of the variety program *The Good Old Days.*

"When I was a kid nobody would speak to me," she said in *Who's Working You Then,* a 1972 documentary, adding, "I wanted to prove that I was as good as, if not better than, anybody else."

Investing sixpence at Woolworths on Professor Foxtone's short pamphlet on ventriloquism, Rogers began her journey to prove it. The showman Carroll Levis discovered her sometime in the 1950s, and she worked the variety circuit for years before finding success.

In the early eighties, she and Shorty Harris appeared on the HBO special *Blockheads,* and the two toured the world, from Bulgaria to the Persian Gulf, packing theaters in Hollywood and Las Vegas and performing three times

Terri Rogers with her sidekick, Shorty. She learned ventriloquism from a pamphlet she bought at Woolworths.

Rogers and Shorty in 1975. Her voice was rich and regal, while his was a crass tenor.

in one year at NATO headquarters in Belgium. She also performed on the men's club circuit, where she featured a far filthier Shorty than could be televised. Sometime in the late 1970s, the Moving Picture Company produced an unreleased film based on Shorty.

Rogers's partner, the magician Val Andrews, once wrote that he remembered the comedian Jimmy Wheeler admonishing her audience: "Blimey, you lot don't realize what you've seen and heard!"

Rogers was transgender, and she leveraged her natural range to create Shorty's voice. "All vents must be able to create another person," the critic Peter Hepple once wrote in a rave review of her performance at Ronnie

Scott's Jazz Club in London. "But Terri Rogers is almost frighteningly good at it, partly through her technical skill in producing a voice," which he described as "a good couple of octaves below her own ladylike tones."

Rogers's act is brilliant independent of its sub-rosa queerness, but knowing it's there adds a special resonance. For instance, the male Shorty was built from a female doll from the Cheeky Girl line by the master dummy maker John Leonard Insull, then installed in a cheap suit.

In one skit, Shorty howls as Rogers—bedecked in jewels and grinning—holds his detached head high above his empty body. "Sadistic bastards, you are," he says as

Rogers's right hand scratches his spine, her left hand visibly working his controls.

Their comic pairing also reflected British discourse around transgender life during Rogers's time. In a 1971 article for *Archives of Sexual Behavior*, the surgical pioneer John Randell writes of his transfeminine patients: "I think if they are going to be ladies they should be ladylike. Conformity, and not making trouble, is what we are looking for."

No one but Rogers ultimately knows whether she sought care through Randell's transgender clinic at Charing Cross; family friends argue that a *Times* of London obituary claiming she did was in error. But whether or not the two met, it is hard to resist the idea that Rogers imagined Randell's infamous words as she built her act about the ladylike operator of a male doll with license to insult the world.

Rogers knew that to be openly transgender would close doors. In 1952, when she was first studying Professor Foxtone, the *Daily Mirror* outed another transgender ventriloquist, Bobbie Kimber, then the popular host of the BBC's variety television show *Music-Hall*. Kimber's contract with the BBC was canceled; by the 1960s she was driving trucks. Possibly because of Kimber, Rogers guarded her transness as an open secret. Janette Page, a family friend who met Rogers as a teenager, said in an interview that Rogers only occasionally raised the subject. Once, she said, at a Christmas dinner, when Rogers and Andrews arrived and kissed the family hello, Page's brother avoided her kiss. Later, in private, Rogers cornered the boy's mother, asking: "Was it because of the way I am?" She assured Rogers it wasn't.

Rogers remained close with many luminaries of the British magic world, including Ken Brooke and Page's father, Pat: "My friends, the greats," Rogers wrote. A lifelong hobbyist magician, her own illusions ranged from raw spectacle—swallowing a handful of razor blades, which she then regurgitated neatly arranged on a thread—to intricate topological tricks, based on the branch of math that involves folding surfaces. She learned by reading Martin Gardner's *Scientific American* column, "Mathematical Games," and developed at least one trick for David Copperfield, with whom she corresponded. She also offered encouragement to others in the field.

Andrews, a prolific writer of magic and Sherlock Holmes mysteries, collaborated with Rogers on instructional videos and on three books of illusions, including *Secrets: The Original Magic of Terri Rogers*. They visited their circuit of magical friends together, Andrews often taciturn until Rogers prompted: "Val, tell them about . . . !"

"It was a love story," Page said.

In Rogers's final years, as she suffered a series of strokes, Andrews remained by her side, pushing her wheelchair as she traveled to give talks at conventions and clubs.

Rogers died of pneumonia on May 30, 1999. She was sixty-two.

"My dearest friend and companion of 25 years," Andrews wrote in an appreciation later that year, adding, "I held her hand and realized that those intriguing voices were stilled."

Rogers's work lives on in YouTube videos and movies, including the 1986 documentary *A Gottle of Geer*, which includes a skit in which a man acting as a neuropsychologist interviews Rogers and Shorty, who say they hate each other shortly before she seals him, cursing, in a suitcase. Shorty now remains silent—wherever he is.

—

**JEANNE THORNTON** is the author of the novel *Summer Fun*, winner of a Lambda Literary award; *The Dream of Doctor Bantam;* and *The Black Emerald*. Her work has appeared in *Wired, n+1, Harper's Bazaar,* the *Evergreen Review,* and other places. She lives in Brooklyn.

While others ducked for cover, Margaret Gipsy Moth charged forward, camera rolling.

# Margaret Gipsy Moth

## 1951–2010

BY NATALIE SCHACHAR

AS THE FORMER YUGOSLAVIA was splitting apart in 1992, the Bosnian capital of Sarajevo came under attack in what has been described as the longest siege of a city in modern warfare.

Margaret Gipsy Moth, a camera operator for CNN, was on the scene that July, tasked with covering the blockade formed by Bosnian Serb troops, who were encircling the city with the intention of taking a portion of it.

But as she and two other CNN journalists were being driven in their white van on a stretch of road known as Sniper Alley, they came under fire.

Moth, who was sitting behind the driver, was hit by a bullet that shattered her jaw and tore through the base of her tongue, grave injuries that nearly took her life and left her speech permanently slurred.

It was one of many attacks against journalists that highlighted the indiscriminate nature of the nightmarish conflict, and it accelerated efforts by the news organization to protect its employees.

"Everybody was a little more careless in the beginning," Stefan Kotsonis, a former CNN correspondent who was in the van with Moth, said in an interview. At the television network, he added, "everything changed."

Within hours of the shooting, CNN began ramping up security for journalists in war zones, ultimately providing armored vehicles, making bulletproof vests and helmets a standard part of equipment, sending staffers to predeployment risk training, and frequently paying security advisers to accompany news teams.

Moth was considered fortunate. After more than a dozen surgeries, she returned to cover the conflict in Sarajevo, joking that she needed to find her missing teeth.

And for another fifteen years at CNN, she continued to cover the cruelty that humans inflicted on one another in hostilities across the globe, including the Chechen war, the US war in Afghanistan, the second Palestinian intifada, and the civil war in Sierra Leone.

"People say, 'People like you—you have a death wish.' And it used to make me so angry," she said in *Fearless: The Margaret Moth Story*, a 2009 CNN documentary. "I don't know anyone who's enjoyed life more or values my life more."

Moth, who consistently held court as the center of a party, was known for taking younger, female journalists under her wing while covering the world's hot spots. She was also daring and mischievous.

In 1991, as gunmen began firing on protesters in Tbilisi, Georgia, some photojournalists took cover behind vehicles. Moth stood up and filmed the militiamen.

# Through it all, she felt lucky to have a job that satiated her hunger to observe critical moments in human history.

In a teeming marketplace of Iraq's Sadr City after the Gulf War, she smacked the cigarette out of the mouth of a man assumed to be a plainclothes security officer who had pushed her camera into her nose.

And in 2002, as Israeli troops encircled Yasser Arafat's headquarters after a Palestinian suicide bombing, Moth scored an exclusive interview with the leader by walking into his compound with a band of medical professionals.

Through it all, she felt lucky to have a job that satiated her hunger to observe critical moments in human history.

She was also committed to her look.

Dressed in black from head to toe, she wore her jet-black hair spiky or teased; rarely, if ever, was seen without her signature black eyeliner; and slept in a pair of black combat boots to be ready for action. She smoked Cuban Montecristo No. 5 cigars, relished the 1969 comedy-drama *Fellini Satyricon* and the 1987 film *Wings of Desire*, and treasured Penguin Classics. Her favorite author was Fyodor Dostoyevsky.

"As dark and real as she would get, she didn't indulge in the dark side of human behavior," said Jeff Russi, her companion in the 1980s. "That's what gave her the strength to witness the atrocities she had to witness."

Margaret Annette Wilson was born on January 30, 1951, in Gisborne, New Zealand. Her mother, Nona (Cammock) Wilson, was a housewife who later worked in a factory; her father, Raymond, was a bricklayer and plasterer.

An avid skydiver who would jump from planes when the weather was fine, young Margaret renamed herself after a series of de Havilland Moth light aircraft powered by Gipsy engines. She obtained her skydiving D license and often used a customized square black parachute, logging more than eight hundred jumps.

While studying photography at the University of Canterbury's School of Fine Arts in Christchurch, she took a course on moving images and became interested in film.

She considered her gender a hindrance to securing many of the jobs she applied for but was ultimately thought to be one of the first woman television camera operators in Australasia.

She moved to the United States in 1979 and was hired by the media department of MD Anderson Cancer Center in Houston the next year. She also painted houses and interned at KPRC-TV before working at KHOU, a CBS affiliate, in 1984.

She was hired by the Dallas bureau of CNN in 1990. Around the same time, hundreds of staffers were being deployed to cover the Gulf War, and the International desk would often rotate in camera operators from other parts of the network.

Moth volunteered to capture the drive to push Saddam Hussein's army from Kuwait.

"CNN, then as now, sends on war zone assignments only the most levelheaded, trustworthy and savvy of staffers," said Eason Jordan, former chief news executive of the organization, in an email. At the end of the Gulf War, Moth returned overseas because, he said, she was the "best-qualified and most impressive prospect for the job."

Her assignment in Sarajevo, the capital of Bosnia and Herzegovina, began in the spring of 1992.

Moth filmed from atop the lead tank as US forces entered Kosovo in June 1999.

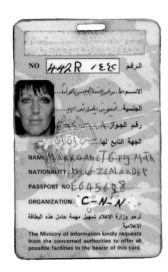

In her seventeen years with CNN, Moth covered conflicts all over the world.

When asked what she would do if she met the sniper who shot her, Moth said she would be interested to know his intentions.

"I would not feel any anger or anything because when you are in a war zone, both sides are fighting each other," she said in *Fearless,* the documentary. "If you're on one side, you're sort of 'with' that side, and you have to take what comes with it."

Moth learned she had colon cancer around 2006.

"I would have liked to have gone out with a bit more flair, but I feel like if I can die with dignity, then that's the main thing," she said in the documentary. "I don't think it matters how long you live, as long as you can say that 'I've gotten everything out of life.'"

She died on March 21, 2010, in Rochester, Minnesota. She was fifty-nine.

Throughout her career, Moth was known for being cynical, pragmatic almost to the point of cold-blooded, and devastatingly harsh toward anyone who showed signs of machismo.

But she earned a reputation for her unshakable sense of morality, rugged individualism, and single-minded focus. In 1992, Moth received the International Women's Media Foundation's Courage in Journalism Award, which recognizes women journalists who have demonstrated extraordinary courage in their careers.

"There's so much interest in her story," said Joe Duran, her lifetime friend and former colleague at CNN, in an interview. "I think her story will only grow."

Moth compared her own life to a game of tennis.

"You have no choice over how that ball comes to you," she said in the documentary. "But it's how you hit it back that counts."

---

**NATALIE SCHACHAR** is a former editor for the Associated Press and was based in Mexico City. Like Margaret, she dislikes business attire and machismo.

# The Evolution of Obituaries

---

## BY AMISHA PADNANI

On Thursday, September 18, 1851, the very first edition of *The New York Times*—then *The New-York Daily Times*—hit newsstands for a price of one cent per copy. The front page displayed news from various parts of Europe. On page four, the last page, and under the simple all-caps headline "DIED" was a brief announcement about the death of Seth E. Sill, a Supreme Court justice, who was 42.

Obituaries, as we know them today, existed long before the *Times* began publishing them. Some historians surmise the first obituaries went as far back as ancient Rome, around 59 BCE, and that they were written on papyrus. Eventually, the *Times*'s first obits felt more like a society page, cramming dozens of brief obits of local people in the community onto a black-and-white page—with no photos. Gradually, the *Times* began limiting obituaries to notable people around the world and devoting more column space to each article, so they read less like a bland notice and more like a distillation of the essence of a person's life.

Today, obits have become their own art form, written "with the touch of an artist rather than a bookkeeper, so that the rays of a subject's personality would shine through," as Clifton Daniel, the *Times*'s former managing editor, said in former *Times* editor Arthur Gelb's book *City Room.* Social mores have also begun to shape obits. People with disabilities now choose how they prefer to be identified, for instance, and we will always use a person's choice of pronoun. Just as society keeps evolving, so too will obituaries.

# Paddling Their Own Canoes

---

The following history makers started out looking to achieve a personal goal and had no idea that they would be opening pathways for others. Here you'll read about people who were often the first to do something, or who broke records against all odds. Today, their stories inspire others to follow in their footsteps.

Major Taylor in 1898. He traveled the globe, becoming known as the "Black Cyclone."

## World-Champion Bicyclist

# Major Taylor

## 1878–1932

BY RANDAL C. ARCHIBOLD

MORE THAN ONE HUNDRED YEARS AGO, one of the most popular spectator sports in the world was bicycle racing, and one of the most popular racers was a squat, strapping man with bulging thighs named Major Taylor.

He set records in his teens and was a world champion at twenty. He traveled the globe, racing as far away as Australia, and amassed wealth among the greatest of any athlete of his time. Thousands of people flocked to see him; newspapers fawned over him.

Major Taylor was the "Black Cyclone," at once the LeBron James and Jackie Robinson of his time. He blew past racial barriers in an overwhelmingly white field bent on stopping him, sometimes violently.

He was the first African American world champion in cycling and the second Black athlete to win a world championship in any sport.

So consider this: he died penniless in 1932, at age fifty-three, and was buried in a pauper's grave.

The head-spinning arc of Taylor's life is a story too seldom told. He endured racial hostility—including a brutal beating at a race and more than one episode of sabotage on the course—yet he persevered and professed to bear no animosity.

"Life is too short for a man to hold bitterness in his heart," he wrote in his self-published 1928 autobiography,

*The Fastest Bicycle Rider in the World: The Story of a Colored Boy's Indomitable Courage and Success Against Great Odds.*

He lived a life of triumph and tragedy seemingly made for Hollywood, yet by the end of his life he could barely sell copies of his book.

"To imagine what he went through in the 1890s is unimaginable," Edwin Moses, an Olympic gold medalist in track and the honorary chairman of the Major Taylor Association, said in a telephone interview. "I could not imagine competing and being a winner with what he put up with."

Major Taylor was not actually a major.

Marshall Walter Taylor was born in Indianapolis on November 26, 1878, one of eight children of Gilbert and Saphronia (Kelter) Taylor. He acquired his nickname as a boy doing bicycle tricks outside a cycle shop while dressed in a military uniform to attract customers.

The shop's owner, Tom Hay, entered Taylor in his first race, a ten-miler, and he won by six seconds. He was thirteen.

But despite his victories and his jaw-dropping times, Taylor was not allowed to join cycling clubs in Indiana and was barred from tracks. So a savvy racing manager and bicycle manufacturer named Louis Munger, known as Birdie, persuaded him to move to Worcester, Massachusetts.

Taylor at the start of a race in 1907. He endured racial hostility yet persevered.

"I was in Worcester only a very short time before I realized that there was no such race prejudice existing among the bicycle riders there as I had experienced in Indianapolis," Taylor wrote in his autobiography.

In 1896, Munger entered Taylor in a grueling six-day race at Madison Square Garden (a television commercial for Hennessy cognac, released in 2018, celebrates his performance in that race). It crushed him physically but catapulted him, just after his eighteenth birthday, into the world of professional cycling.

"He had to be terrified," said Karen Brown-Donovan, his great-granddaughter, in an email, adding, "especially since he was the only person of color on the track.

"The fact that he lasted for the duration of the six-day race was astonishing," she said.

In 1899, he shocked the world by winning the one-mile sprint at the world championship in track cycling, the second Black athlete, after the Canadian bantamweight boxer George Dixon, to win a world title in a recognized sport.

But for all his newfound celebrity, racism still held him back, even in Worcester.

When he moved into a new house, his neighbors at first tried to get him to relocate.

And with Jim Crow laws in full force, he wasn't spared on the track, either.

Ice water was thrown at him and nails were laid in the path of his bicycle by members of rival racing teams. Riders routinely jostled and elbowed him—and he still won.

Perhaps the worst incident, covered in *The New York Times,* was in September 1897. After a one-mile race in which Taylor placed second, the third-place finisher, William Becker, "wheeled up behind Taylor and grabbed him by the shoulder. The colored man was thrown to the ground, Becker choked him into a state of insensibility, and the police were obliged to interfere."

Becker accused Taylor of crowding him, something nobody else saw. He was later fined $50 but was allowed to continue racing.

The hotbed of cycling was Europe, but it took some time before Taylor would compete there. Many of the races were on Sundays, and Taylor, a devout Baptist since his mother's death in 1898, refused to race then—a conviction that inspired the Otis Taylor blues song "He Never Raced on Sunday."

Still, Taylor had become so famous that race organizers eventually moved events to weekdays to accommodate him. He was embraced in France and beat every European champion, further sealing his iconic status.

"Major Taylor had a proud and confident identity in Europe and was not a crushed or threatened black man," Andrew Ritchie wrote in his 1988 biography, *Major Taylor: The Extraordinary Career of a Champion Bicycle Racer.*

The *Times* marveled during a 1903 tour in Australia, "He has won many big prizes and is making money at a rapid rate."

Eventually, age and younger competitors caught up with Taylor. He retired in 1910, then struggled to capitalize on his success. Interest in cycling was fading as the automobile captivated the public. He made bad investments—including the self-published autobiography—and his savings were further devastated by the 1929 stock market crash, all but erasing his fortune. His health declined and his marriage, to Daisy Victoria Morris in 1902, fell apart.

"Once he was done as a sports person his opportunities dried up," said Todd Balf, author of *Major: A Black Athlete, a White Era, and the Fight to Be the World's Fastest Human Being,* published in 2008. "I can only imagine the stress and strain of trying to make a go of it."

He moved to Chicago, rented a room at a YMCA, and tried going door-to-door to sell the book, "but there was no second chance after he retired from racing," Ritchie said.

He died on June 21, 1932, alone and largely forgotten, his body unclaimed in the morgue. There was a short obituary in the African American newspaper *The Chicago Defender.*

"This was a tragic event for someone who had received so much acclaim during his lifetime," said Brown-Donovan, his great-granddaughter. Her grandmother Sydney Taylor Brown (named for the city she was born in) was his only child.

"My grandmother always hated that he died this way," she said. "She didn't know he was so ill."

Before he left for Chicago, Taylor gave his daughter "every tangible memory of his cycling career—his journals, scrapbooks, photos, trophies, medals, letters, etc.," Brown-Donovan continued. "This is why my grandmother became a fierce protector of his legacy for the rest of her own life. People know about Major Taylor today because of Sydney Taylor Brown."

Cycling today remains a predominantly white sport, though a number of athletes have come to know and be inspired by Taylor's story and several cycling clubs have adopted his name.

Still, "at the pro level, there has never been anybody who walked in his shoes," Balf said.

Taylor's body was in a pauper's grave for years in Mount Glenwood Memory Gardens, near Chicago. In 1948, a group of former racing stars had him reburied, with financial assistance from Frank Schwinn of the Schwinn Bicycle Company, in the cemetery's Garden of the Good Shepherd. There is now a memorial outside the Worcester Public Library as well.

The plaque on his grave reads:

*Worlds champion bicycle racer*
*who came up the hard way*
*without hatred in his heart*
*an honest, courageous and God*
*fearing, clean living gentle-*
*manly athlete. A credit to his*
*race who always gave out his*
*best gone but not forgotten*

———

**RANDAL C. ARCHIBOLD** is the sports editor of *The New York Times.* He thinks of Major Taylor every time he rides but still doesn't cycle like him.

# Bette Nesmith Graham

## 1924–1980

BY ANDREW R. CHOW

BETTE NESMITH GRAHAM didn't tell anyone about the first few bottles of her whitish concoction. She had mixed it in her kitchen blender and poured it into nail polish containers, then hid it in her desk, furtively applying it only when needed to avoid the scrutiny of a disapproving boss.

In due time, her mix would be in virtually every office desk and supply cabinet around the world. The substance was Liquid Paper, the correction fluid that relieved secretaries and writers of all stripes from the pressure of perfection.

Graham later brought it to market and was soon leading an international business, based in Dallas, that produced twenty-five million bottles of Liquid Paper a year at its peak, with factories in Toronto and Brussels. She would sell the company for $47.5 million in 1979 and donate millions to charity—six months before she died at fifty-six.

But in 1954, Graham was a divorced single mother supporting herself and her son from paycheck to paycheck, earning $300 a month (about $2,800 in today's money) as a secretary for a Texas bank. She was a bad typist to boot. And then she was forced to use a new typewriter model that had sensitive key triggers and a carbon ribbon instead of one made of fabric. The typos piled up, and when she tried to use an eraser, carbon ink would smear all over the page.

Graham was also an artist who observed that painters covered up mistakes not by erasing their work, but by painting over it.

So she sneaked some fast-drying white tempera paint into work and concealed her typos with a watercolor brush. This was much faster and cleaner than an eraser, and barely noticeable on the page. Soon the other secretaries wanted their own supply, and she found herself staying up late, filling bottles in her kitchen.

Bette Clair McMurray was born in Dallas on March 23, 1924. Her mother, Christine Duval, was an artist and a businesswoman who opened her own knitting store and taught Bette oil painting. Her father, Jesse McMurray, worked at an automotive parts store.

Bette was passionate about painting and sculpting, if not particularly skilled. "When I found out that talent wouldn't support me, then I realized that I would have to give that up," she said in an interview for the Business Archives Project at the University of North Texas in 1980.

She left school at seventeen to become a secretary and married her high school sweetheart, Warren Nesmith, two years later. When Nesmith went off to fight in World War II, Bette was pregnant with a boy. The son, Michael

Graham with her son, Michael, who later achieved success as a musician, actor, writer, and member of The Monkees.

Nesmith, would find fame as a member of the rock band The Monkees.

The marriage ended in divorce shortly after Warren returned, in 1946.

Graham—the name she took after a subsequent marriage—struggled to make ends meet, taking on side jobs like painting lettering on bank windows, designing letterheads, and modeling furs.

"She would often burst into tears of panic," Michael Nesmith wrote in his autobiography, *Infinite Tuesday: An Autobiographical Riff* (2017).

Graham's invention of correction fluid gave her a glimpse of a potential way out of her troubles, and she tried to form a business, calling it the Mistake Out Company, but could not afford the $400 patent fee. She moved forward anyway, poring over books in the public library to study formulas for tempera paint and working with a chemistry teacher to improve the consistency of her product.

"Our lab is working on a faster drying solution," Graham wrote to one customer (the "lab" being her kitchen and her blender).

Every evening she returned home from work to tinker with the formula, write letters to potential buyers, and send samples.

"During that time, I often became discouraged," she told the magazine *Texas Woman* in 1979. "I wanted the product to be absolutely perfect before I distributed it, and it seemed to take so long for that to happen."

She solicited wholesalers and traveled from Dallas to San Antonio and Houston on weekends to market her product.

Her first employees were her teenage son and his friends. For a dollar an hour, they worked out of her garage, using plastic ketchup bottles with funnel-like spouts to squeeze the substance into small nail polish bottles, applying labels by hand, and cutting the tips of the brushes inside the caps at an angle.

Graham became so devoted to her venture that she accidentally signed a letter at her job with the notation "The Mistake Out Company." She was promptly fired, giving her a chance to become a full-time small-business owner in 1958. That year she applied for a patent and changed the name to the Liquid Paper Company.

Graham's product began to catch on. She was written about in an office supply magazine, had a meeting with IBM, and received a large order from General Electric.

Each new breakthrough required more employees and more space. She moved her operation from her kitchen to a trailer, then to a four-room house, and finally to a shiny new headquarters in downtown Dallas. In 1968, she opened an automated plant. By 1975, Liquid Paper was producing twenty-five million bottles a year and holding a vast share of a multimillion-dollar market that had spawned several competitors, like Wite-Out.

Bette Graham was now wealthy, with fabulous jewelry and a Rolls-Royce. She established two foundations, the Gihon Foundation, which gave grants and financial support to promote women in the arts, and the Bette Clair McMurray Foundation, which did the same for women in business.

But her wealth and influence came with setbacks. In 1962, Graham married a frozen-food salesman, Robert Graham, who took an increasingly active role in the company, including a seat on the board. In 1975, they went through an acrimonious divorce.

The bitterness remained, and Robert Graham maneuvered to have the company bar her from making any corporate decisions.

"They wouldn't let me come on the premises or let anyone there have anything to do with me," Bette Graham said. To add insult to injury, they tried to change the very formula for Liquid Paper, thus removing her right to royalties from it.

Amid the power struggle, and despite declining health, Graham managed to wrest back control of the company and engineer its sale to Gillette for $47.5 million in 1979 in a deal that restored her royalties. She died on May 12, 1980, of complications of a stroke.

She left her fortune to her son, who took over her foundations and continued to dole out money to striving women.

"Most men are ignorant—they don't really understand," she said in an interview with the Business Archives Project in 1977. "And so women have to just keep on with their determination and be relentless. We have to not relent."

---

**ANDREW R. CHOW** is a correspondent for *Time* magazine. In the sixth grade, he made an enemy by spilling Wite-Out all over another student's desk.

A 1971 advertisement for Liquid Paper in *Glamour* magazine.

## Doctor Who Was "Different from Others"

# Dr. Margaret "Mom" Chung

## 1889–1959

BY NINA CHHITA

MARGARET CHUNG KNEW FROM AGE TEN that she wanted to become a medical missionary to China. Her mother had been placed in a mission home as a young child after she immigrated from China to the United States and had flourished there. She named Margaret after the home's superintendent and told her daughter stories of her life in the home.

Religion was an important part of young Margaret's life. She was raised in a Presbyterian household, where her father insisted that the family pray before every meal, even a snack, and sang hymns with the children before bed.

So it was a blow when she graduated from medical school in 1916 and her application to be a medical missionary was rejected three times by the administrative boards. Though she had been born on United States soil, she was regarded as Chinese, and no funding for Chinese missionaries existed.

Still, following that dream led her to a different accolade: she became the first known American woman of Chinese ancestry to earn a medical degree.

She opened a private practice in San Francisco's Chinatown. It was one of the few places that would provide Western medical care to Chinese patients, who were often scapegoated as the source of epidemics and turned away by hospitals. (Her own father died after he was denied treatment for injuries he sustained in a car accident.)

As a physician and surgeon during the Second Sino-Japanese War and World War II, she was regarded highly for her patriotic duties, founding a network for pilots, high-ranking military officials, celebrities, and politicians that she leveraged to recruit pilots and lobby for the women's naval reserve.

Every Sunday she hosted dinners for men in the military, feeding crowds of up to three hundred people who called her "Mom." Her efforts grabbed the attention of the press: she represented unity between China and the US, allies in the war; one headline, in *The Gustine Standard*, read, "Dr. Chung Proves East and West Can Meet."

Margaret Jessie Chung was born on October 2, 1889, in Santa Barbara, California. At the time, the 1882 Chinese Exclusion Act was in full force. Her parents, who had emigrated from China in the 1870s, were barred from obtaining US citizenship under the act. They faced limited job opportunities, so the family moved around California as they looked for work. Her father, Chung Wong, was a former merchant who toiled on California farms and sold vegetables. Her mother, Ah Yane, also worked on farms and sometimes as a court interpreter.

Margaret Chung was the first known American woman of Chinese ancestry to earn a medical degree.

In medical school, Chung reinvented herself as "Mike" and dressed in a blazer and tie.

Margaret herself was no stranger to hard labor. She took on farming duties when her parents were unwell and helped raise all ten of her siblings. Her duties at home disrupted her schooling, and she did not complete the eighth grade until she was seventeen. To secure the rest of her education, she spent summer evenings knocking on doors to sell copies of the *Los Angeles Times* as part of a competition for a scholarship. That scholarship funded preparatory school, which enabled her to gain acceptance to the University of Southern California College of Physicians and Surgeons in 1911.

"As the only Chinese girl in the USC medical school, I am compelled to be different from others," she said in a 1913 interview with the journalist Estelle Lawton Lindsey. She reinvented herself as "Mike," slicking back her black hair and dressing in a long blazer draped over a shirt and tie, completing the outfit with a floor-length skirt. Between classes, she shot craps with the guys, hoping to win a couple of cents. Her crude one-liners in conversations left the other students roaring with laughter. She worked throughout college and could be found scrubbing dishes at a restaurant while simultaneously studying medical textbooks propped up on a shelf.

After she graduated and was rejected as a medical missionary, she turned to surgery, performing trauma operations at Santa Fe Railroad Hospital. She was at her best operating under intense pressure, a handy skill for the long days of emergency work. Touring musicians and actors also used the hospital; most famously, she removed the actress Mary Pickford's tonsils. Chung established her own private practice, and her dedicated patient following included actors from the early Hollywood industry.

While accompanying two patients to San Francisco, Chung fell in love with the city's landscape. With its dramatic hills cloaked in fog, it looked nothing like Los Angeles. After learning that no doctor practiced Western medicine in the city's Chinatown, home to the largest Chinese American population in the country, she left her Los Angeles practice and set up a clinic on Sacramento Street in 1922.

San Francisco was isolating. People from the community invited Chung out, but she declined, writing in her unpublished autobiography, "I was embarrassed because I couldn't understand their flowery Chinese." Rumors persisted that because she was single, she must have been interested in women. She was protective of her personal life, but her biographer, Judy Tzu-Chun Wu, said that Chung frequented a North Beach speakeasy with Elsa Gidlow, who openly wrote lesbian poetry, and that she likely had a relationship with the actress Sophie Tucker.

Chung's practice initially had difficulty attracting patients. But as word spread, her waiting room filled up with people seeking treatment, including white tourists curious to see her Chinese-inspired furniture and her consultation room, whose walls were plastered with pictures of her celebrity patients.

Years of planning and community fundraising culminated in the opening of San Francisco's Chinese Hospital in 1925. Chung was selected as one of four department heads and led the gynecology, obstetrics, and pediatrics unit while still running her private practice.

Chung earned the nickname "Mom" after hosting dinners for hundreds of
military men during World War II.

When Japan invaded the Chinese province of Manchuria in 1931, an ensign in the United States Naval Reserves looking to support the Chinese military visited Chung at her practice. She invited the man and six of his friends for a home-cooked dinner. It was the first of many that she would host almost every night for months. It was, she wrote in her autobiography, "the most selfish thing [she'd] ever done because it was more fun than [she] had ever known in all [her] life."

The pilots thought of her as an adoptive mother, but, as one of them pointed out, she had no father for them. "Well," she quipped back, "that makes you a lot of fair-headed bastards, doesn't it?"

Every Sunday, "Mom" personally catered suppers for hundreds of her boys. By the end of World War II, her family had swelled to around 1,500. To help keep track, everyone had a number and group: leading pilots were the Phi Beta Kappa of Aviation, those who did not fly (including celebrities and politicians) were Kiwis, and the submarine units were Golden Dolphins.

The movers and shakers of America packed into her home, and with them, influence. She called upon her network to secretly recruit pilots for the American Flying Tigers, an American volunteer group that pushed back against Japan's invasion of China. She also enlisted two of her Kiwis to introduce a bill in the House and Senate that led to the creation of Women Accepted for Volunteer Emergency Service in 1942. Eager to support her country, she wrote asking to join WAVES in whatever capacity, but her application was rejected.

Despite her efforts, no official recognition of her contributions ever came. After the war ended, attendance at her Sunday dinners dwindled. Nevertheless, her schedule brimmed with practicing medicine, visiting her military sons, and writing her memoir.

She died of ovarian cancer on January 5, 1959. She was sixty-nine.

———

**NINA CHHITA** is the creator of the Instagram account @nina.draws.scientists, where she chronicles the contributions of women in science. She successfully attempted Dr. Chung's stuffing recipe from 1931, though she had to cut down the serving size.

Miki Gorman in 1976 after finishing first among women in the New York City Marathon.

# Miki Gorman

## 1935–2015

---

BY AMISHA PADNANI

MIKI GORMAN WAS SITTING ALONE at a corner table of a Magic Pan restaurant in Manhattan on October 23, 1976, when her food arrived: not one but two large crepes stuffed with mushroom and spinach soufflé.

A couple sitting nearby gawked at her. Gorman, at five feet tall or so, weighed only ninety pounds, and the plates of food covered her table.

"I'm running the New York City Marathon tomorrow!" she told them. "And I'm going to win."

And so she did, the first woman to cross the finish line the next day. Even more, she won again the following year. No other American woman would take the title for the next four decades.

"We've gone so long without winning, I can't believe it," Gorman told *The Washington Post* in 2004, long after her retirement in 1982. "My win was a lifetime ago."

In 2017, Shalane Flanagan finally ended the drought, crying, cursing, and pumping her fist as she broke the finish line tape at 2:26:53. It was no small feat; by then the New York City Marathon had become the world's largest race, with more than fifty thousand participants.

Gorman was not around to see Flanagan's victory; she died on September 19, 2015, at eighty, in Bellingham, Washington. The cause was metastasized lung cancer, her daughter, Danielle Nagel, said.

Despite Gorman's accomplishments, news of her death was not widely reported. Had it been, readers would have learned of record-breaking achievements that landed her in several halls of fame. One feat, in 1978, was a world best for a woman in the half marathon, at 1:15:58. She also won the Boston Marathon in the women's category in 1974 and 1977, the latter victory coming, remarkably, the same year that she won in New York. She is the only woman known to have won both races twice.

"She ran everything, from track races and really quick stuff all the way to these hundred-mile races," said George Hirsch, chairman of New York Road Runners, a nonprofit running group that organizes the marathon. "There's no one that I know of to this day who has that kind of a range and excelled in them all."

Her success followed a life of hardship.

Gorman was born Michiko Suwa on August 9, 1935, to Japanese parents in occupied China, where her father was working for Japan's imperial army. They later moved to Tokyo; after World War II, she helped care for her younger twin brothers there.

"My father returned from the military looking like a skeleton," she wrote in a first-person account for *The New York Times* in 2005. "Well, we all looked like skeletons. We were always hungry."

Gorman ahead of the 1974 Boston Marathon.
She went on to win in the women's division.

In the 1960s, she met and married Michael Gorman, a stockbroker from Cleveland. Miki Gorman worked as a secretary during her running years and afterward, retiring in 1994. She and her husband separated in 1982.

Not long after their marriage, she confided in him that she felt insecure about her looks. "I was embarrassed that I was so small," she told *Runner's World* magazine in 2010.

Her husband suggested that she accompany him to an athletic club, thinking that if she exercised she would be hungrier and would eat more and put on weight. Though she didn't gain weight, she returned to the club regularly to run along an indoor track.

The club offered a prize for the member who ran the most miles for a month, and in October 1968 Gorman set her sights on winning. "I got a huge trophy," she told *The New York Times* in 2010. Another competition included a hundred-mile race that would involve running 1,075 laps on the track. She began training. "The first year I stopped at eighty-six miles," she said. "I cried." She returned the next year and finished all one hundred miles, then competed in the race again the next three years.

Gorman started running in cross-country races and found that she could win easily. Once she began passing taller and younger women, she realized that her height and weight were not disadvantages.

"I gained so much confidence from my running," she said. "I finally realized that being small didn't have to hold me back."

Laszlo Tabori, the celebrated Hungarian coach who was then based in Los Angeles (he died in 2018), took notice of her wins and began training her.

By the time Gorman signed up for the New York City Marathon in 1975—five years after its inception—she was an unlikely candidate to win. She was already forty, considered old for an elite runner, and had given birth to a daughter, her only child, at the start of the year.

But while most runners train to build up to the 26.2-mile distance, Gorman had been running hundred-mile distances. She wound up finishing second among women, behind Kim Merritt.

Their diet, she wrote, had consisted of soybeans that had been soaked for a couple of days, along with a little rice.

She was twenty-eight when an American army officer stationed in Japan offered her a job in the United States as a nanny. He brought her to Pennsylvania, where she worked long hours doing chores for his family.

A few years later she answered an ad from California seeking a secretary who could speak both Japanese and English. She got the job and moved to Los Angeles. There she earned $300 a month (about $2,400 in today's money), sending some of her pay home to her mother in Japan.

The next year was the first time the marathon course would traverse all five boroughs of New York City, having until then been confined to loops through Central Park. Some 2,090 runners lined up at the start on Staten Island, by the Verrazzano-Narrows Bridge. Only eighty-eight of them were women.

Gorman quickly lost sight of Merritt ahead of her. Still, she zipped along the course, dodging obstacles, according to the book *First Ladies of Running* (2016) by Amby Burfoot.

Few roadside barriers protected the route in those days, and at one point a St. Bernard dog bounded right up to her. ("He was almost as tall as I was," Gorman said.) Then there was the metal grating, now covered, on the Queensboro Bridge. ("My toes felt like they were on fire.") The wind blowing against the runners was no help, either. ("I tucked behind the bigger runners whenever I could.")

But then she caught sight of Merritt and zeroed in on her. As they entered the hills of Central Park, the final stretch of the race, she rolled past Merritt, barely giving her a glance, and kept her pace all the way to the end. Her time was 2:39:11, a course record for women.

A surprise awaited at the finish: the couple from the night before at the Magic Pan restaurant had come to watch the race.

"She was happy to see them," her daughter said. "And the couple was shocked that this little Japanese woman actually won."

Just as she said she would.

By the time Gorman signed up for the New York City Marathon in 1975, she was forty and a mother.

---

**AMISHA PADNANI** is a journalist and an avid runner. She has completed the New York City Marathon four times and agrees that the Queensboro Bridge was one of the biggest challenges.

Gil Cuadros in 1993. In his era, to be Chicano and gay seemed an impossible existence.

## Chicano Writer and AIDS Activist

# Gil Cuadros

## 1962–1996

BY ROSA BOSHIER

THE AUTHOR GIL CUADROS had his creative awakening at the age of seventeen, when he and a friend, the photographer Laura Aguilar, pored over art and erotica at Chatterton's Bookshop in Pasadena, California.

"The bookstore we went to was like a country," he wrote in 1992 in *LA Weekly,* "and we wanted to emigrate."

Cuadros had grown up in Montebello, California, where to be Chicano and gay seemed like an impossible existence. "We never said 'gay' or 'lesbian,'" Cuadros wrote in *LA Weekly,* "we used 'attraction,' 'tendencies,' 'desires.'" In his book, *City of God,* a collection of short stories and poems published by City Lights Publishers in 1994, Cuadros treated these desires as holy. Weaving together memoir, fiction, and poetry, the book affirms and complicates Chicano and queer identity, and challenges the stigma of AIDS.

Though *City of God* has gained a cult following, it remains unknown to a broader audience. The artist Luis Alfaro described the book in *LA Weekly* as "both a celebration and a memorial—a beautifully devastating blow-by-blow account of life before and after diagnosis."

Cuadros came of age in the 1970s, during the height of the Chicano movement. He started writing in the late eighties, when Los Angeles was in a stage of molting— the English-only movement, which protected English as the unifying language in the United States, attacked bilingual education, and the city's rapid gentrification further segregated communities of color. It was also at this time that AIDS activists took to the streets to demand access to health care.

Cuadros heralded the intersections of his identities, but he was also wary. He addressed this tension in his short story "My Aztlán: White Place," in which he describes West Hollywood white men who "ask where [he's] from, disappointed at [his] answer, as if *they* are the natives."

"Gil's career was about confronting the reality that he was facing," Rafael Perez-Torres, an English professor at the University of California, Los Angeles, said in an interview, "and reflecting his conflicting feelings about how and who he belonged to in this world."

Gil David Cuadros was born on July 22, 1962, in Montebello. His father, Daniel Cuadros, worked at an Anheuser-Busch bottling plant in east Los Angeles County; his mother was a homemaker. Gil attended Schurr High School and East Los Angeles College, where he discovered authors who addressed queer themes, like Jean Genet and Tennessee Williams. At twenty-one, Cuadros came out to his mother, at whose hands he suffered cigarette burns and mouth-bleeding blows. She

Cuadros in 1983, the year he moved to Pasadena with his partner, John Edward Milosch.

kicked him out of the house. Both displacement and the desire for family acceptance color *City of God*. In Cuadros's short story "Reynaldo," a young gay man discovers letters that his grandmother wrote to her late husband's male lover to make amends after a long estrangement.

In 1983, Cuadros moved to Pasadena with his partner, John Edward Milosch, and attended Pasadena City College. Tragedy followed this newfound freedom; Milosch's health deteriorated from AIDS, and he died in 1987. Cuadros learned he had AIDS the next year. Doctors gave him six months to live. He was twenty-five.

Cuadros grew more serious about writing while taking Terry Wolverton's class at the Los Angeles Gay and Lesbian Center. He found community amid fellow students, all men living with HIV, who shared information about medical treatments and social services. Cuadros credited the class with giving him purpose and extending his life. He lived to be thirty-four.

"Nobody really expected to survive," Wolverton said of Cuadros and other students in a phone interview. "They took beautiful risks."

Cuadros also critiqued the health care system. He wrote about moving to Hollywood to be closer to doctors, the food bank, housing, and legal aid. He clawed through complex bureaucracy to nurse his new partner, Marcus A. Wagoner, as he himself diminished. In the poem "Conquering Immortality," Cuadros writes, "before the time of lovers' funerals / and we only used first names on their quilts"—a heartbreaking acknowledgment of the daily death toll from AIDS, and the government's insufficient response.

"You couldn't have AIDS and not be involved in AIDS activism," Wolverton said. "Anything you had to fight for, a bus pass or a housing voucher, was advocacy."

Cuadros worked with VIVA, a queer Latinx arts and advocacy group. He fought for representation alongside writers like Wanda Coleman, who included him in a special edition of *High Performance* magazine that featured Los Angeles writers responding to the 1992 Rodney King verdict.

"Gil's activism is embedded in his writing," Kevin Martin, the executor of Cuadros's estate, said in an interview. "He was angry at his life being torn apart."

In 1991, Cuadros received the Brody Literature Fellowship and two grants from the City of Los Angeles Department of Cultural Affairs. He earned a PEN American Center grant for writers with AIDS. His work was featured in the anthologies *His: Brilliant New Fiction by Gay Writers* (1995), *Blood Whispers: LA Writers on AIDS* (1991), and *Grand Passion: The Poets of Los Angeles and Beyond* (1995). Cuadros's poem "There Are Places You Don't Walk at Night, Alone" was adapted into a 1994 public service announcement on hate crimes for MTV.

Cuadros named his collection *City of God* for a scene from Federico Fellini's 1963 film *8½*, in which a cardinal delineates anything outside of the city of God as unholy.

By accepting Los Angeles in all of its contradictions, "the poverty and the richness," as he once described it, Cuadros authentically portrayed the city as a splintered mirror, a maze of stories.

"He was dedicated to the idea of truth," Perez-Torres said in a phone interview, "as hollow and glorious as that sounds." But it was precisely the hollow and the glorious that fascinated Cuadros, the way that Los Angeles, the body in pain, or one's sexuality can be a thing of beauty and site of grief. By confronting these contradictions of being alive, Cuadros allowed readers to contend with their own multifaceted identities.

Cuadros died on August 29, 1996, six months after Wagoner.

"Gil wrecked himself trying to find someone who could care for Marcus," Wolverton said, "and in the end they both succumbed."

Cuadros ends his article "The Emigrants" with an anecdote about confronting a born-again Christian at a gay pride parade. "I told him I had AIDS, like it was a weapon," Cuadros wrote, "that I wasn't ashamed of the

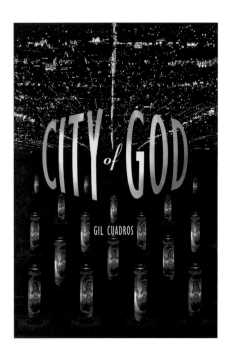

*City of God* (1994) is a collection of poems and short stories that gained a cult following.

illness." However, he is soon swept up by celebration: "Laura and I waved to friends along the route, tossing confetti, dancing together to the music we claimed as common heritage of our family."

———

**ROSA BOSHIER** is a freelance writer and educator. Originally from Los Angeles, she now reads and writes from the sweltering heat of Houston, Texas.

## Mountain Climber Who Defied Tradition

# Alison Hargreaves

## 1962–1995

BY MAYA SALAM

WHEN ALISON HARGREAVES reached the peak of Mount Everest on May 13, 1995, she sent a radio message to her son and daughter: "To Tom and Kate, my dear children, I am on the highest point of the world, and I love you dearly."

With that triumph, she became the first woman in history to conquer the Earth's apex—29,032 feet high—alone and without bottled oxygen. Hargreaves, one of the world's greatest alpinists then and of all time, also did without the fixed ropes set by others on that Himalayan climb. Only the Italian mountaineer Reinhold Messner had ascended Everest in a similar manner before.

Her homeland, Britain—stoked by a front-page headline in *The Times* of London that read, "One of the Greatest Climbs in History"—rejoiced.

"The rest of Fleet Street followed, keeping the story in the air" until her return, her daughter, Kate Ballard, said.

The celebrations were "just unbelievable," Hargreaves recalled in what is thought to be her last interview. "These guys were leaping all over me and the trolley, trying to take pictures," she said of the photographers who awaited her at Heathrow Airport in London. "It was just frantic."

But the excitement did not last long. Exactly three months after Everest, in the late afternoon of August 13, Hargreaves reached the summit of K2 in Pakistan, the world's second-highest peak. Just hours later, she and five others died when they were engulfed by a storm with fierce winds that rose up the mountain. She was thirty-three.

After her death, a backlash—fueled by a media frenzy around her death—began to mount. Some called her selfish and criticized the choice to leave behind young children to put herself in harm's way. Similar denunciations were not leveled so harshly against the fathers who died on the mountain alongside her.

"The media wheeled out the psychologists who asked why I didn't break down," Hargreaves's husband, James Ballard, said in a 2002 interview with *The Guardian*. "The next stage was everyone saying she shouldn't have left the children."

Those who criticized Hargreaves were "wrong and incredibly shortsighted," her daughter said. "Twenty years later with more equality and thinner glass ceilings, would they have written the same? No."

In the 2002 interview, James Ballard expressed disappointment in how women and mothers are judged for succeeding in their careers, particularly dangerous ones. "How could I have stopped her?" he said of his wife. "I loved Alison because she wanted to climb the highest peak her skills would allow her to. That's who she was.

"I just hope that there was a point to Alison's death and that, in the long term, what she achieved will help shift attitudes," he said.

Some would say she did just that. Hargreaves was a "trailblazer," Molly Schiot, who profiled Hargreaves in her 2016 book, *Game Changers: The Unsung Heroines of Sports History*, told the online magazine *Ozy* last year.

Her courageous Everest climb helped in "breaking down social constructs of what it means to be a mom," Schiot said.

On July 28, 2017, the mountaineer Vanessa O'Brien conquered K2, becoming the first American woman to do so. (She also holds a British passport.) And at fifty-two, O'Brien was also the oldest woman to reach the peak.

Two days later, on July 30, she paid tribute to Hargreaves in a Twitter post. "I respect & acknowledge Julie Tullis (1986) & Alison Hargreaves (1995) who lost their lives on descent of #K2—I thought of them often #RIP," she wrote. Tullis, a British climber, died during a storm while descending K2.

In her final interview, Hargreaves, who began rock climbing at thirteen, said that Everest was "always at the back of [her] mind."

"It was never, ever at the front of it," she continued. But that changed when she started considering the prospect of taking it on alone: "I'd started to do a lot of solo climbing and then thought it would be great to try and do Everest totally independently, totally under my own steam, without oxygen."

Everest was not her only record. In the summer of 1993, Hargreaves became the first person to climb the notoriously perilous six great north faces of the Alps solo in a single season. The undertaking inspired her book, *A Hard Day's Summer*.

In 2015, her son, Tom Ballard, who was six years old when she died, became the first person to climb the north faces alone in a winter season. (He died in 2019 while climbing Nanga Parbat in Kashmir.) Her daughter is also a mountaineer.

In a way, Tom's first Alps ascent was with his mother. In July 1988, Hargreaves scaled the treacherous north

Hargreaves with her children, Kate and Tom, in May 1995, three months before her death.

face of Eiger while six months pregnant with him. The trek was to commemorate the fiftieth anniversary of the first ascent of Eiger.

In her last interview, Hargreaves addressed the challenges and inequality female mountaineers faced. The interview was conducted on July 27, 1995, at K2's base camp by Matt Comeskey, a fellow climber who went on to survive the storm after turning back early. It was obtained by *The Independent* and published that September.

"I think women climb before they get married, before they have boyfriends and babies, then they lose interest," Hargreaves told Comeskey. "Having children is very fulfilling, and a lot of people don't feel the need for anything else.

"For me, that was a conscious decision," she said. "I actually wanted children, and I also wanted to carry on with the climbing."

When asked if a female climber needed to be tougher than a man, she said: "I think that women in general have to work harder in a man's world to achieve recognition."

She recalled an exchange in which she was diminished by a colleague. "I was at a climbing dinner once when a very well-known climber came up to me and said: 'Are you a roadie?'" she said. "For me, that was the worst thing he could have said.

"I've always had a chip on my shoulder, I'm sure," she added.

Alison Jane Hargreaves was born on February 17, 1962, in Derby, England. She was the second of three children of John Edward Hargreaves, a senior scientific officer at British Rail Derby, and Joyce Winifred Hargreaves.

At 28,251 feet, K2 in the Karakoram Range of Pakistan is just less than the height of Everest but is regarded as far more demanding and dangerous. Hargreaves was a member of an American expedition led by Rob Slater. Also on the mountain was a team from Spain and a New Zealand expedition led by Peter Edmund Hillary, son of Sir Edmund Hillary, the first man to conquer Everest.

Extreme weather sent most of the climbers back before reaching the top, including Hillary and some members of his team, like Comeskey. But Hargreaves and Slater teamed up with Bruce Grant and Jeff Lakes from the New Zealand group, and the Spaniards Javier Escartin, Javier Olivar, and Lorenzo Ortíz, for another try. It would prove fatal.

All but Lakes, who had turned back, reached the summit. Hargreaves did so without artificial oxygen. Lakes died from exposure on his descent.

Hargreaves had intended to attempt the third-highest peak in the world, Kanchenjunga in the Himalayas, next.

"If you are given two options, take the harder one because you'll regret it if you don't," Hargreaves said in her final interview. "At least if you take the harder one and fail, you'll have tried."

———

**MAYA SALAM** is a senior staff editor on the Culture desk of *The New York Times,* where she previously worked as a gender reporter and a breaking-news reporter. Salam is a lover of the outdoors, especially the mountains, and thinks of Hargreaves's grit and passion every time she sets out on an adventure.

# Regina Jonas

## 1902–1944

BY GABRIEL POPKIN

WHEN REGINA JONAS STUDIED at the Academy for the Science of Judaism, a seminary in Berlin, in the 1920s, every officially ordained rabbi the world had ever known had something in common: they were all men.

To be sure, women had held prominent roles in Judaism, including as scholars and teachers. The Talmud, the central text of Jewish law, mentions female sages. Osnat Barzani, a Kurdish Jewish scholar and teacher in the 1600s, took on roles traditionally reserved for men, as did various women in nineteenth- and early-twentieth-century America. A long line of Jewish women developed prayers and traditions.

But Jonas was unsatisfied with these options. She sought official rabbinical ordination, or *smicha,* which conferred the highest status in Judaism. She later explained: "God planted in our heart skills and a vocation without asking about gender. Therefore it is the duty of men and women alike to work and create according to the skills given by God."

In 1930, Jonas completed a thesis at the seminary that directly posed the question "Can women serve as rabbis?" Drawing on sources from Jewish law, or Halacha, she argued that the answer was yes—that only custom and tradition had limited *smicha* to men.

But bad luck then dealt her ambitions a cruel blow: The rabbi she studied under, who gave her thesis a grade of "good," died suddenly, before he could ordain her. Although Jonas had other prominent supporters, including Rabbi Leo Baeck, who later led a Nazi-era organization for German Jews, none would ordain her.

Finally, on December 27, 1935, the liberal rabbi Max Dienemann of Offenbach agreed to do it. He wrote, "She has passed the exam I have given her in religious legal topics," adding, "I testify to her that she is capable to answer questions of religious law (the Halacha), and that she is suitable to serve as a rabbi."

That statement shattered an almost two-thousand-year-old glass ceiling. It was "an earthshaking event," one observer said.

Even Baeck ultimately signed the German translation of her ordination letter.

Jonas began to teach in Berlin, but because no synagogue would employ her, she joined the Jewish Community of Berlin to minister to Jews in hospitals and old-age homes. She also found work in a women's prison.

Jonas sought not to reform or revolutionize Judaism, but rather to promote Jewish traditions and counter assimilationist trends that she felt were threatening the religion's survival.

"She made a radical point to be the first woman rabbi, but for conservative reasons," Elisa Klapheck, a rabbi

Regina Jonas in 1936, the year after she was officially ordained the world's first woman rabbi.

# "For me it was never about being the first. I wish I had been the hundred thousandth!"

who wrote *Fräulein Rabbiner Jonas: The Story of the First Woman Rabbi* (2004), said in an interview.

Former students of Jonas whom Klapheck interviewed recalled her "modern pedagogic" teaching style; she would, for instance, mount annual performances of a Hanukkah play she wrote, to bring Judaism alive. And she was renowned for her "oratorical skills" and "sonorous voice," Klapheck wrote.

Elizabeth Sarah, rabbi emerita of Brighton & Hove Progressive Synagogue in England, who has written about Jonas, described her as "a very strong, authoritative voice, very pious, very devoted, very, very serious."

But not all were thrilled; some found Jonas too strident or eccentric. And some male rabbis opposed granting her the pulpit in synagogues.

While Jonas's career was ascending, conditions for Jews in Germany were going downhill fast. The Nuremberg Laws, excluding Jews from German society, were passed the same year that Jonas received her ordination. As other rabbis fled, Jonas gained prominence, traveling to communities whose rabbis had left.

Jonas, too, was urged to leave Germany. But, she said, she could not abandon people who were suffering or leave her mother, with whom she lived. In the spring of 1939, she wrote in a rabbinical commentary in a Jewish newspaper that the Nazi persecution was a "trial by fire, testing the strength of our love for children, gratitude, the mutual support of family and friends in these alien conditions."

In early November 1942, Jonas and her mother were deported to the Theresienstadt concentration camp in Czechoslovakia. In her deportation file she identified herself as a *"rabbinerin,"* or female rabbi. The file also contained her thesis.

The documents made their way to an archive of German Jews, where they sat untouched for nearly fifty years, until unearthed by a German religion scholar, Katharina von Kellenbach, after the Berlin Wall fell.

The Nazis had established Theresienstadt as a model concentration camp to try to fool the outside world about how they were treating Jews. There Jonas worked for Viktor Frankl, a psychologist who later found worldwide fame with his autobiographical book *Man's Search for Meaning*. At the camp, Jonas greeted new arrivals by train, orienting them and trying to dissuade thoughts of suicide. Her rabbinical sermons urged prisoners to find meaning in their lives, even under dire circumstances. One moved Frankl so deeply that he recalled it nearly fifty years later when contacted by von Kellenbach.

"What I find most extraordinary about her," von Kellenbach said in an interview, "is that she decided to deny the Nazis the power to define Jewish life."

Jonas was deported to Auschwitz on October 12, 1944. It is believed that she was killed the day she arrived, on October 14. She was forty-two.

Several prominent male survivors, including Frankl and Baeck, could have told her story but didn't—a choice that has baffled scholars. A belated surge of interest in Jonas owes itself instead to von Kellenbach, who published an article about her in 1994, bringing her to the world's attention.

There is now a children's book, a documentary film, and an opera about Jonas. She is memorialized at Theresienstadt; at Yad Vashem, the memorial to Holocaust victims in Israel; and at the Jewish Museum in Berlin, among other places. Female rabbis worldwide now embrace her as the founder of their lineage.

"We really cannot help but stand in awe of her courage," said Sally Priesand, the second woman to be ordained a rabbi, at Hebrew Union College in Cincinnati in 1972. "All female rabbis stand on her shoulders."

Regina Sara Jonas was born in Berlin on August 3, 1902, and grew up in the Scheunenviertel, a poor and crowded district near Berlin's grand New Synagogue. Her father, Wolf, a businessman, died of tuberculosis when Regina was eleven, leaving her mother, Sara, to raise her and her brother, Abraham. Abraham also became a religious teacher; he and Regina often worked together.

During the period when Jonas was born, German Judaism was swept up in an extraordinary period of creative ferment. Germany in the 1800s gave birth to the Jewish enlightenment and the Reform and Modern Orthodox movements, both of which later became prominent in the United States. German Jews, while still barred from certain positions in German society, were far more integrated and emancipated than most of their European peers.

Jonas's thesis embraced this spirit of innovation within Jewish tradition, arguing not that Halacha needed reform to accommodate female rabbis, but rather that it already had room for them. It "remains one of the most comprehensive attempts ever to justify the female rabbinate on the basis of Halacha," Klapheck wrote.

Jonas believed that female rabbis shouldn't marry. But in 1939 she began a romantic relationship with Rabbi Joseph Norden of Hamburg, then a widower. Letters they exchanged suggest that they became engaged; they also show a more humorous and playful side of Jonas.

In recent decades, Jonas has been recognized as a trailblazer, though she herself chafed at that status. She told *Berna,* a Swiss women's newspaper: "For me it was never about being the first. I wish I had been the hundred thousandth!"

Still, her story poses a "what if": If the Nazis hadn't devastated European Jewry, would she have inspired a generation of female rabbis the world never got to know? Instead, it was another thirty-seven years before Priesand was ordained. That event, covered in *The New York Times* and elsewhere, opened a door, and the number of women stepping through it continues to grow.

Women now make up more than half of the students in many rabbinical schools in the United States and Britain, and occupy some of the most prominent positions in Reform, Reconstructionist, and Conservative Judaism. Several years ago, women started to be ordained as rabbis in the Modern Orthodox tradition as well.

"We can only ask the very important question: If the Holocaust hadn't happened, would we be dating the modern women's rabbinate from 1935?" Sarah said. "I'm sure we would."

———

**GABRIEL POPKIN** is a half-Jewish, half-German writer who contributes to *The New York Times* and *The Washington Post.* He became intrigued by Regina Jonas's remarkable story during an Arthur F. Burns Fellowship in Berlin.

George Braithwaite, shown in 1971, has been described as "the Magic Johnson of table tennis."

# George Braithwaite

## 1934–2020

BY ANDREW KEH

GEORGE BRAITHWAITE WAS STANDING on a railway bridge, nerves jangling. The year was 1971. He and his group, all fifteen members of the United States national table tennis team, stood in Hong Kong, then a British colony. Across the bridge from them was mainland China.

As classical music droned from the speakers arranged outside, the players picked up their luggage and strode across the bridge, becoming the first group of American citizens admitted into mainland China since the Communist government had taken over in 1949.

The moment marked the opening chapter of a geopolitical drama known as Ping-Pong diplomacy, a series of table tennis exhibitions that marked the end of China's decades-long isolation from much of the rest of the world. The first trip—an impromptu detour for the Americans after a tournament in Japan—was hastily arranged. The players, now accidental diplomats, were venturing anxiously into what felt like a hidden world.

These Ping-Pong pilgrims were a motley group: there was a college professor, a dental assistant, two high school girls, a self-proclaimed hippie, and Braithwaite, an immigrant from Guyana who worked at the United Nations.

In the decades after the group's trip to China, Braithwaite would become a ubiquitous character in American table tennis—a late bloomer who ascended to the top ranks of the sport in the country, a smiling presence in the freewheeling underground Ping-Pong world of New York—until he died on October 26, 2020, at eighty-six.

But Ping-Pong, any player will tell you, is not a big-time sport in America. So while Braithwaite, or "the Chief," as he was known, was a luminary in that world—the sort of person everyone knew, everyone had a story about—he was relatively unknown outside of it.

"If you didn't know the Chief, you weren't really playing Ping-Pong, you were not really part of the community," Wally Green, a friend and practice partner in New York, said in an interview. "I think everyone in the country who played knew the Chief."

George Hugh Braithwaite was born on April 15, 1934, in Georgetown, Guyana. A gifted athlete, he competed for the Guyanese track team at the 1958 Caribbean Games. His love affair with Ping-Pong began after his arrival in the US in the 1960s. Soon after finding a job as a clerk at the UN, he was introduced to the organization's modest table tennis club. He became a mainstay, spending his lunch hours with a paddle in his hands.

New York, his new home, was a colorful hotbed for the game, and he started playing relentlessly in clubs up and down Manhattan, across Queens, and out in Brooklyn,

Braithwaite in 1971 during the geopolitical drama that came to be known as "Ping-Pong Diplomacy."

honing the metronomic playing style that would become his calling card through his career.

"He was a machine. He was Rafael Nadal on clay," Sean O'Neill, a five-time national singles champion, said in a phone interview, referring to the Spanish professional tennis player. "He was happy to play thirty-five-shot rally after thirty-five-shot rally because he was physically superior to everyone."

Having joined the game so late, in his thirties, Braithwaite, who became a US citizen in 1971, seemed to be making up for lost time, playing table tennis competitively into his seventies and winning dozens of regional and national tournaments at various age levels.

In 1985, in his fifties, he won the Amateur Athlete of the Year award from the US Table Tennis Association. In 1989, he was inducted into the US Table Tennis Hall of Fame, becoming one of very few Black players bestowed that honor. In 2007, he won the table tennis federation's lifetime achievement award.

"He had a bigger-than-life personality," Tahl Leibovitz, who has represented the US in five Paralympic Games, said by phone. "In table tennis, when you have someone like George, he stands out."

Still, not everyone, especially the younger players Braithwaite befriended or coached, knew about his unlikely place in geopolitical lore. When asked, he was happy to recount the mind-boggling details.

He and his teammates were competing at the World Table Tennis Championships in Nagoya, Japan, when they were invited by the Chinese to play some exhibition matches in the hermetic country. China, which had largely sealed itself off from the international community for more than two decades, had been looking for a way to reenter the global stage. The US was eager, too, to engage again with China. The Ping-Pong players, then, were the messengers sent forth to break the ice.

It was a dizzying experience for the unwitting diplomats. The American players were accustomed to playing matches in relative silence, in empty halls. In Beijing, they played for a spirited crowd of eighteen thousand, and a few days later they played for another five thousand spectators in Shanghai. The teams were mismatched—the Americans were amateurs, the Chinese had just won gold medals in four of the seven world-championship events—but the matches had a friendly tenor.

"I knew their significance and my responsibilities," Zheng Minzhi, a member of the Chinese team, told *The New York Times* in 1997. "I knew I was not only there to play, but more important, to achieve what cannot be achieved through proper diplomatic channels."

In between, the Americans were shuttled to a traditional opera, elaborate banquets, and sightseeing tours. They met Zhou Enlai, the Chinese premier. Some of them, including Braithwaite, battled illness along the way.

The Americans were regarded as curiosities by the locals, but Braithwaite, in particular, attracted a crowd wherever he went, according to Connie Sweeris, who was twenty-three when she made the trip as a member of the team.

When a photo of the players lined up along the Great Wall made the cover of *Time* magazine that year, Braithwaite stood out not only for his warm smile and stylish cardigan sweater, but also because he was the only Black person in the traveling party.

"A lot of those people, I don't know if they'd ever seen a Black man," Sweeris said in a phone interview. "He'd be talking with them, laughing with them, trying to communicate. We didn't have enough interpreters. We just tried to smile and use hand gestures."

Upon returning home, Braithwaite and his teammates were bombarded with interview requests by television and radio shows. There was hope among the players and officials that they could capitalize on the ensuing buzz by raising Ping-Pong's stature.

"It would be a good thing if we have made the whole country aware of table tennis as a sport and not just a game," Braithwaite told *The New York Times* a couple weeks after returning home.

That never happened. Ping-Pong in America remained a curiosity, a recreational pastime. But Braithwaite kept competing.

He eventually served as vice president of USA Table Tennis, the national governing body of the sport. He gave private lessons and coached in local schools through a nonprofit organization—anything to be around the game, to spread its gospel.

Everyone knew Braithwaite as the Chief. There is some disagreement, though, on where the nickname originated.

Thomas Hu, who worked with Braithwaite as head of the nonprofit American Youth Table Tennis Organization, called him Chief simply because Braithwaite greeted everyone else as Chief. Connie Sweeris's husband, Dell—another Hall of Fame player—said it was because people thought Braithwaite resembled Robert Parish, the Boston Celtics great, who was himself nicknamed the Chief.

Others insisted the name was dreamed up by amused opponents who thought Braithwaite's customary midgame celebrations resembled a Native American dance.

"He had kind of an annoying manner, if you were his competitor," Dave Sakai, a longtime friend and doubles partner, said in a phone interview. "After winning a big point, an important point, he'd kind of do a little dance with his right hand in the air. After that, people called him the Chief, and it stuck."

Braithwaite had a way of making people feel close to him. O'Neill described him as "the Magic Johnson of table tennis"—always smiling, always giving people a thumbs-up, always working as an informal ambassador of the sport.

"He sucked twenty-four hours out of every day, and he had the nine lives of a cat," he said. "If you were around George enough, he made you love the sport even more, based on what it could do to bring people together."

———

**ANDREW KEH** is a sports reporter for *The New York Times*. He previously worked as a correspondent in Germany, where he battled colleagues on an outdoor Ping-Pong table at the Berlin bureau—and sometimes won.
ALAIN DELAQUÉRIÈRE and SHEELAGH MCNEILL contributed research.

Audrey Sutherland estimated she covered 8,075 solo miles in Alaska and British Columbia over nearly twenty-five years.

# Audrey Sutherland

## 1921–2015

———

BY JEN A. MILLER

WHEN AUDREY SUTHERLAND MADE a plan to set out in an inflatable kayak, alone, and paddle 850 miles from Ketchikan to Skagway in Alaska, she was not what most would have considered a typical candidate for the feat, especially in 1980. She was a woman. She was sixty years old. And most of her paddling experience—extensive as it was—had been in Hawaii, where the waters were warmer, calmer, and more inviting.

Also, there was a holdup: her request for a two-month leave from her job had been rejected.

"I walked into the bathroom and looked at the familiar person in the mirror," she wrote in *Paddling North* (2012), about her decision to take the trip. " 'Getting older, aren't you lady? Better do the physical things now. You can work at a desk later.' "

She resigned the next day and set out for Alaska two months later.

She made the paddle in eighty-five days, split over two summers, and decided to keep going. In *Paddling North,* she estimated that she had covered 8,075 solo miles in Alaska and British Columbia over nearly twenty-five years.

"But it is never enough," she wrote.

Solo adventure travel, now a trend among women like Cheryl Strayed, the author of *Wild* (2012), was hardly common at the time. Sutherland was a pioneer, and a resourceful one at that.

In 1964, for instance, while making her way along the northern coast of Molokai, a largely untouched Hawaiian island that was home to a leper colony, she kept her food and gear (and wine, which she stored in thirty-five-millimeter film cans) in a Styrofoam box repurposed from the packaging of a Royal typewriter. She secured the box by latching it to an aluminum pack frame, which is typically used by backpackers to carry their gear.

She had no boat, raft, or kayak, but swam, towing her belongings behind her with a ten-foot rope. She also brought a camera and took pictures of herself that became the basis for illustrations done by her sister, Dorothy Schufeldt Bowles, for Sutherland's first book, *Paddling My Own Canoe* (1978).

When she went back, in 1967, Sutherland brought along a ride: an inflatable kayak that she saw in a catalog from the Smilie Company of San Francisco, which made products for backpackers and mule packers. It became her mode of transportation for the rest of her trips, including in Samoa, Norway, Greece, Scotland, and Maine.

Her books recorded her adventures, becoming guides for generations of solo travelers. She encouraged readers

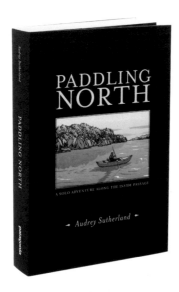

In *Paddling North* (2012), Sutherland chronicled
her decision to kayak long distances alone.

never to wait for the right opportunity or the right person
to travel with—just go. Her mantra was "Go simple, go
solo, go now."

Once, when asked by the travel writer Paul Theroux
why she traveled alone, she replied: "I don't. I have three
people within me—the paddler, sizing up the conditions.
The critic, nagging me and telling me I'll never make it.
And the writer, standing back and trying to remember
it all."

She took the book title *Paddling My Own Canoe* from
another bold woman who became a role model for future
generations, Louisa May Alcott, who wrote in her journal, "I'd rather be a free spinster and paddle my own
canoe."

"Her legacy," her son, Jock Sutherland, said, "is one of
appreciation and realization that you need to be capable
with not only your mind but your heart and your soul and
your body. You need to be able to take these challenges

and have a feeling of confidence—to have a good sense
you're going to make it."

Adventure started early for Sutherland.

She was born Audrey Helen Schufeldt on February 11,
1921, in the Los Angeles neighborhood of Canoga Park.
Her father, Charles Lee Schufeldt, built a cabin in the San
Bernardino National Forest. He died when Sutherland
was five. But her mother, Alice (Horton) Schufeldt, continued staying there with Audrey and her two sisters every
summer. Audrey would often head out into the woods
alone.

"I stalked deer at dusk and fireflies at night, ran wet
and exultant in cloudbursts and thunderstorms, and
climbed to the tops of young pine trees to swing them in
whipping circles," she wrote in *Paddling My Own Canoe*,
which was republished, along with all her other books, by
Patagonia Books in 2018.

She enrolled at University of California, Los Angeles
when she was sixteen and graduated with a degree in
international relations. She and her sisters worked as
riveters building airplanes during World War II.

In 1942, she married John Lauren Sutherland, a Coast
Guard officer who became a commercial fisherman. They
moved from California to Hawaii, settling in 1954 in a
house on the water near Haleiwa, on the North Shore of
Oahu. It became her lifelong home.

When Sutherland and her husband divorced, he
returned to California and she stayed in Hawaii with their
four children. She earned a master's degree in education
counseling from the University of Hawaii at Manoa and
taught swimming and worked as a substitute teacher
before getting a job with the army as an adult education
counselor.

She had been drawn to Alaska after traveling there for
work, trips that showed her "some gorgeous territory,"
her daughter Noelle Sutherland said.

"I don't think any of us had the sense of 'you're too old
to be doing that,'" her daughter said. "If she was still doing
it, then she wasn't too old to be doing it."

Between her adventuring, Sutherland was a
frequent keynote speaker at kayaking symposia hosted

by L.L.Bean and taught continuing education at the University of Hawaii. For her ten-week course on adventuring, the final exam was "going out and spending the night on one of the outer islands," said Rusty Lillico, a former student. "For a lot of us, it was the first time we'd done that."

The experience, he said, changed his life. In 1982, he helped start the Hui Wa'a Kaukahi Kayak Club of Hawaii, now the oldest and largest recreational kayak club in the state. He arranged for Sutherland to meet regularly with the group to talk about her experiences and offer kayaking instruction.

When Sutherland died, at ninety-four, on February 23, 2015, Lillico helped the club organize a memorial service for her. Her death was not widely noted outside of the outdoors world, in part because she had lived a quiet life.

"I wouldn't say she was reclusive, but she was not a public figure at all," Lillico said. "She talked very quietly, so you had to really pay attention to what she was saying or you wouldn't get it at all."

Her written words, however, will continue to resonate—among them, "What we most regret are not the errors we made, but the things we didn't do."

Sutherland with a freshly caught salmon.
She was a pioneer, and a resourceful one at that.

JEN A. MILLER is the author of *Running: A Love Story* and has been writing about health, fitness, and New Jersey for *The New York Times* since 2006.

Artist Behind a Famous Tarot Deck

# Pamela Colman Smith

## 1878–1951

BY EMILY PALMER

IN 1904, when Pamela Colman Smith was twenty-six, the *Brooklyn Daily Eagle* pronounced her a romantic: "There is not a page of her life, not an incident, that is not overflowing with romance."

But hers was not the life of traditional romance. In fact, she may never have even had a romantic partner. Rather, her life was filled with a different kind of romance: all the excitement, the mystique, and even, at times, the magic that can be stuffed into a single lifetime.

She is best known as an artist, whose hand-painted designs illustrate the world's bestselling deck of tarot cards; around one hundred million of what is known as the Rider-Waite deck have sold in more than twenty countries.

But she was also an author, publisher, once-incarcerated women's suffragist, world traveler, prolific letter writer, party hostess, public entertainer, storyteller (dabbling also in theater), mystic, and, in her later years, converted Catholic who brought back to life a withering chapel in the English countryside.

While Colman Smith was not a tarot card reader herself, she had always flirted with the idea of magic, at one point joining the secret-society occultist group the Hermetic Order of the Golden Dawn.

There she met Arthur Edward Waite, an occult scholar who commissioned Colman Smith to illustrate the tarot deck he was creating in 1909. Colman Smith was paid a small one-time fee for her many months of work and research, ultimately creating eighty drawings for Waite's deck, one of the first to be fully illustrated (the deck has seventy-eight cards).

"Her deck transcends time and space," Mary K. Greer, author of *Tarot for Your Self: A Workbook for Personal Transformation* (1984), said in an interview. "Even using her own motifs, it transcends the personal so that there's something universal about it. One hundred years later, it has multicultural overlays that work for everybody."

Colman Smith spent part of her childhood in Jamaica and grew up hearing West African tales, which profoundly impacted her artistic style, said Tamara Scott-Williams, an illustrator who has researched Colman Smith's life.

"You can read her tarot deck because each card possesses a complete story, each card has its symbolism, its imagery, its colors, its characters, its dream, its imagination," Scott-Williams said in an interview. "And so Pamela Colman Smith becomes the bridge between the tarot cards of the past—which are very simple playing cards—and the tarot that would become the future."

Some of the landscapes Colman Smith drew on her cards resembled the places where she stayed; the faces mirrored the people she befriended. And her illustrations

Pamela Colman Smith in the early 1900s. Her designs illustrate the world's bestselling tarot cards.

When the Rider-Waite tarot deck was mass marketed, Smith's name was left off the packaging.

allowed for nuance. The Five of Pentacles, for instance, depicts two people, one of whom uses crutches to walk. They are bundled up in the snow, a towering church with warmly lit stained glass behind them. The card has a variety of interpretations, from outcast to sanctuary, depending on one's perception of whether or not they are welcome inside.

When the Rider-Waite deck, published by William Rider & Son in London, was mass-marketed in England, Colman Smith's name was left off the packaging (some have been trying to reclaim her work by renaming the deck Waite-Smith or Rider-Waite-Smith), but she ensured her legacy in the coiling initials she inked in the corner of each card.

She used the same serpentine sigil—or magical symbol—on most of the paintings and drawings she created over her lifetime.

Corinne Pamela Colman Smith, who sometimes went by Pam, Con, or Pixie, was born on February 16, 1878, in Middlesex, England, to American parents. Her father, Charles Edward Smith, was a merchant plagued by debt who was embroiled in court cases, and her mother,

Corinne Colman Smith, acted in drawing room plays. The family lived between the United States, Europe, and the Caribbean.

Colman Smith attended the Pratt Institute in New York to study art but eschewed formal instruction and left after two years.

"It was found absolutely impossible to hold her down, fetter her or even guide her," the *Brooklyn Daily Eagle* wrote. "Some of the best American artists, on seeing her work, said that she could not be curbed in any way or she would accomplish nothing."

Colman Smith, following her own erratic schedule of sleeping until noon, found success in New York and London.

She wrote and illustrated *Annancy Stories* (1899), a collection of folktales that she learned when listening to nighttime stories told in the Jamaican patois.

From 1902 to 1903, she published poems and drawings with Jack B. Yeats in what they called *A Broad Sheet,* before creating her own *The Green Sheaf,* a literary magazine for which she painstakingly hand-painted each copy in color. From 1904 to 1906, she and a friend, Ethel Fryer-Fortescue, ran the Green Sheaf Press, exhibiting work by women writers and publishing Colman Smith's second set of Jamaican folktales in a book called *Chim-Chim* (1905).

After Colman Smith's parents died, she painted *The Wave* (1903), depicting seven mourning wave-women, their grief-sloped blue bodies alternately turned in angles of agony, compassion, and reflection, their dress trains foaming hearts over an otherwise calm sea.

*The Wave* was prominently displayed from 2022 to 2023 in an exhibit at the Whitney Museum of American Art, where it is part of the permanent collection.

"It's a magical, beautiful, very intuitive work—a lyrical presentation anthropomorphizing nature as women in states of mourning, and that's immediately engaging," the curator Barbara Haskell said in an interview. "Her work hits a nerve in today's world: in the face of crisis people really do yearn for an authentic connection to the soul."

Women as trees and waves are recurring themes in Colman Smith's art. By the time she was twenty-four, she had been on twenty-five voyages, doing much of her traveling by sea.

In 1907, she became the first artist who wasn't a photographer to have her work displayed by Alfred Stieglitz in his experimental 291 gallery in Manhattan, where a sizable crowd of high society packed the cramped gallery to see her seventy-two drawings, mostly what she called "music pictures"; Colman Smith could see images in music, a form of synesthesia. She had another solo show at his gallery two years later.

Also in 1907, she wrote a manifesto, *A Protest Against Fear,* in which she argued "that fear has got a hold of all this land. Each one has a great fear of himself, a fear to believe, to think, to do, to be, to act." In protest, she urged younger artists: "Try to feel truly one thought, one scene, and make others feel it as keenly as you do—thus is art born."

After completing her tarot illustrations, Colman Smith turned her attention to the suffragist movement, designing posters and cartoons for London's militant artist collective known as the Suffrage Atelier. She later joined the executive council of the Pioneer Players, a theater society that produced plays written by women, where she illustrated playbills and designed costumes. She also joined suffragists in protests and was jailed at least once.

Later in life she converted to Catholicism, moved to Cornwall, and wrote and directed a children's Nativity play at a chapel she helped resurrect, naming it Our Lady of the Lizard. She spent her remaining days in the English seaside town of Bude.

Throughout her life, she kept up a voluminous correspondence with friends and relatives, her letters filled with exclamation points, underlined intonations, conversational dashes, and drawings in the margins. She seemed to be a wily motormouth—hardly finding use for a comma or period, one thought running into the next, without breaking for breath.

In her writing, as in her life, she verged on the romantic, suggesting in an effusive letter to a cousin that she

*The Wave* (1903) depicts seven mourning women, which Smith painted after her parents died.

should visit her in Jamaica: "And we'd play croquet by moonlight! It's quite light enough!"

Her outfits, too, were expressive, with her "love for bizarre and barbaric colors," according to the *Brooklyn Daily Eagle,* that accentuated her dark features.

Her ethnic background eluded friends who seemed intent on defining her; her longtime friend, the famous English stage actress Ellen Terry, called Colman Smith a "Japanese toy," while her portraitist Alphaeus Philemon Cole said he believed she was Afro-Caribbean. While the parents listed on her birth certificate were white, historians say dubious parentage or a secret adoption cannot be ruled out.

Such lingering questions will likely remain unanswered. So, too, will questions about her sexual orientation. No romantic relationships are recorded, though she spent the last two decades of her life with her widowed housekeeper, their relationship close if not intimate.

By the time she died of a heart ailment on September 18, 1951, at the age of seventy-three, she was destitute, having spent whatever little money she had on lavish dinner parties and church renovations. To this day she is buried in an unmarked grave. But her legacy lingers beyond the confines of an English countryside cemetery.

Smith's peripatetic life included becoming an author, publisher, suffragist, world traveler, and mystic.

Alex V. Cipolle, a distant relative of Colman Smith's and a journalist who has written for *The New York Times*, spent her childhood summers in a mountain home in Keene Valley, New York, where about a dozen of Colman Smith's paintings still hang on the walls: a grove of tree people swaying and dancing, or women whose legs turn to mountains and waterfalls and whose bodies become waves.

"I would fall asleep looking at these paintings and wake up looking at these paintings," Cipolle said in an interview.

Her paintings—with "very interesting, bold, unapologetic lines," Cipolle said—are reflective of how Colman Smith lived her life.

"She was this radical feminist—an iconoclast—who was so ahead of her time," Cipolle added. "I think she would still be radical today."

———

**EMILY PALMER** is an investigative reporter covering courts and crime. While she has witnessed many futures divined by the jury, she has never had her tarot read. She now owns two of Pixie's decks and is looking to change that.
SUSAN C. BEACHY contributed research.

## Musician Who Defined Oakland's Hip-Hop Sound

# Joe Capers

## 1957–2002

BY THERÍ A. PICKENS, PHD

WHEN PEOPLE THINK ABOUT California's music, many only consider Los Angeles. But music insiders know the Bay Area, and Oakland, specifically, as a powerhouse of sound. From the late 1980s until the mid-nineties, a slew of Oakland hip-hop artists released classic records: Digital Underground's *Sex Packets*, MC Hammer's *Please Hammer Don't Hurt 'Em*, Too $hort's *Short Dog's in the House*, and Tony! Toni! Toné!'s *The Revival*. Their regional sound was as distinctive as Sean "Diddy" Combs's New York, Jermaine "JD" Dupri's Atlanta, or Missy Elliott and Timbaland's Virginia. Just like in those locales, there was one musician whose ear helped shape it all in Oakland: Joe Capers.

Capers worked tirelessly from the basement of his home, the headquarters of J-Jam Recording, which he established in August 1989. As a producer, he pushed artists to fulfill their potential. His roster included locals like Cassidine and Pooh-Man along with those nationally known, like Dawn from En Vogue, MC Hammer (when he was with the Holy Ghost Boys), X Clan, Yo-Yo, Tony! Toni! Toné!, and Milli Vanilli. His official credits include work on Digital Underground's "Sex Packets" and "Doowutchyalike" and Tony! Toni! Toné!'s *Sons of Soul* and *The Revival*.

As a sound engineer, Capers was renowned for his ear. Naru Kwina, a hip-hop artist and the coproducer of the documentary *Blind Joe: The Legacy of Joe Capers* (2021), recounts that Capers forced him to memorize his rhymes rather than read them from a paper.

"I'm blind! I ain't deaf!" Capers joked to him after hearing papers rustling.

In fact, most artists in the documentary echo the refrain that Capers did not have "these," pointing to their eyes, but he had "these," pointing to their ears.

The ethnomusicologist Birgitta Johnson explains his expertise this way: "He's attuned to the sound culture of Black people and Black life."

Capers acutely understood the Oakland sound, which was heavily influenced by funk music, with its strong bass lines and syncopated beats; 1970s and '80s dance music; psychedelic soul, with its Black rock origins; and the amalgamation of jazz and soul repertoires. Oakland artists drew inspiration from live instrumentation, bands like Parliament-Funkadelic, Sly and the Family Stone, and Earth, Wind & Fire. Capers duplicated the vibe in clubs, discos, and skating rinks.

Joe Edward Capers was born on November 6, 1957, in Houston, to Webb Capers and Ella Darby, and began playing the guitar and keyboard when he was six.

He lost his sight in 1965 at eight years old, after having been burned by a household cleaning agent. (Capers

The music producer Joe Capers with his guide dog, aptly named Tenor.

and his mother won a lawsuit against Drackett Products Company, which awarded $800,000 in compensatory damages to Capers and $5,550.40 to his mother.)

In April 1978, he married Jeanetta Bigham Capers; they had one daughter.

Capers learned to rely on his sense of touch to build his musical career. The musician and educator James Richard met Capers at the Lucky Lion club, where his band the Sekret Service played regularly. After a set, Richard spoke to Capers about his band's gear. Capers touched the keyboard, saying, "No, wait. Don't tell me!" Then he called out the instrument's make and model.

Capers never referred to himself as "Blind Joe," but other artists gave him the nickname out of affection.

He belonged to a long history of Black blind or visually impaired musicians, including Blind Tom Wiggins, Blind Lemon Jefferson, the Blind Boys of Alabama, Art Tatum, Rahsaan Roland Kirk, Ray Charles, and Stevie Wonder, as well as the rappers Question and Fetty Wap. The scholar Terry Rowden wrote in *The Songs of Blind Folk: African American Musicians and the Cultures of Blindness* (2009) that "it's clear that many blind individuals have out of sheer necessity achieved prodigious development in the area of music performance. For centuries, music has been one of the few respectable careers available for the blind (as it was for African Americans)."

Rowden also warns that "we must be wary of the tendency to endow blind people as a group with special characteristics." Leroy F. Moore Jr., the founder of Krip-Hop Nation, a network of musicians, and a coproducer of the *Blind Joe* documentary, agrees, suggesting that this narrative is common but incomplete—people with disabilities don't regard a disability as an obstacle to overcome, but rather as part of their identity.

Instead of assuming blindness heightens other senses, it would be more accurate to think of Capers's skills as honed over years of experience as a multi-instrumentalist and musical aficionado. Capers managed the technical equipment used to record, enhance, mix, and reproduce music. Like the best sound engineers, he had a facility and dexterity with the machines and understood the physics, flexibility, and possibilities of sound.

At a time when few, if any, accessible studios existed, Capers put thought into how he built J-Jam Recording Studios. It had a ground-floor-level entrance. In addition, Joe situated the equipment so that he could navigate it himself and ensured it was soundproofed. He moved through the studio with such ease that MC Hammer said it was only after he had been recording with Capers that he realized he was blind.

The studio was also a welcome respite for an ever-present cadre of musicians with whom Capers shared his love of seafood and his mother's annual Christmas gumbo, Capers's daughter said. Since they played at nightclubs where fights could erupt, Capers carried a knife. Once, Wiggins remembered Capers's saying, "It's time to even the score: I'm gonna turn out the lights."

MC Hammer described Capers in *Blind Joe* as a "real Oakland cat" who was "always talking crazy to you, making you laugh, always got a joke, always had a heart of gold."

Toward the end of his life, Capers had to close his studio because of dwindling finances. He acquired a guide dog, aptly named Tenor, who afforded him some more independence.

Capers died on November 27, 2002, in Lithonia, Georgia. In Oakland, his virtuosic ear is remembered every August, which is celebrated as Joe Capers Month.

——

**THERÍ A. PICKENS, PHD,** is a professor, editor, and freelance writer. Her neighbors alternately bemoan and applaud her enthusiastic enjoyment of 1980s and '90s hip-hop.

Capers in his early teenage years. He lost his sight at age eight.

## Beyond the Obit: What I Know About Joe

### AS TOLD TO AMISHA PADNANI

Leroy F. Moore Jr., the founder of Krip-Hop Nation, and Naru Kwina, a musician and film-maker who created a documentary about Joe Capers, remember Joe Capers's legacy.

**NARU** I first heard about Joe when my good friend Taj (aka Turntable T) worked as an intern at his studio and brought me in to record some of my songs. Taj told me that Joe was blind.

It only took about ten minutes for me to realize what a great teacher and engineer he was. Among the things he told me: I needed to learn my rap lyrics and not read out of my notebook.

When I came back the next day, I tried to trick him, because how would a blind man know I was reading from a paper? He asked if I was still reading from my book, and I lied, saying I wasn't. He told me he was blind but not deaf, and that he could hear the pages turning. He kicked me out and wouldn't let me return until I had learned all of my lyrics.

He made me take my music seriously.

**LEROY** I never got to meet Joe Capers, but in 2009, after I did a radio show about disabled/deaf hip-hop artists on KPFA in Berkeley, California, I received a phone call from a friend of Joe's who told me what he did for the music scene in the 1980s and '90s. I realized this was a man worthy of more attention.

I partnered with Bethany Stevens, a queer disabled sexologist who was a professor at Georgia State University at the time, to hold a Joe Capers award ceremony the next year to recognize his music and advocacy work. We gave the award to Joe Capers's family, who live in Georgia.

When I came back from that event, I hooked up with Naru and told him about it. He then helped me get Joe's name out to the public.

**NARU** Leroy and I coordinated with the film-maker Dedoceo Habi and the videographer Quentin Scales to create a documentary about Joe. It took over six years, but the film finally came out. It's called *The Joe Capers Project*.

**LEROY** We also pushed for Oakland's mayor to make the month of August Joe Capers Month, which was huge for Krip-Hop Nation—to have a Black disabled musician honored in this way. After all, it's our role to highlight disabled artists like Joe who came before us; it's their legacies we follow and build upon today.

Bold and unpredictable, Lilí Álvarez was also a figure skater, Alpine skier, and tango dancer.

Multitalented Tennis Champion from Spain

# Lilí Álvarez

## 1905–1998

—————

BY CHRISTOPHER CLAREY

LILÍ ÁLVAREZ, A BOLD and unpredictable Spanish tennis player, became an international star in the 1920s by reaching three consecutive Wimbledon singles finals. She later established new social codes in the sport by becoming the first woman to wear a divided skirt—a forerunner of shorts—at the tournament.

But her talents and interests extended far beyond the tennis court. Álvarez was one of the most extraordinary multisport athletes of her era: a prizewinning figure skater, Alpine skier, automobile racer, and tango dancer who was also an accomplished equestrian, hiker, fencer, and billiards player.

She was ahead of her time, but Spain, long socially conservative and with few elite female athletes, was slow to celebrate her achievements, most of which occurred outside the country.

She was also a journalist who wrote for Britain's *Daily Mail* newspaper and other publications as a correspondent during Spain's civil war and wrote several books about feminism, spirituality, and the fundamental role of sports in building character and bolstering well-being. And she was one of the first Spanish women journalists to write about sports.

"I always understood sports—and more generally everything that was physical—as a base, as the foundation of a richer and fuller life in every sense," she wrote in her book *Plenitud* (1946).

Sports, she wrote, were "the ground floor" on which "an individual's psychological structure was constructed."

That was certainly her experience.

Elia María González-Álvarez y López-Chicheri was born on May 9, 1905, at the Hotel Flora in Rome to affluent expatriate Spanish parents of aristocratic descent who were on an extended visit to the city. Her mother, Virginia López-Chicheri, had left Spain after separating from her first husband. In Switzerland, Virginia met Emilio González Álvarez, a lawyer by training, and the couple continued to travel extensively after the birth of their daughter, Elia María, soon nicknamed Lilí.

Lilí, who was educated by private tutors, including her mother, learned to speak five languages: Spanish, French, English, German, and Italian.

"She always had governesses, her education was tremendously individual," her nephew Jaime López-Chicheri Dabán said in a 2021 interview with *El País,* one of Spain's leading publications. "She was a very cultured woman, very cultured, very cultured, who had great admiration for herself. She was nice and a bit vain but rightly so."

Álvarez grew up primarily in Switzerland, with her father determined to pass on to her his newfound passion for sports and, in particular, for figure skating, which she started at age five.

Though she excelled and won competitions, she resisted the sport's rigid guidelines that required skaters to etch patterns into the ice that were judged for precision. In 1923, while she was training to compete in the first Winter Olympics the next year in Chamonix, France, she suffered an injury that ended her figure skating career.

Álvarez shifted her focus to tennis, which she also had begun playing at an early age, receiving coaching in Switzerland and, later, on the French Riviera.

In 1919, the year she turned fourteen, she won the Swiss indoor title. In 1924, despite missing out on the figure skating competition, she became one of Spain's first two female Olympians, reaching the quarterfinals in singles tennis at the 1924 Summer Olympics in Paris and the round of sixteen in doubles with her partner Rosa Torras.

She played in her first Wimbledon in 1926, upsetting Molla Mallory, the Norwegian American star and future inductee of the International Tennis Hall of Fame, in the semifinals of the singles before losing to Kitty Godfree of Britain 6–2, 4–6, 6–3 in the final.

Álvarez also lost in the Wimbledon final in 1927 and 1928, both times in straight sets to Helen Wills, the powerful, poker-faced Californian who was on her way to becoming one of the greatest players in history with nineteen major singles titles, eight at Wimbledon.

Wills wrote about Álvarez and her movement in her book *Tennis* (1928): "Lilí is an interesting opponent because of the fact that she plays swiftly, with more of a man's than a woman's speed. She is animated and full of life and her game is an unusually daring one. She frequently chooses a more difficult shot when an easier one would do. For this reason she is capable of the unexpected and can surprise a player completely with her acutely angled swift forehand drive, and her equally sharply angled backhand. She is one who gets a great deal of pleasure from her game."

Álvarez was ranked second in the world in 1927 and 1928 by the British journalist A. Wallis Myers, then the definitive source on tennis rankings. The British press nicknamed her "the Señorita."

"She was considered a tennis star, a celebrity of the 1920s," said Richard Hillway, an American tennis historian who wrote, with Robert T. Everitt, *The Birth of Lawn Tennis* (2018). "When she first came to Wimbledon, all the newspapers were chasing her everywhere, just in her first year. She was very attractive to look at, and she had a beautiful and stunning style of play."

In 1929, she earned her only Grand Slam title, winning the women's doubles at the French Championships with her partner Kea Bouman. She also reached the mixed doubles final at the French Championships in 1927 with the American star Bill Tilden, who later called her "the most interesting personality in women's tennis" in his book *Shooting Stars* (1930).

"She is a sportswoman unique in athletic annals," Tilden wrote. "Miss Álvarez does too many things well to be a champion tennis player. Her interests are too divided. She cannot give the amount of concentration to tennis that is necessary to turn out a champion. Ah! But what a game Álvarez has developed. It is one of grace, daring and beauty, transcending that of Lenglen at her most picturesque."

He was referring to Suzanne Lenglen, the balletic French superstar. But the Señorita did come excruciatingly close to winning Wimbledon and made more headlines in 1931 when she took to center court in a daring, calf-length trouser skirt designed by the couturier Elsa Schiaparelli that was a major and practical departure from the tennis skirts of the day. The fashion statement, which divided opinion at Wimbledon, was a gateway to liberating women to wear pants in and outside of the workplace.

In 1934, Álvarez married Count Jean de Gaillard de la Valdène, a French aristocrat who had been a World War I fighter pilot. Álvarez miscarried and the couple ultimately separated after five years of marriage. She moved back to Spain after the civil war was over in 1939, at the beginning of Francisco Franco's dictatorship. She bristled at the subordinate role of women in Spanish society

Álvarez competing at Wimbledon in 1928. She reached the singles final in three consecutive years.

but pulled off one last athletic coup: winning the Spanish national title in tennis in 1941, the same year she won the national downhill and slalom titles in Alpine skiing, which was still her favorite sport after a childhood spent largely in the Alps.

But the Spanish sporting authorities stripped her of the skiing titles and barred her from competition, according to Spanish news reports, because she criticized championship organizers for making the women wait to race until the men had finished, leaving the women with subpar conditions.

She was soon reinstated but, now in her late thirties and upset at her treatment, did not compete again at an elite level.

"She walked through life with her head held high and with the pride felt by pioneers, those women who had to make their way through the hostile and reactionary reality of much of the 20th century," *El Pais* wrote in 2021, emphasizing how little recognition she had received in Spain during most of her lifetime.

This pained Álvarez.

"Arriving in your country and seeing that you don't count for anything in the entire sports movement despite your career, it hurts a lot, that's the truth," she said in a 1979 interview with *El País*. "I think I should be something like the grande dame of women's sports. I think that I could have possibly helped the younger generations of athletes a lot."

Acclaim did arrive, but very late. The success of Spanish women's tennis stars Arantxa Sánchez Vicario and Conchita Martínez in the 1990s put the spotlight back on Álvarez's achievements. There are streets named for her in Málaga and Valdemoro, near Madrid.

In 1998, the Spanish government announced that she would receive the Royal Order of Sports Merit gold medal, but Álvarez, diminished by Alzheimer's disease, died on July 8, 1998, at age ninety-three, shortly before the awards ceremony.

Nearly twenty years later, in 2017, Spain's Instituto de la Mujer y para la Igualdad de Oportunidades began awarding annual prizes named for Álvarez to honor journalistic work that contributes to equality between men's and women's sports.

———

**CHRISTOPHER CLAREY** played junior tennis, high school tennis, and Division III tennis at Williams College before writing about those who could really play the game. Now, as *The New York Times*'s tennis correspondent, he has covered more than one hundred Grand Slam tournaments and was long based in Spain, land of Rafael Nadal and Lilí Álvarez.

Joe Carstairs at Whale Cay, an uninhabited island in the Bahamas that she bought in 1934.

## Lesbian Speedboat Racer and Eccentric

# Joe Carstairs

## 1900–1993

BY ANNABELLE WILLIAMS

"ENGLISH WOMAN HAS FAST BOAT," the Associated Press proclaimed in a 1928 article leading up to the annual Harmsworth Trophy boat race in Detroit. The woman in question would have bristled at the characterization: Joe Carstairs, an avowed masculine lesbian, preferred to shake the gendered strictures of the time.

While the Harmsworth title went to an American racer, Garfield Wood, Carstairs had some success in racing, winning several other British races, including the 1926 Duke of York boating crown.

Carstairs led a relatively short career—retiring from boat racing in the early 1930s—but still received news attention for leading an eccentric lifestyle: as an ambulance driver, quasi-ruler of a private island in the Bahamas, and proud owner of a doll companion known as Lord Tod Wadley. An innate desire to rebel against traditional ideas of gender and sexuality also cemented Carstairs as a seminal figure in the annals of queer history.

Marion Barbara "Joe" Carstairs was born on February 1, 1900, in Mayfair, an upscale district of London, to Albert Carstairs, a Scotsman who served in the British Army's Royal Irish Rifles regiment, and Evelyn Bostwick, an heiress to Standard Oil, of which her father, Jabez Abel Bostwick, was a founding partner.

Albert and Evelyn divorced when Joe was young, with Evelyn remarrying and having two more children, whom she toted around Europe while following the social scene.

In 1911, young Joe boarded an ocean liner bound for the Low-Heywood School for Girls, a boarding school in Stamford, Connecticut.

In 1916, Carstairs got a job driving an ambulance in Paris, discovered a need for speed, and began to identify as a lesbian.

Paris's relatively permissive social atmosphere and changing sexual mores of the Roaring Twenties gave Carstairs the freedom to explore relationships with women with little scrutiny. Joe mingled with queer bohemians including Dolly Wilde, the niece of Oscar, and eschewed dresses and heels for men's clothing.

But when Carstairs's mother found out, she insisted Carstairs get married to secure access to the family's inheritance. In 1918, Carstairs wed a friend, Count Jacques de Pret; it was a marriage on paper only and was later annulled.

At the end of World War I, Carstairs moved to Ireland to drive ambulances for the Women's Legion Mechanical Transport Section, supporting the British Army during a time of unrest. In 1919, Carstairs went to France to

# "A great love story (of a woman and her doll) or a cautionary tale about the dangers of wealth and madness."

help reconstruct towns and transport bodies for burial. Then it was back to London, where Carstairs and another ambulance driver founded the X-Garage in Kensington, taking visitors on tours, including the *Peter Pan* author J. M. Barrie.

In 1925, around the time Carstairs received inheritances from her mother and grandmother, she began building and racing boats.

After retiring from boat racing in the early thirties, Carstairs still longed for the open sea and went to the Bahamas, buying an island known as Whale Cay in 1934. The total cost was reported to be $40,000 (more than $880,000 in today's dollars).

Whale Cay, which sits where the Caribbean Sea and the Atlantic Ocean meet, was just nine miles long and four miles wide.

In *The Queen of Whale Cay*, a 1997 biography of Carstairs, the author Kate Summerscale described the island as initially uninhabited, save for one couple who operated a small lighthouse. Carstairs cleared the island and rendered it into a functioning plantation, growing palms, fruits, and vegetables. Her island resembled a feudal kingdom, in which she essentially ruled as a monarch and funded the economy with the family's wealth, as well as with support from a shipping operation that ran supplies from the island to mainland America. Soon, locals from other islands came to work there, and at its peak, Whale Cay housed around five hundred Bahamians.

The property's centerpiece, the Great House, was completed in 1936. It included a swimming pool, small school, church, and housing for construction workers. The island also had a power plant, general store, and museum.

Carstairs traveled to Europe every year but mostly stayed on the island, seeking companionship in a doll that had been gifted by a girlfriend, Ruth Baldwin. The doll, Lord Tod Wadley, was about one foot high and had been produced by the German toymaker Steiff.

"I was never entirely honest to anyone, except to Wadley," Carstairs was quoted as saying in Summerscale's biography. The doll had Cartier accessories and fur coats, enjoying the same sort of opulent life as Carstairs.

The *New York Times* critic Carolyn T. Hughes, in a 1998 review, said she couldn't tell if *The Queen of Whale Cay* was "a great love story (of a woman and her doll) or a cautionary tale about the dangers of wealth and madness."

Newspapers and magazines gained additional interest in the British eccentric when Carstairs hosted the Duke of Windsor, formerly King Edward VIII, and his wife, Wallis Simpson, in 1941, on the island. More media attention came the next year, when Carstairs rescued dozens of stranded Americans off the coast of Nassau.

Carstairs also crossed paths with the actress Marlene Dietrich, building a friendship—and rumored affair—that soured later in life. Dietrich visited Whale Cay, as did many of Carstairs's girlfriends.

Carstairs set up programs benefiting local Bahamian youth, including a boys' summer camp. But the founding ethos of Whale Cay was a colonial and classist one, in which Carstairs exercised control over residents' daily lives, Summerscale wrote in her book, and as social

Carstairs in 1928 with Lord Tod Wadley, a doll given to her by a girlfriend.

Carstairs's rebellion against traditional ideas of gender and sexuality made her a seminal figure in queer history.

mores around racial inequality evolved, it became difficult to continue operating the small society.

By the late 1950s, Carstairs began experiencing health problems. By the 1960s, fewer Bahamians remained on Whale Cay, and Carstairs sold it in 1975 (it has been sold multiple times since) and began splitting time between New York's Sag Harbor and the Florida coast. Carstairs kept in touch with former friends and lovers and often provided them with financial support.

Over time, Carstairs amassed more dolls as companions for Lord Tod Wadley. By this time, the leather on Wadley's face had deteriorated; Carstairs patched him up with Band-Aids as one would a child.

Carstairs died at ninety-three on December 18, 1993, in Naples, Florida.

In 2016, the auction house Doyle hosted a sale of many of Carstairs's personal effects, including photographs of lovers and one of Wadley's companion dolls. But Wadley himself was cremated along with his owner and buried in England, in a grave so simple that it belied the eccentric life it represented.

———

**ANNABELLE WILLIAMS** is a former fellow on *The New York Times*'s Obituaries desk. She wrote this article primarily from her 275-square-foot Brooklyn studio, which is almost as nice as Joe Carstairs's private island.

116

# Getting an Obituary Right

BY AMISHA PADNANI

Obituaries are land mines for potentially incorrect facts. Among the details one must uncover are:

- name (more complicated than one might expect in some cases)
- claim to fame
- day and place of death
- age
- where they were born and lived
- names of parents and occupations
- educational/military background
- names of survivors
- information on marriages/children, if any

Getting these details right is key and can take some detective work. Luckily, many states keep records that can help with uncovering the date and places of birth and death, along with parents' names. Ancestry.com keeps census records that may also reveal a person's occupation and marriages, as well as draft cards that could show when the subject may have served in the military. Websites like LinkedIn can be helpful in learning about places the person has worked. Obit writers and editors are also extremely cautious about getting what we call "confirmation"—proof that the subject is gone, along with information about where, when, and how the death occurred—from a relative, an agent, a funeral home, or someone close to the deceased. There's a good reason for this practice: a newspaper's biggest nightmare is publishing an obituary for someone who is not actually dead.

That happened in 1980, when a professional hoaxer named Alan Abel faked his own death to trick *The New York Times.* He had one person pose as a grieving widow, another as an undertaker who answered calls from the *Times* to confirm the death. The next day, he held a news conference to essentially say, "Ha ha! I fooled you all—I'm here, and I'm alive," and the *Times* was forced to run an embarrassing correction. I learned about all of this in 2018, when we heard that Abel had actually died. "Is it for real this time?" my colleagues and I wondered. It was, and we had a little fun with the headline, which read: "Alan Abel, Hoaxer Extraordinaire, Is (on Good Authority) Dead at 94."

# Envisioning
# New Possibilities

---

When we think of movers and shakers, we imagine
people with influence. The people in this section were
not born into positions of power. But by questioning
the way things were, they created opportunities to
make change—not only for themselves but also for
the people around them.

Condemned Code Breaker and Computer Visionary

# Alan Turing

## 1912–1954

BY ALAN COWELL

ALAN TURING'S GENIUS embraced the first visions of modern computing and produced seminal insights into what became known as "artificial intelligence." As one of the most influential code breakers of World War II, his cryptography yielded intelligence believed to have hastened the Allied victory.

But, at his death several years later, many of his secretive wartime accomplishments remained classified, far from public view in a nation seized by the security concerns of the Cold War. Instead, by the narrow standards of his day, his reputation was sullied.

On June 7, 1954, Alan Turing, a British mathematician who has since been acknowledged as one the most innovative and powerful thinkers of the twentieth century—sometimes called the progenitor of modern computing—died as a criminal, having been convicted under Victorian laws as a homosexual and forced to endure chemical castration. Britain didn't take its first steps toward decriminalizing homosexuality until 1967.

Only in 2009 did the government apologize for his treatment.

"We're sorry—you deserved so much better," said Gordon Brown, then the prime minister. "Alan and the many thousands of other gay men who were convicted, as he was, under homophobic laws were treated terribly."

And only in 2013 did Queen Elizabeth II grant Turing a royal pardon, fifty-nine years after a housekeeper found his body at his home at Wilmslow, near Manchester, in northwest England.

A coroner determined that he had died of cyanide poisoning and that he had taken his own life "while the balance of his mind was disturbed."

At his side lay a half-eaten apple. Biographers speculated that he had ingested the poison by dousing the apple with cyanide and eating it to disguise the toxin's taste. Some of those who studied his personality or knew him, most notably his mother, Ethel Turing, challenged the official verdict of suicide, arguing that he had poisoned himself accidentally.

To this day Turing is recognized in his own country and among a broad society of scientists as a pillar of achievement who fused brilliance and eccentricity, moved comfortably in the abstruse realms of mathematics and cryptography but awkwardly in social settings, and was brought low by the hostile society into which he was born.

"He was a national treasure, and we hounded him to his death," said John Graham-Cumming, a computer scientist who campaigned for Turing to be pardoned.

Above all, Turing's name is associated for many people with the top-secret wartime operations of Britain's

Alan Turing is regarded today as one of the most innovative thinkers of the twentieth century.

Turing, front, in 1939 in Bosham, England, with his friend Fred Clayton, rear, among others.

code breakers at Bletchley Park, a sprawling estate north of London, where he oversaw and inspired the effort to decrypt ciphers generated by Nazi Germany's Enigma machine, which had once seemed impenetrable. The Germans themselves regarded the codes as unbreakable.

At the time, German submarines were prowling the Atlantic, hunting Allied ships carrying vital cargo for the war effort. The convoys were critical for building military strength in Britain and eventually enabled the Allies to undertake the D-Day landings in Normandy in 1944, heralding the collapse of Nazi Germany the next year.

Only by charting the submarines' movements could Allied forces change the course of their convoys, and for that they relied on the cryptologists of Bletchley Park to decode messages betraying the Germans' deployments.

The enduring fascination with Turing's story inspired the 2014 movie *The Imitation Game*, starring Benedict Cumberbatch and Keira Knightley. But his scientific range went far beyond the limits of cinematic drama: he laid down principles that have molded the historical record of the relationship between humans and the machines they have created to solve their problems.

Even before World War II, Turing was making breakthroughs.

Credit for the creation of the first functioning computer in 1946 went to the researchers John Presper Eckert and John W. Mauchly for their machine, the Electronic Numerical Integrator and Computer, or ENIAC, which they had developed at the University of Pennsylvania during World War II.

But Turing's notions preceded ENIAC. He conceived what became known as the universal Turing machine, which envisioned "one machine for all possible tasks"—essentially the computer as we know it today, Andrew Hodges, Turing's biographer, wrote in a condensed version of his 1983 book, *Alan Turing: The Enigma.*

Turing's vision, Hodges said, was that one machine could "be turned to any well-defined task by being supplied with the appropriate program."

He added, "The universal Turing machine naturally exploits what was later seen as the 'stored program' concept essential to the modern computer: It embodies the crucial twentieth-century insight that symbols representing instructions are no different in kind from symbols representing numbers."

Later, technology that emerged from the Manhattan Project, the United States–led effort to develop the atom bomb, also relied on Turing's ideas.

"What had begun as a British idea was scaled up to industrial size by the Americans," David Kaiser, a professor at the Massachusetts Institute of Technology, wrote in 2012 in the *London Review of Books.*

Turing's postwar work at the University of Manchester on the first functioning British computers was also significant: it reflected the emerging power of electronic computing in the Cold War race for nuclear supremacy. And he remained fascinated by the interplay between human thought processes and their computerized inventions. Even in 1944, Hodges wrote, Turing had spoken to a colleague about "building a brain."

In an article published in 1950 in the academic journal *Mind*, Turing developed a method that came to be known as the "Turing test," a sort of thought experiment to determine whether a computer could pass as a human. As part of his experiment, a human interrogator would ask questions and try to figure out whether the answers had come from a computer or a human.

Many years later, on a visit to London, President Barack Obama placed Turing in a transatlantic pantheon of innovation and discovery, saying, "From Newton and Darwin to Edison and Einstein, from Alan Turing to Steve Jobs, we have led the world in our commitment to science and cutting-edge research."

Alan Mathison Turing was born in London on June 23, 1912, the second of two sons of Ethel Sara Stoney and Julius Mathison Turing, who had met in imperial India, where Julius was a senior colonial administrator. After Alan's birth they left him and his brother, John, in the care of foster parents in England while they returned to India so that Alan's father could continue his work.

"Alan Turing's story was not one of family or tradition but of an isolated and autonomous mind," Hodges wrote.

In his early days, Turing's education reflected the overwhelming social requisite of his class to secure a place at a reputable private boarding school. Alan, at age thirteen, enrolled at Sherborne School, in southern England, where his fascination with science raised alarms in an educational system based on the study of what were called the classics—works in Latin and ancient Greek.

"If he is to be solely a scientific specialist, he is wasting his time at a public school," Nowell Smith, Sherborne's headmaster, wrote to his parents, as recorded in Hodges's book.

Nonetheless, he secured a place at King's College in Cambridge to study mathematics, graduating in 1934 with a first-class honors degree. With remarkable academic precocity he was made a fellow of the college in 1935. A year later, he published the groundbreaking paper "On Computable Numbers, with an Application to the Entscheidungsproblem" (or "decidability problem"), a reference in German to a celebrated riddle that the American logician Alonzo Church had also explained.

The rear wiring of the Bombe, which Turing and other code breakers used to decipher German communications.

Both Turing and Church reached the same conclusion—a basis for computer science—that there is no single algorithm that could determine the truth or falsity of any statement in formal logic (though Turing's thinking was more direct).

Turing completed a doctoral thesis at Princeton in 1938 before returning to Cambridge. With Britain's declaration of war on Germany in September 1939, he joined the Bletchley Park code breakers at the Government Code and Cypher School, working in makeshift huts clustered around a mansion.

Their greatest initial challenge was figuring out the method of encryption of the German Enigma device, which had been invented twenty years earlier by Arthur Scherbius, a German electrical engineer who had patented it as a civilian machine to encrypt commercial messages. The machine involved entering letters on a typewriter-like keyboard and then encoding them through a series of rotors to a light board, which showed the coded equivalents. The machine was said to be capable of generating nearly 159 quintillion permutations.

The British were helped initially by a Polish mathematician who had been studying the Enigma machine and had provided vital details after Hitler's forces invaded Poland in 1939. But under the direction of Turing and another Cambridge-educated mathematician, W. G. Welchman, the Bletchley Park code breakers greatly expanded and accelerated those early efforts. Using a huge contraption called the Bombe, they mimicked the operations of the Enigma machine to break its codes.

"The critical factor was Turing's brilliant mechanization of subtle logical deductions," the biographer Hodges wrote.

In 1942, Turing was assigned to visit the United States for several months of high-level consultations on the encryption of conversations between President

Franklin D. Roosevelt and Winston Churchill. His wartime work earned him a high civilian award, and he was named an officer of the Most Excellent Order of the British Empire.

In the postwar years, Turing's fascination with computers led him to design the Automatic Computing Engine. Although it was never built, Turing believed that "the computer would offer unlimited scope for practical progress toward embodying intelligence in an artificial form," Hodges wrote.

In October 1948, Turing began working at Manchester University's computing laboratory. He bought a house in nearby Wilmslow in 1950. Among his enthusiasms were his work on various scientific themes, including morphogenesis, the theory of growth and form in biology; his continued secret ties to Britain's postwar code breakers; and long-distance running.

He was also, Hodges said, beginning to explore the homosexual identity he had hidden when he proposed marriage in 1941 to Joan Clarke, a Bletchley Park cryptanalyst. He later withdrew the offer after explaining his sexuality to her, and the two remained friends.

About ten years later, the police were investigating a burglary at his home when he admitted to having had a physical relationship with a man named Arnold Murray. Murray told Turing that he knew the thief's identity, and detectives, in their questioning, asked Turing about his relationship to Murray.

In March 1952, Turing and Murray were charged with "gross indecency" and both pleaded guilty in court. Murray was given a conditional discharge, but Turing was ordered to undergo chemical castration by taking doses of the female hormone estrogen to reduce sex drive.

Two years later, the motive for his apparent suicide, at age forty-one, remained unclear and left many questions. At the time, Hodges wrote, known homosexuals were denied security clearances, which meant that Turing could not be involved in secret work during the Cold War, leaving him excluded and embittered. While a coroner deemed the death a suicide, the telltale apple at Turing's side was never forensically examined.

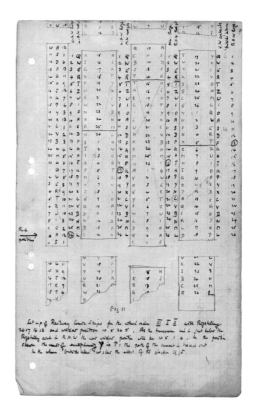

A sampling of Turing's mathematical theory of the Enigma machine.

"Eccentric, solitary, gloomy, vivacious, resigned, angry, eager, dissatisfied—these had always been his ever-varying characteristics," Hodges wrote, "and despite the strength that he showed the world in coping with outrageous fortune, no one could safely have predicted his future course."

——

**ALAN COWELL** is a freelance writer based in London after a long career as a foreign correspondent for *The New York Times.* He was born in Manchester, England, near where, coincidentally, Alan Turing lived and worked in the final tragic days of his life.

## The Woman Behind the Man Who Built the Brooklyn Bridge

# Emily Warren Roebling

## 1843–1903

BY JESSICA BENNETT

IT WAS NOT CUSTOMARY for a woman to accompany a man to a construction site in the late nineteenth century. Petticoats tended to get in the way of physical work.

But when Washington A. Roebling, the chief engineer of the Brooklyn Bridge, fell ill, it was his wife, Emily Warren Roebling, who stepped in—managing, liaising, and politicking between city officials, workers, and her husband's bedside to see the world's first steel-wire suspension bridge to completion. She would become the first person to cross the bridge, too. She carried a rooster with her, as the story has it, for good luck.

Emily Warren Roebling was not an engineer. But she was a woman of "strong character," as the biographer Hamilton Schuyler once described her, who was instrumental to one of the greatest architectural feats of the nineteenth century. Connecting Brooklyn and Manhattan for the first time, the Brooklyn Bridge was then the world's longest suspension bridge. Fourteen years in the making, its construction was complicated by corrupt politicians and crooked contractors. Upon completion, it was immediately proclaimed the "Eighth Wonder of the World."

"I don't think that the Brooklyn Bridge would be standing were it not for her," said Erica Wagner, the author of *Chief Engineer: Washington Roebling, the Man Who Built*

*the Brooklyn Bridge,* a biography of Emily Roebling's husband. "She was absolutely integral to its construction."

Emily Warren was born in 1843 in Cold Spring, New York, one of twelve children of Sylvanus Warren, a New York State assemblyman, and his wife, Phebe Lickley Warren. In her teens, she traveled to Washington to attend the prestigious Georgetown Academy of the Visitation, where she studied history, astronomy, French, and algebra, among other subjects—in addition to housekeeping and needlework. "Her intelligence, liveliness and charm were always apparent to those around her," Wagner writes in *Chief Engineer.*

She met her husband, the civil engineer Washington A. Roebling, through her brother G. K. Warren, a general in the Civil War under whom he served. The son of John A. Roebling, a German American engineer known for building suspension bridges, the younger Roebling was struck by Warren right away, Wagner said. After they were married, he would describe his wife as "a woman of infinite tact and wisest counsel."

The Roeblings married in 1865 and soon set off for Europe, where a pregnant Emily would accompany her husband in the study of caissons, the watertight structures filled with compressed air that would later enable workers to dig beneath the East River. Back home, the

Emily Warren Roebling, who studied law at New York University and supported equality in marriage.

Top: an advertisement for the Brooklyn Bridge in 1883.
Bottom: a plaque dedicated to Roebling hangs on the
Brooklyn Bridge today.

elder Mr. Roebling was preparing for construction of a suspension bridge across the East River that he boasted would be "the greatest bridge in existence." In those early days, it was called the "Great East River Bridge."

The Brooklyn Bridge would go on to become, at least according to lore, the most photographed structure in the world, a gateway to that "shining city," as Thomas Wolfe once described it, whose granite towers and thick steel cables have inspired countless artists, musicians, engineers, and architects.

But its construction was far more treacherous than most casual pedestrians know.

Just a few days in, while surveying the construction site, the elder Mr. Roebling had his foot crushed in the pilings of a Brooklyn pier when a barge came in to dock; he contracted tetanus and died less than a month later. His son succeeded him as chief engineer—only to later become incapacitated by a mysterious illness that left him partially paralyzed, blind, deaf, and mute, according to reports at the time. (It was later believed that Mr. Roebling suffered from "caisson disease," or the bends, a kind of decompression sickness caused by changing air pressure not uncommon on bridge-building sites.) At least two dozen other men died working on the bridge, according to David McCullough's *The Great Bridge.*

"It was a struggle physically, it was a struggle politically, it was a struggle financially," said Richard Haw, the author of *The Brooklyn Bridge: A Cultural History* and *Engineering America: The Life and Times of John A. Roebling.* "The bridge was built by hand, so there were a lot of lost fingers. There were falls, and no safety net to catch you. There was a huge amount of undocumented injuries."

Enter Emily Warren Roebling, who would study law at New York University and argue in an Albany law journal article for equality in marriage. She became her husband's "eyes and ears," Haw said.

She began as secretary, taking copious notes. She went back and forth to the construction site. She negotiated the supply materials, oversaw the contracts, and acted as liaison to the board of trustees. Eventually, she became a kind of "surrogate chief engineer," according to a biography of Warren by the historian Marilyn Weigold, a professor at Pace University. She used her "superb diplomatic skills" to manage competing parties—including the mayor of Brooklyn, who tried to have her husband ousted from the project.

During the final years of the bridge's construction, her husband looked out from his bedside window in Brooklyn Heights—using a telescope and binoculars to watch the bridge grow.

"All along, he is present," Wagner said. "But he is not able to go to the bridge, and he's not able to see anyone. But amazingly, he holds this extraordinary structure in his head. And she is able to help him transmit his thoughts."

As Emily Roebling put it, years later, in an 1898 letter to her son: "I have more brains, common sense and know-how generally than have any two engineers, civil or uncivil, and but for me the Brooklyn Bridge would never have had the name Roebling in any way connected with it!"

The bridge finally opened on May 24, 1883, to great fanfare. On that day, thousands crossed, under a sea of fireworks, with the *Times* declaring that "no one man can be given the credit of this colossal undertaking." In another article, the *Times* reported on "how the wife of the Brooklyn Bridge engineer has assisted her husband."

Today, there is a plaque on the bridge honoring all three Roeblings. It reads: "Back of every great work we can find the self-sacrificing devotion of a woman."

Emily Roebling died on February 28, 1903, in the Roeblings' Trenton home, of stomach cancer.

———

**JESSICA BENNETT** was *The New York Times*'s first-ever gender editor and is the author of two books. She lives in Brooklyn, a stone's throw from the Williamsburg Bridge, which is much less beautiful but took half the time to construct.

Adefunmi I in 1998. He created the Oyotunji village for practitioners of the Yoruba religion.

# Adefunmi I

## 1928–2005

———

BY DIONNE FORD

WHEN HE WAS GROWING UP in Detroit, Walter King wondered why his family didn't celebrate cultural holidays like his Jewish and Polish classmates. So he went to his mother.

"Who is the African God? That's what I want to know," he asked her when he was fifteen.

His mother didn't have the answer. "Blacks didn't really have any knowledge of their history and culture before slavery," she explained, as recounted in *Yoruba Traditions and African American Religious Nationalism* (2012), by the Harvard Divinity School scholar Tracey E. Hucks.

The exchange was pivotal. King's quest to answer his own question became the young man's raison d'être. He read everything he could about Africa, taking an African name that would eventually evolve to Efuntola Oseijeman Adelabu Adefunmi I.

It was while reading *National Geographic* magazine that he learned of Yoruba. The Yoruba people are one of the largest ethnic groups in Africa and trace back to the ancient city of Ile-Ife in Nigeria. The slave trade spread their religion throughout the African diaspora, where it is recognized by a variety of names, including candomblé in Brazil, Santería in Cuba, and voodoo in Haiti.

But according to *Making the Gods in New York: The Yoruba Religion in the African American Community*, by Mary Cuthrell Curry (1997), "the religion ceased to exist" in the United States—if it ever existed at all. That is, until Adefunmi I created a branch called Orisa-Vodun and the one-of-a-kind village in South Carolina that embodies it, Oyotunji.

"His mission was to bring the African gods to African Americans," Hucks, the scholar, said in an interview. She spoke with Adefunmi I extensively for her book and lived at Oyotunji, which she called "a core space for African Americans" and "a Mecca where one could go to get initiated." About twenty-five people live there today, but the population reached a few hundred at its height in the 1980s. Scholars estimate that thousands of people globally have been initiated into Yoruba priesthoods through connections to the village.

Between 1956 and 1961, Adefunmi I established three temples in Manhattan; a festival on the Hudson River to honor Osun, the Yoruba river goddess that Beyoncé channels in her album *Black Is King;* and a parade that included Black nationalists on horseback clad in African garb.

The Ujamaa African market he founded in 1962 sold every kind of African ware, from *ileke* waist beads and *gele*s (head wraps) to drums and dashikis—loose-fitting tops, which he made himself.

Scenes from the Oyotunji village in South Carolina in 1973.

"He started a cottage industry of producing, selling, and making African attire," his wife, Queen Mother Iya Orite Olasowo Adefunmi, said in a phone interview.

The first time she saw him in New York City, he was preaching about the cosmos and African deities from a soapbox on 125th Street in Harlem, dressed in a flowing robe. Visitors to the 1964 World's Fair may have seen him drumming in the African Pavilion. Anyone who tuned in to watch the 1977 TV show *Roots* saw Olasowo and other Oyotunji residents dancing in a scene that Adefunmi produced.

In 1996, the *Miami Herald* called him the "father of the Yoruban cultural restoration movement" and said that he was central to the practice's spread around the United States and beyond. In recognition of his work, Adefunmi was crowned *oba,* or king, of the Yoruba in North America by the *ooni,* the spiritual leader of the Yoruba people in Nigeria.

Walter Eugene King was born on October 5, 1928, in Detroit to a Baptist family. He was one of five children. His mother, Wilhelmina Hamilton, worked for the Works Progress Administration, the New Deal agency, and his father, Roy King, owned and operated a furniture reupholstery and moving company. They were followers of the Black nationalist leader Marcus Garvey and were committed to his "Back to Africa" movement. But Walter was more interested in learning about Africa's cultures and religions than emigrating there.

By the time Walter graduated Cass Technical High School, he had stopped going to church. At twenty, he joined Katherine Dunham's dance company in New York City. Dunham's performances often included songs for the orishas, Yoruba deities, and took the company to places like Egypt and Haiti. On August 26, 1959, in Matanzas, Cuba, Adefunmi became the first African American fully initiated into Santería. The next year, he founded the Yoruba Temple in Harlem, which the *Amsterdam News* called the "center of African culture."

He grew uncomfortable with Santería's Catholic influence and its slave context, Kamari Clarke wrote in *Mapping Yorùbá Networks: Power and Agency in the Making of Transnational Communities* (2004). So he incorporated Black nationalism into his practice and renamed his expression of the religion Orisa-Vodun.

The Yoruba Temple attracted Black activists like the poet and playwright Amiri Baraka and Queen Mother Moore. The three served together in the Republic of New Africa, a Black nationalist organization formed on the idea that a self-governed Black nation should be created out of five Southern states. The group also sought reparations of $4 billion. In 1968, *Ebony* magazine referred to it as "the newest and perhaps boldest innovation in the history of Black separatism."

"He was a territorial nationalist," Hucks said, "and really wanted to know, how do we build a nation for ourselves in this country?"

The answer was Oyotunji Village, the community that Adefunmi I established in 1970 as "a place of rehabilitation for African Americans in search of their spiritual and cultural identity," he told *Essence* magazine. The name refers to the African Yoruba kingdom of Oyo and means "Oyo rises again." He felt the Yoruba religious movement needed a rural setting, so he chose a location in Sheldon, South Carolina, in the heart of the Gullah Geechee Cultural Heritage Corridor, where descendants of enslaved West Africans retained their Indigenous African traditions in the remote sea islands dotting the South Atlantic coast.

A sign posted in both Yoruba and English welcomes visitors to the village: "You are leaving the United States. You are entering Yoruba Kingdom . . . Welcome to Our Land!"

Walking through the village, replete with life-size carvings and shrines, "you see the magnificence of the buildings," Clarke said in an interview, adding that "you would hear the roosters crowing in the mornings" and see "people walking just in their lappas wrapped around them to go and get water, and only the Yoruba spoken." She lived at Oyotunji and traveled with its community members to Nigeria. Its evolution from a Black-only space to a site of pilgrimage and learning open to all is one of the things that has sustained it, Clarke said.

The creation of Oyotunji is, to Clarke, "a phenomenal story" of "trying to aspire to something else, something more, and rectifying the challenges with African colonialism by trying to redo it in a different way in the contemporary period."

In the process of living this ideal, "some people had to turn their back on families" who were critical of the movement and its beliefs.

African religions have traditionally been stigmatized as demonic, Hucks said, and have been sensationalized in the media, especially when it comes to the village's practice of polygamy. When Adefunmi and his wives appeared on *The Oprah Winfrey Show* in 1988 alongside Mormons and other polygamous people, "what [got] eclipsed," Hucks said, "is all of the culture and religion."

Yet Adefunmi's son Oba Adejuyigbe Adefunmi II said in an interview, "Growing up in a polygamous family, it was very easy for a child to be taken care of." His father had seventeen wives and twenty-three children in Oyotunji, and six children from previous marriages.

When Adefunmi II went to public school, before the village established its own, he was sometimes ridiculed for his African clothing and tribal markings.

"We lived in two different worlds," Adefunmi II said. "We would say, 'Why can't we just be regular?' Our parents would tell us we're not regular."

The divination he received at birth ordained that he would be the next king of their village, which for Adefunmi II "was a terrible thought [his] whole life." "I wanted to be a rapper," he said. The family traveled around the country to his father's speaking engagements in "zebra vans," old VW buses painted with black and white stripes. He remembers the zebra vans zooming down their village road to cheers when he was four. It was 1981 and they were returning with his father from a trip to Nigeria, where he had been crowned Oba Adefunmi I, the first in a line of New World Yoruba kings. (*Adefunmi* means "crown for me.")

Adefunmi I died on February 11, 2005, of heart disease. He was seventy-six.

Adefunmi II was appointed the new *oba* of the village later that year. He estimates that Oyotunji receives about twenty thousand visitors annually (with the exception of two years during the coronavirus pandemic), ranging from Yoruba practitioners to curious travelers and online visitors seeking spiritual counseling and divinations.

"Everybody's practicing Yoruba culture today," he said. "I can hear the language that people laughed at us for talking back in Savannah when we were kids. I can hear it on Spotify. I hear it all over the radio," he noted, referring to artists like India Arie, Future, and Beyoncé.

"That makes us proud," he added. "All of this is the residual effect of what our elders did and what my father did."

———

**DIONNE FORD** is the author of the memoir *Go Back and Get It: A Memoir of Race, Inheritance, and Intergenerational Healing.* She and her family have vacationed an hour south of Oyotunji on the South Carolina Sea Islands for the past two decades.

Florence Merriam Bailey pioneered modern bird-watching techniques.

## Activist Who Defined Modern Bird-Watching

# Florence Merriam Bailey

## 1863–1948

BY JONATHAN WOLFE

IN 1886, Manhattan was one of the richest bird-watching areas on the planet.

One ornithologist from the American Museum of Natural History counted forty distinct species on two walks in the city, including California quail, scissor-tailed flycatchers, and at least one green-backed heron.

But these species were not seen flitting between buildings or filling the streets with song. Rather, their earthly remains were adorning the hats of women who had succumbed to a fashion craze.

Milliners used the birds' feathers, heads, and even entire carcasses to decorate increasingly elaborate hats. The fashion trend led to the deaths worldwide of about five million birds a year.

To its devotees, the trend was fabulous. To Florence Merriam Bailey, it was murder.

"The birds must be protected; we must persuade the girls not to wear feathers in their hats," she wrote in 1889 in *Bird-Lore,* an illustrated magazine published by the National Audubon Society.

A student at Smith College at the time, Bailey decided to start a grassroots effort with a simple step: she took her fellow classmates outdoors.

"We won't say too much about the hats," she wrote in *Bird-Lore.* "We'll take the girls afield, and let them get

acquainted with the birds. Then of inborn necessity, they will wear feathers never more."

It was the beginning of an animal rights campaign that evolved into a lifelong crusade of ecological conservationism and promotion of what would become modern-day bird-watching. Bailey eventually traveled around the country to write about the pursuit.

Back then ornithology was generally practiced by examining "skins," or dead birds preserved in universities or museums. Ornithologists typically trapped or shot birds and then decamped indoors to identify the bodies. Bailey, on the other hand, urged that birds be observed quietly in their natural habitat.

"Florence was one of the first bird-watchers to actually watch birds instead of shoot them," Marcia Bonta, a naturalist and author of *Women in the Field: America's Pioneering Women Naturalists* (1991), said in a phone interview.

In 1889, at the age of twenty-six, Bailey published *Birds Through an Opera-Glass,* considered the first field guide to American birds. The book, one of many travelogues and field guides she would publish, suggested that the best way to view birds was through the lenses of opera glasses, not a shotgun sight. Her approach, now commonly practiced with binoculars, helped form the basis of modern bird-watching.

Pages from *Birds Through an Opera-Glass*, which Bailey published in 1889.

"When going to watch birds," she wrote, "proceed to some good birdy place—the bushy bank of a stream or an old juniper pasture—and sit down in the undergrowth or against a concealing tree-trunk, with your back to the sun, to look and listen in silence.

"The student who goes afield armed with opera-glass," she added, "will not only add more to our knowledge than he who goes armed with a gun, but will gain for himself a fund of enthusiasm and a lasting store of pleasant memories."

Soon hundreds of other women were protesting the millinery industry's use of birds, an effort that led to the passage in 1900 of the Lacey Act, which prohibited trade in illegally acquired wildlife, and the Migratory Bird Treaty Act of 1918, which protects migratory birds.

Florence Augusta Merriam was born on August 8, 1863, in Locust Grove, in northern New York State, to Clinton Levi Merriam, a banker and Republican congressman from New York, and Caroline Hart Merriam. Her father, who was friends with the naturalist John Muir, encouraged his four children to go outdoors and study the surroundings of Homewood, the family's estate.

Her older brother Clinton spent his childhood ensnaring animals in the woods and stuffing them. (One of Florence's pet cats became a victim when it accidentally fell into one of his traps.) Clinton Hart Merriam later became the director of the United States Biological Survey (now the United States Fish and Wildlife Service) and a founder of the National Geographic Society.

Bailey left Smith College to work for her father and later moved to New York City to do social work.

"That she had a social consciousness was unusual," Bonta said. "Most of the naturalists were entirely focused on the natural world."

While in New York, Bailey learned she had tuberculosis and decided to take the "West" cure, traveling to California, Arizona, and Utah, where she wrote travelogues and bird field guides like *My Summer in a Mormon Village* (1894), *A-Birding on a Bronco* (1896), and *Birds of Village and Field* (1898).

Her health was restored, and she moved to Washington, DC, to live with her brother Clinton, who introduced her to the naturalist Vernon Bailey. They married in 1899 and began traveling to explore the natural

Bailey, observing birds with her husband, Vernon, in Netarts, Oregon, in 1920.

world. Using a simple tent, the couple went camping every spring, summer, and fall, with Texas, California, Arizona, North and South Dakota, the Pacific Northwest, and New England among their destinations.

"By all accounts their marriage was idyllic," Bonta said. "It was collaborative, egalitarian, and they supported each other's projects and efforts."

On a trip to the Grand Canyon in 1937, Bailey described coming across a cabin after days of traveling with the couple's old white pack mule, Queen.

"How eagerly we went to work to make camp," she wrote in *Among the Birds in the Grand Canyon Country* (1939). "Our first real camp of the season, stoning up a safe camp fire, gathering snakebush for a quick blaze to cook by, bringing out cot beds left in the cabin for wayfarers, leveling their feet with stones on the downside of the slope and rolling down our sleeping bags—under the sky! How good it seemed to have heavens for a roof once more!"

Bailey and her husband went on their final camping trip, in upstate New York, in 1941, when he was seventy-eight; their aim was to see the aurora borealis. He died a year later.

Bailey died of heart failure in Washington, DC, on September 22, 1948. She was eighty-five. A small, gray mountain chickadee native to Southern California, *Parus gambeli baileyae*, had been named in her honor in 1908.

"No woman and very few men had ever known so much about all the birds of the United States," Bonta wrote in *Women in the Field: America's Pioneering Women Naturalists*. "And none had tried as hard as Florence to teach everyone—man, woman and child—about the joys of watching birds and the beauty of the natural world."

——

**JONATHAN WOLFE** is an editor at *The New York Times*. As a young Boy Scout, he collected nature field guides—mostly for the colorful animal photos.

Engineer Who Helped Save *Apollo 13*

# Judith Love Cohen

## 1933–2016

BY SHANNON HALL

WHEN JUDITH LOVE COHEN went to the hospital in labor, she took a sheet of paper with her: a printout of a pesky work problem. Later that day, she called her boss to inform him that she had found a solution—oh, and she had delivered a healthy baby boy.

Cohen, a rare woman aerospace engineer in the second half of the twentieth century, undertook several NASA projects, including ones on the Apollo space program and the Hubble Space Telescope. And she loved to solve problems.

"She was a force," said the actor Jack Black, the son who was born that day. "She would come home from work with a head full of steam—of ideas and passions.

"That was the reason she was able to bust through the walls and glass ceilings in a world that wasn't usually experienced by women," he added in a phone interview.

Cohen worked on the Apollo Abort Guidance System, a computer that lived on board the Lunar Excursion Module. During the last stage of the trip to the moon, two astronauts would move from the Command Module into the Lunar Excursion Module and drop down onto the lunar surface while a third astronaut would pilot the spacecraft. But there was a caveat: if they couldn't find a suitable place to land, the Abort Guidance System would kick into action—automatically returning them to the Command Module before they ran out of fuel. In a perfect world, it would never have been used. But when disaster struck the *Apollo 13* mission, the astronauts relied on the Abort Guidance System to bring them home. In short, it saved their lives.

Once back on Earth, the *Apollo 13* astronauts traveled to Southern California to thank the team of scientists and engineers. Cohen must have stuck out like a sore thumb: not only was she a woman, but she also did not dress in the typical work attire of the time, instead opting for loose-flowing skirts with scarves in her hair—a look that her colleague Ann Maybury described in an interview as "bohemian." When Maybury asked Cohen about her outfits, she said, "I'm a woman and they won't recognize me, so I may as well be happy the way I am."

Cohen's work didn't end there; she became a social activist for women's rights, and she founded a publishing company, where she wrote more than thirty books encouraging young girls to consider careers in math and science.

It was an unexpected path given her upbringing.

Judith Love Cohen was born on August 16, 1933, in Brooklyn to Maurice and Sarah (Roisman) Cohen. Her Jewish parents had escaped to the United States from Russia before World War I. Much of her extended family

Judith Love Cohen, shown in 1959 with an early Pioneer spacecraft, took on several projects for NASA.

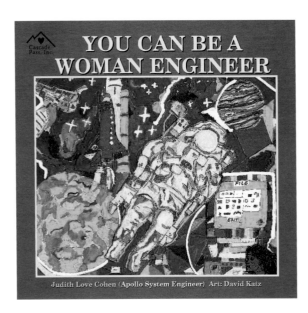

YOU CAN BE A WOMAN ENGINEER

Judith Love Cohen (Apollo System Engineer) Art: David Katz

Cohen published children's books about women in science, including *You Can Be a Woman Engineer* (1991).

was killed during the Russian Revolution and ensuing civil war and World War II.

Although her parents, who settled in Brooklyn, considered themselves lucky, they continued to face discrimination and worked hard to earn a living; Cohen's father sold seltzer water from a wagon.

The women in Judith's family worked at a dress factory, and she was expected to follow their path. But her father taught her basic geometry and encouraged her to learn math and science. At the age of eight, she would take the subway by herself to Manhattan to attend ballet lessons and visit the science museum. By the time she was nineteen, she was dancing with the Metropolitan Opera's ballet company and studying engineering at Brooklyn College.

After Cohen attended college for two years, she married her first husband, Bernard Siegel, and moved

to California. During the next decade, she worked as a junior engineer for North American Aviation, had her first three children, and attended the University of Southern California's engineering school—where she never encountered another female student; in fact, she had to go to another corner of campus just to find a women's restroom.

"It was definitely a man's world," David Katz, her third husband, said in an interview. "And it was a real struggle to get respect for what she was doing."

But she rarely complained.

"She didn't need permission, she didn't need mentors, and she didn't need role models," said her son Neil Siegel. "She was her own guidance system."

Cohen graduated with a master's degree in electrical engineering in 1957 and began working at Space Technology Laboratories, which eventually became TRW. Although her résumé later included working on the Minuteman missile during the Cold War and the Hubble Space Telescope, she considered the Apollo program to be the highlight of her career.

Cohen divorced Bernard Siegel in the mid-1960s. She then married Thomas William Black and had her fourth child, but they divorced in the late 1970s. She married Katz in the early 1980s. Together thirty-five years, they had a happy marriage. "I really looked up to her tremendously," Katz said. "To me, she was like a goddess."

Cohen worked as an advocate for women's rights, encouraging TRW to post job openings inside the company and write formal descriptions for every position—a change that made those positions more accessible to women. "She and they became kind of pioneers for better treatment of women in the workplace," Siegel said.

She retired in 1990, but even then she wasn't the type of woman to sit still. The next year she wrote a children's book called *You Can Be a Woman Engineer,* which traced her career trajectory. And when she couldn't find a publisher, she and Katz started their own company—ultimately publishing an entire series featuring female professionals in science positions.

"By the time she was done," Siegel said, "she must have influenced tens of thousands of girls."

She had that same influence on those close to her. "I think she taught her children, her peers, and me, of course, to go for your dreams," Katz said.

Black agreed, adding that he would often find a job, lose that job, and move back home—a cycle that repeated throughout his twenties before his acting career took off.

"She never kicked me out on my can," he said. "I would come crawling back and she would always take me in. My bedroom was always kept the same."

Cohen died of cancer on July 25, 2016. She was eighty-two.

Toward the end of her career, she worked on the Hubble Space Telescope, whose iconic images have shaped our view of the cosmos. She was the deputy system engineer on Hubble's ground system—a massive database that handled mission planning, observation support, and routine data processing. The last step was particularly complex since that data first went through an editing pipeline, where instrumental artifacts—defects introduced by the camera itself—for example, were removed.

"Her résumé was pretty shiny to a little kid," Black said. "And the cool thing about the Hubble is that, you know, we still get photos from deep inside the universe. And every time we get a new one that I see on the internet, I think of my mom and it's kind of a beautiful thing."

A yearbook photo of Cohen when she graduated as the only woman from the University of Southern California's engineering school.

**SHANNON HALL** is an award-winning freelance science journalist based in the Rocky Mountains. Hubble's iconic photographs encouraged her to study astronomy and ultimately write about it for a living.

# Fannie Farmer

## 1857–1915

BY JULIA MOSKIN

RECIPES IN NINETEENTH-CENTURY cookbooks relied on measurements like a "handful" of rice or a "goodly amount" of molasses—on the assumption that women largely knew how to cook.

Fannie Merritt Farmer changed all that. Widely credited with inventing the modern recipe, Farmer was the first professional cook to insist that scientific methods and precise measurements—level teaspoons, cups, and ounces—produce better food; she was also the first to demonstrate that cooking classes could be mass-market entertainment.

These were just a few of her contributions as the foremost cooking teacher, writer, and lecturer of her day. Chiefly, she was responsible for *The Boston Cooking-School Cook Book*. First published under her name in 1896, it was a bestseller and remains in print, with more than seven million copies sold. The book's popularity and longevity has made Farmer a primary source for generations of American cooks.

"Correct measurements are absolutely necessary to ensure the best results," Farmer famously wrote.

Julia Child, one of the only American cooks to become as widely influential as Farmer, said that *The Boston Cooking-School Cook Book* was the primary reference in her own mother's kitchen and that she cut her teeth as a cook on its pancakes, popovers, and fudge recipes.

Both women were famous as teachers and writers, not as brilliant cooks. Child and Farmer were considered unusual in their time: both were ambitious, charismatic media titans; purveyors of domestic wisdom who led unconventional domestic lives; and privileged women from old New England families with a strong sense of how things ought to be done.

Born in Boston on March 23, 1857, Farmer was raised in nearby Medford by genteel but financially struggling parents, John Franklin Farmer, a printer and editor, and Mary Watson Merritt. A great-niece described them as "Unitarian and bookish." The eldest of four daughters, Fannie planned to attend college and become a schoolteacher, one of the few professional avenues open to women at the time. But after she suffered some paralysis in her lower body at age sixteen, probably from polio, the prevailing medical wisdom dictated that she could not leave home or apply herself intellectually.

In her twenties, Farmer was finally allowed to work, becoming a kind of governess in the home of a wealthy family friend. It was her employer who encouraged Farmer to expand her culinary knowledge, according to Laura Shapiro, author of *Perfection Salad: Women and Cooking at the Turn of the Century* (1986).

Farmer, seated at bottom left, joined the staff of the Boston Cooking School just after graduating.

At thirty-one, Farmer enrolled in the august Boston Cooking School, which was founded as a philanthropic venture to enable women of modest means to find work as cooks in private homes and institutions. Its stated promise was "to lift this great social incubus of bad cooking and its incident evils from the households of the country at large." She joined the staff just after graduating, in 1889.

The concepts of "domestic science" and "home economics" were in their infancy, but these factors—bolstered by the work of women like Farmer and her colleagues Mary Lincoln, Maria Parloa, and Ellen Swallow Richards, the first woman to be admitted to the Massachusetts Institute of Technology—were already shaping the field.

This new scientific approach to cooking made culinary expertise accessible to anyone willing to study. And as Farmer's knowledge of food deepened throughout her career, she became a respected expert on the topic of diet and health.

She became a multimedia culinary force, a frequent figure on the lecture circuit whose weekly lectures were published in the *Boston Evening Transcript*. (She was one of the first women to lecture at Harvard Medical School.)

Her charisma and energy at the podium brought women of higher social strata under her sway, and she expanded her knowledge to encompass dishes for dinner parties, ladies' luncheons, and more.

In 1902, she started Miss Farmer's School of Cookery, which was not only educational but also profitable, allowing her to buy land, build a house, and support her parents, sisters, and other family members.

She also acted as food editor for the influential magazine *Woman's Home Companion* and promoted standards of detail and precision that survive to this day.

Measuring cups and spoons were already available, suggesting that she was not the inventor of such standards but rather an effective evangelist for them. And powerful new products like baking powder and compressed yeast were making precision in recipes much more important.

"I'm sure the fact that her cake and pie recipes actually worked was a huge part of her success," Shapiro said in an interview.

Farmer died of complications of a stroke on January 15, 1915. She was fifty-seven.

Even after her death, her cookbook was frequently revised, most thoroughly and successfully in 1979 by Marion Cunningham, who took its classic recipes into the modern era.

Earlier books, including previous editions of *The Boston Cooking-School Cook Book*, assumed that all women were taught basic culinary skills at home and that they did not need to be told what pie dough should feel like or how to roast beef. But much of that changed after the Industrial Revolution. Traditional skills like preserving, cheese making, and bread baking ebbed, and Boston and other cities became magnets for new kinds of Americans: single women, young people, and immigrant families, all in need of homes, jobs, and food.

Under a new name, *The Fannie Farmer Cookbook* has sold three million more copies; many cooks still rely on it for basics like Parker House rolls, scalloped potatoes, and waffles. (*The Joy of Cooking,* with its more cosmopolitan and friendly tone, gradually displaced the Farmer cookbook as the standard kitchen bible after it was published in 1931.)

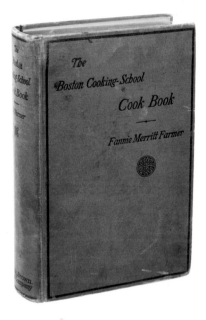

*The Boston Cooking-School Cook Book* was originally published by Farmer in 1896.

But Farmer's enduring legacy is a simple one: exactitude in cooking.

"She made it possible for any woman to put a meal on the table, even if she couldn't cook at all," Shapiro said. "There's nothing more democratizing than that."

———

**JULIA MOSKIN** has been a food reporter for *The New York Times* since 2004 and was a recipient of the 2018 Pulitzer Prize for Public Service. Her first culinary project was Fannie Farmer's griddlecakes.

Lillias Campbell Davidson encouraged women to bicycle
when they were considered "by nature physically unfit."

# Lillias Campbell Davidson

## 1853–1934

BY AMANDA HESS

WHEN WE TALK ABOUT "MOBILITY" for women, these days, we're often speaking metaphorically about social and economic opportunities. But in the late 1800s, the writer Lillias Campbell Davidson dedicated herself to advocating for women to become literally mobile—to travel alone in carriages and in trains; to embark on long walks and climb mountaintops; and especially, to experience the freedom and thrill of riding a bicycle.

Davidson started riding in the early 1880s, when she was in her late twenties, and quickly styled herself as an advocate and expert. Women cyclists were viewed as so improper in her neighborhood in the south of England that she rode in the early morning, when the streets were empty; she once turned down a side street to avoid being spied riding by the town vicar. Soon, Davidson was publicly advocating for women to join her, in ladies' columns for the *Scottish Cyclist* and *The Cyclists' Touring Club Gazette.* In 1892, she founded the Lady Cyclists' Association, an early cycling organization for women, and served as its president for the next five years. In 1896, she published her collected wisdom in *Handbook for Lady Cyclists.*

"A new world of enjoyment is unlocked to the woman who finds herself a-wheel," Davidson wrote. Cycling "is a door that leads to many paths of pleasure."

One such pleasure was simply physical. Davidson championed "the feeling of active movement, of the power of free locomotion, the thrill of healthful exertion, and the bounding of the pulses." But bicycling also allowed middle-class women to escape their homes—"the lives of women have been unnaturally cramped and contracted within doors," she wrote—and travel to see new country-side sights and tour other towns alone.

Cycling also helped radicalize the female wardrobe. The rise of cycling dovetailed with the rational dress movement, and Davidson encouraged women to shed corsets and petticoats in favor of more practical attire. In an 1894 issue of *The Cyclists' Touring Club Gazette,* Davidson dismissed the "war against rational dress" as not "very convincing or very full of logic" and quoted one Baltimore woman's response to those who would shame her for wearing bloomers on her bike: "I can ride faster than people can talk."

As the suffragist Susan B. Anthony told the journalist Nellie Bly in 1896, bicycling "has done more to emancipate women than anything else in the world." That made the bike a controversial accessory for a lady up until the turn of the century. As late as 1893, as Julie Wosk details in her history *Women and the Machine, Cycling* magazine discouraged women from riding, writing that "for feats of speed

502   *Home Notes.*   JULY 4, 1896.

## THE LADY CYCLIST.

BY LILIAS CAMPBELL DAVIDSON. *(President of the Lady Cyclists' Association.)*

THERE has been an effort in the cycling page of a certain well-known paper to combat the idea that long gear is undesirable for ladies. The writer scouts the suggestion, and advocates cranks of from six and three-quarters to seven inches on a lady's machine, if her gearing is sixty-three or sixty-six. She bases her opinion on some recent experiments of her Osmond, which, I would like to remark, is better suited to the needs of men than of my own sex. Decidedly, if the gearing is high, longer cranks can be used, but neither high gearing nor long cranks suit feminine needs as well as a lower gearing and shorter cranks, nor are they as desirable. The ordinary woman, unless upon the racing track, does not go in for great speed. While long cranks in no wise undesirable affect a man's appearance awheel, they have undoubtedly that effect upon a woman who wears a skirt. The longer the crank-throw, the more pronounced the movement of the knees, and to overcome this is the desire of every woman who aims at being a graceful rider. With short cranks the revolutions are more rapid, but the ugly threshing movement of the knees becomes far less apparent, and no woman, unless exceptionally tall, should be led away by such advice, to indulge in seven inch cranks, unless she wants to make herself look conspicuously ugly.

Too many writers on cycling subjects are apt to overlook the fact that a woman's costume calls for many modifications in her machine, unnecessary to a man. Miss Lillian Russell's golden bicycle is making the mouths of some envious women water, and so is the description of another just turned out, in which the handle bar is studded with gems. It is needless to point out the ostentation of such motiveless adornment of the cycle, which no one need be anxious to copy. Of course Miss Lillian Russell's mount was presented by a host of admirers, and is an exceptional thing; but the be-gemmed and be-gilded cycle can answer no sensible purpose, that anyone can guess at, beyond that of inciting to further effort the already active cycle thief, and of causing its unhappy owner perpetual anxiety when it is out of her sight for more than an instant.

A great many riders who ordered their new mounts early this season, so as to be provided with a means of enjoyment from the time country roads got into condition, have been desperately disappointed not to have received them even yet. The orders were so enormous that they have not yet been executed, though the manufacturers are working their hardest to get them done.

Two ladies I know of, ordered their new bicycles in March, and have not got them yet, and the firm, one of the best and most dependable in the country, have announced weeks ago that no more orders could be received before the autumn, though those in hand were being executed with all the speed possible to employ.

It is amusing to see how steeped in pride some novices become as soon as they are able to achieve a little finish on their cycles. The other day the public on a certain promenade, much frequented by fashionable strollers, was kept in a state of amusement by a girl who had just mastered the art of taking both hands off. They were not taken far, but curved with an apprehensive readiness close to the handles, and the care with which the rider managed her mount verged on the agonised. Yet to judge by her air of elation, and the number of times she rode up and down that promenade, casting looks of triumph on either side, she apparently believed herself to have invented the accomplishment she had just acquired, and to be astonishing an admiring world by its display.

Cycling has claimed for it that it is one of the finest steadiers of feminine nerve ever invented. Women who have previously found it impossible to brave the terrors of a crossing, now project themselves into crowded traffic with an absolute recklessness of risk that amazes and alarms the bystanders. A cycle agent told me that his little daughter will ride between the wheels of carts and drays with a disregard of consequences which makes him tremble, and yet, till she took to cycling, she was the victim of nerves which failed her at the most imaginary perils. It is one more thing that women in general have to thank cycling for.

I have so often to use my pen in warning enthusiastic cyclists that cycling, like all good things, needs to be cultivated with temperance, that I should be glad to think my warnings were no longer required. But I have just heard of a young and perfectly healthy girl, who has strained her heart from over indulgence in her beloved exercise, and, after three weeks in bed, has been forbidden to ride again for months. Lest anyone should think it is the use of the bicycle and not its abuse that brought about such consequences, I may say that she used to boast she could spend the entire day on her bicycle, only getting off for meals, and that she prided herself on never giving in, however much fatigue possessed her. It is a thousand pities that girls should be so foolish, for by abusing cycling they not only injure themselves, but it, by creating a reasonless prejudice against it.

An 1896 article by Davidson in *Home Notes.*

and protracted endurance, she is by nature physically unfit, and bound morally, if she respects her sex, to avoid anything in the nature of deleterious excess of exertion."

Davidson herself emerged as a moderate, sometimes even a traditionalist, on the subject of gender. She discouraged women from racing, writing in her handbook that "a woman's nervous system suffers a hundred times more than a man's from this excitement."

She wrote that housewives who took up cycling could return to their work "cheered, refreshed and braced to take up the burden of daily commonplace life once more." And while she encouraged each woman cyclist to understand how every nut and spoke worked on her machine, she warned that "there is no necessity for her to be constantly airing her knowledge in conversation."

Davidson also occasionally revealed herself as a casual and cruel elitist. When she spoke of assisting her "sisters in their wanderings," she was speaking exclusively to women of the middle and upper classes. In *Hints to Lady Travellers,* a travel guide she published in 1889, she schooled women on how to purchase train tickets, pack for a trip, and embark on long-distance hikes. But she also warned her readers to be careful around servants, who are "drawn from a very inferior class"; referred to a maid as a "feather-headed domestic"; and wrote that "the most unpleasant fellow-travellers" are "ladies' maids and footmen." She also cautioned against traveling in certain women-only carriages, which she said attracted "aggressive-looking females."

She wrote as a woman afraid that her newfound freedom would be seized from her if women failed to bike and travel in a way that ultimately reified traditional gender roles and class structures.

"Every woman should look upon herself as, in certain measure, an advocate, so to speak, of the pastime among the members of her own sex," she wrote of cycling. "If she rides in a slovenly, awkward style, and sits her saddle ungracefully—if she dashes frantically along, hot, dusty, and purple of visage, she will surely not win many recruits to the paths of cycling, but frighten them instead, from doing as she has done."

Davidson's own life was marked by travel. Though she didn't write much about herself, surviving census and probate records etch out the contours of her movements. She was born in Brooklyn in 1853 and later moved to England, where she shared an apartment with a couple of other young women, Ménie Muriel Dowie and Alice Werner, at a time when it was still provocative for women to live without men.

The writer Ethel F. Heddle novelized their experience in her 1896 book, *Three Girls in a Flat,* in which she described the ambivalent experience when the freedom of living alone collides with "the sordid, matter-of-fact worries incident on having very little money." Davidson later settled in Southsea, which *The Wheelwoman* called "that ideal place for cyclists."

In her fiction—she'd ultimately publish fourteen novels and many more short stories—Davidson wrote of women who struck out on their own in their youth, only to come around (and, often, return home) to the traditional role of marriage. Davidson herself never did. When she died, in her eighties, in 1934, a probate listing of her estate described her simply as a "spinster."

**AMANDA HESS** is a critic-at-large. She writes about internet and pop culture for *The New York Times* Arts section and contributes regularly to *The New York Times Magazine.*

# Beyond the Obit: A Complex Life

### BY AMANDA HESS

When I started my research for my obituary about Lillias Campbell Davidson, I fell in love with her a little bit. I collected her sharp-witted nineteenth-century quips and gutsy anecdotes like treasures. I envisioned her as a woman who cannily took up a new technology that had been invented just for men and used it to secure her own freedom.

Then I read her 1889 handbook, *Hints to Lady Travellers: At Home and Abroad,* and learned that Davidson was not, after all, the champion of women I had held in high esteem. She was an elitist who warned wealthier women riders against the "very inferior class" of servants and "aggressive-looking females" they might meet while on the road. And even while encouraging middle- and upper-class white women, like herself, to travel far afield, she insisted that they maintain an air of grace and subservience to men, writing, "If there is a man at the head of affairs, he had better be left to manage matters without the hampering interference of feminine physical weakness."

At first, I felt embarrassed about my initial admiration for Davidson. Then I realized that I had approached her life story with a bias of my own—I had wanted her to be likable; instead, she was complicated. She was both an activist and an egoist, a feminist and a classist, ahead of her time yet resolutely retrograde. In the end, I didn't exactly love her, but I came to love her story and how it exemplifies the contradictory, and even limiting, impulses hidden beneath the fight for social progress.

Margaret McFarland's father died when she was five, an event that piqued her interest in child psychology.

Child Psychologist and Mentor to Mister Rogers

# Margaret McFarland

## 1905–1988

BY CHRISTINA CARON

NEARLY EVERYONE KNOWS about Fred Rogers, the beloved host of *Mister Rogers' Neighborhood* who taught millions of children about love, kindness, and the magic of make-believe. But far fewer people are familiar with Margaret McFarland, the child psychologist who mentored him and helped shape his groundbreaking television show.

Rogers first met McFarland in the 1950s, when he was a puppeteer and a producer on a Pittsburgh public television show called *The Children's Corner.* During lunch breaks he attended classes to earn a master's degree in divinity.

When Rogers expressed an interest in learning about the psychology of children, one of his professors recommended that he meet McFarland, who was regarded as one of the most respected child psychologists in Pittsburgh.

She saw great potential in Rogers.

"Fred Rogers is a man who has not closed off the channels of communication between his childhood and his manhood," McFarland told *The Washington Post* in 1982. "Repression, you see, is not his major defense."

But she felt it was a disservice that "he worked off-camera, behind the scenes, manipulating his various puppets." So she told him: "Fred, the children need to see you. They need you to help them distinguish between reality and fantasy."

Rogers was ordained as a minister and was invited to appear as Mister Rogers on a show in Canada in the early 1960s. He returned to Pittsburgh in 1966 to start *Mister Rogers' Neighborhood* on WQED-TV. The show aired for the first time nationally, on public television stations, in 1968. McFarland became his chief consultant.

She and Rogers met nearly every week to discuss scripts and songs that Rogers had written. According to Arthur Greenwald, a producer and writer who worked with Rogers, McFarland's advice became so valuable to Rogers that he took "extensive handwritten notes" and recorded their meetings on audiocassettes, which Greenwald said he "often overheard him replaying in his office."

She would work on the show for twenty years and spoke regularly with Rogers until around her death in 1988. (Rogers died in 2003.)

"She will make just one suggestion, and it raises the whole level," Rogers told *The Pittsburgh Press* in 1987, adding that she was "an enormous influence on" him.

His book *Mister Rogers Talks with Parents* (1983, with Barry Head) is dedicated to McFarland. And the creators of *Daniel Tiger's Neighborhood,* the modern-day animated spinoff of *Mister Rogers,* honored McFarland by naming the main character's little sister Margaret.

Even though the show first aired more than a half century ago, it still resonates. In 2018, a documentary about Rogers grossed more than $22 million, and in 2019, he was portrayed by Tom Hanks in the acclaimed movie *A Beautiful Day in the Neighborhood.*

Margaret Beall McFarland was born on July 3, 1905, in Oakdale, Pennsylvania, a suburb of Pittsburgh, the youngest of three girls of Robert and Gertrude (Messer) McFarland. Her father died when she was five, an event that would later pique her interest in child psychology.

"All of the subsequent phases of what it means to be loved by a male and loving to a male were lost to me," she told *The Pittsburgh Press* in 1987. "I wanted a kind of fathering."

She graduated from Goucher College in Towson, Maryland, in 1927, received her master's degree from Columbia University in 1928, and later earned her PhD from Teachers College at Columbia University.

After graduating, she became principal of the Kindergarten Training College of Melbourne, Australia, then returned to the United States to serve as director of the children's school at Mount Holyoke College, a women's college in South Hadley, Massachusetts, where she was promoted to associate professor of psychology in 1948.

She returned to her hometown in 1951 and was an associate professor at the University of Pittsburgh when she met Rogers.

At the time, she was also working as the executive director of the Arsenal Family and Children's Center, a training ground for pediatric students to study child development; it was founded in 1953 by Benjamin Spock, the pediatrician and bestselling author. He and McFarland collaborated with Erik Erikson, the developmental psychologist known for coining the phrase "identity crisis." (Arsenal is now a preschool and social service agency.)

McFarland believed that an adequate understanding of child development was, as she wrote, "crucial in the solution of many of the problems with which man is grappling." She would often bring in a mother and child to her classroom, ask her students to observe their behavior, then spend hours afterward discussing their interactions.

McFarland was also fond of teaching by parable, gently guiding her students toward clarity by telling stories and asking questions rather than providing critiques. Her methods made a lasting impression.

"There was something very unique about the way she connected with people," said Judith A. Rubin, a therapist who helped people deal with trauma through art. Rubin worked with McFarland at the Arsenal center and appeared as the "art lady" on *Mister Rogers' Neighborhood* in the show's early years.

"I think she had Fred Rogers's capacity to make the person feel as if they were extremely important and interesting," she added.

Serious and reserved, McFarland was content to avoid the spotlight, even as Mister Rogers became a staple for generations of children. She preferred to be a "counterpart to the creative person," said Hedda B. Sharapan, a senior fellow at the Fred Rogers Center and a child development consultant at Fred Rogers Productions.

"She gave him the road map of child development and then said, 'Now you take the journey in the way that's right for your creative spirit,'" Sharapan said. "Fred somehow, with Margaret's help, was able to tap into his own childhood."

In 1979, during a symposium honoring Rogers, Erikson surprised her in front of more than one thousand people at a banquet by acknowledging her research with a special presentation.

"We almost had to drag her out of the chair to stand up," Douglas Nowicki, a friend who is the chancellor of Saint Vincent College in Pennsylvania, said in a phone interview. "She would never have come if she had known in any way she was going to be recognized or honored."

Greenwald, the producer who often worked with Rogers, once suggested that they go out to lunch with friends to celebrate McFarland's birthday.

Fred Rogers and McFarland in 1978.

"Almost predictably, Margaret wouldn't hear of us making such a fuss, and instead invited us to her house, where she would prepare the lunch," he said. "We agreed, because why not? And because beneath that frail exterior was hundreds of years of stubborn Scottish-Presbyterian willfulness that you'd be crazy to mess with."

She loved to feed others. "How she found the time to create the fanciest cookies (in her own kitchen) I'll never know," Rogers wrote in an obituary about her.

McFarland never married or had children. She lived alone in the home in which she grew up, surrounded by her extensive book collection.

Later in life she learned she had myelofibrosis, a rare bone marrow disease, but she continued conducting research and was absorbed in the study of ego development as late as 1987.

News reports of her death at eighty-three, on September 12, 1988, were modest, much like McFarland herself. *The New York Times*, like several other major newspapers, published a brief obituary by the Associated Press. In Pittsburgh, however, original obituaries appeared in the *Pittsburgh Post-Gazette* and *The Pittsburgh Press*.

Her books, which numbered in the thousands, were donated to Saint Vincent College, where the Fred Rogers Center was established in 2003, the year of Rogers's death.

———

**CHRISTINA CARON** is a mental health reporter on the Well desk at *The New York Times*. She attended undergraduate school at Mount Holyoke College, where Margaret McFarland had taught psychology decades earlier.

## Inventor of an Early E-Reader

# Ángela Ruiz Robles

## 1895–1975

BY CINDY SHMERLER

MORE THAN SIXTY YEARS before Kindles, Nooks, iPads, and other electronic devices revolutionized reading, there was a gadget invented in a small village in Spain that had the potential to do the same.

The Enciclopedia Mecánica, or Mechanical Encyclopedia, as it was known, was not the brainchild of a multinational corporation like Apple or Amazon; it was invented by Ángela Ruiz Robles, a widowed teacher who wanted to make learning easier for her students and her three daughters.

Her invention, a pale green box about the size of a textbook with an intricate interior, allowed a user to read any book in any language and on any topic, and was intended to lighten the load of a student's backpack. Today it is seen by many as an analog ancestor of the e-reader.

"What she invented carried on into the future," said Daniel Gonzalez de la Rivera, Ruiz Robles's grandson, in a phone interview from his home in Madrid.

"Each time I see one I am reminded of my grandmother," he added.

Within the Mechanical Encyclopedia's covers were three sets of spools that held scrolls that could be swapped out. The scrolls held text, elaborate line drawings, and ornamental figure sketches, and the encyclopedia contained a small lightbulb, so users could read in the dark. Ruiz Robles created the device, she told the newspaper *Pueblo* in 1958, "to get maximum knowledge with minimum effort."

The machine, which Ruiz Robles called "a mechanical, electrical and air pressure procedure for reading books," received Spanish patent 190,698 in 1949. A prototype received another patent, 276,346, when it was assembled in 1962.

Decades later, in November 2007, Amazon introduced the Kindle, with a six-inch electronic-ink screen that allowed users to download and read some 88,000 books and magazines. The devices sold out in less than six hours. By 2018, Amazon reported selling close to 90 million e-readers. According to Statista, which specializes in market and consumer data, 191 million e-books were sold worldwide in 2020.

Ruiz Robles was ahead of her time. The technology available to her was nowhere near as versatile as e-ink, and touch screens did not exist. Despite repeated efforts, she failed to convince financiers to fund her creation, and it was never widely produced.

Today, the prototype of Ruiz Robles's Mechanical Encyclopedia is displayed prominently at the National Museum of Science and Technology in A Coruña, Spain,

a source of pride for her country and a testament to what might have been.

Ángela Ruiz Robles was born on March 28, 1895, in Villamanín, a small town in the province of Leon in northwestern Spain. Her father, Feliciano Ruiz, a wealthy pharmacist, and mother, Elena Robles, a homemaker, ensured that she had a top-notch education. She graduated from a teachers college in Leon, then taught there until 1916.

In 1918, Ruiz Robles moved to Santa Eugenia de Mandiá, a village in Galicia near the coast, where she worked as a teacher until 1928. She then moved to nearby Ferrol and founded the Academia Elmaca.

The school, located in her home and named for her three daughters, Elena, Elvira, and Maria Carmen, offered classes by day and at night served as a training ground for students of few means. She also developed effective educational methods for students with disabilities, sometimes showing up at their homes to offer extra help.

In 1934, Ruiz Robles became manager of the Escuela Nacional de Niñas del Hospicio, a national school for orphans in Ferrol, where she helped girls who might otherwise have been disadvantaged to thrive in society.

She found great meaning in working on behalf of others.

"We come to this world not only to live our life as comfortable as possible," she told *Pueblo* in 1958, "but to worry about others so that they can benefit from something offered by us."

Between 1938 and 1946, Ruiz Robles published sixteen textbooks, including tutorials in spelling, grammar, syntax, shorthand, and phonetics. But in 1946, her husband, Andrés Grandal, a merchant marine, died of a heart attack, leaving her to raise her three daughters alone.

Despite Ruiz Robles's considerable domestic and teaching duties, she devoted what spare time she had to inventing a modern, interactive approach to education.

Gonzalez de la Rivera described his grandmother as driven, noting that she preferred the solitude of her office and the clacking of her typewriter keys to sitting in cafés or playing cards with friends.

"She never wasted time," he said. "She didn't look at the birds. She was always working."

"Can a good inventor be a good housewife at the same time? Yes, yes, but it is necessary that the servants or people around her do not force her into extensive conversations of ordinary things," she told *Pueblo*. "Silence is essential as it facilitates the gestation of those ideas which then favor the progress of the world."

In 1947, Ruiz Robles was awarded the Cross of Alfonso X the Wise for her innovations in the field of education, research, and social work. In 1952, she was awarded a gold medal at an exhibition for Spanish inventors.

She spent the last few years of her life in Madrid with her daughter Maria Carmen, and she never gave up on having her invention manufactured. Ruiz Robles had offers to produce it in the United States, but she shunned them, saying her creation had to be made in Spain.

"I went with her to different organizations and lawyers to push her mechanical book," said Gonzalez de la Rivera. "I explained how the product worked and how to make the book less heavy. We made the rounds without success. But my grandmother was never frustrated. I never remember her telling me, 'What a pity' or 'What a disaster.' She was never frightened away."

Ruiz Robles died on October 27, 1975. She was eighty.

In 2018, Madrid's city council approved the naming of a street for her in the Spanish capital.

"She was one lady with three daughters and without a husband," said Gonzalez de la Rivera, adding, "It is incredible, what she did."

———

**CINDY SHMERLER** is a freelance writer and frequent contributor to *The New York Times International* sports section. Though she sometimes uses an e-reader, she still cherishes the feel of newsprint on her fingers.

Robles with her Mechanical Encyclopedia.

Reproductive Rights Advocate

# Barbara Waxman Fiduccia

## 1955–2001

BY DENISE GELLENE

BARBARA WAXMAN FIDUCCIA took pride in her identity as a disabled woman. Her stylish dress, whether a kimono-sleeved jacket, leather miniskirt, or leopard-print shoes, was more than an expression of personal taste. To Fiduccia, a reproductive rights activist who used a ventilator and maneuvered her wheelchair with a sort of regal command, her clothing was part of a political statement, a demand to be seen in full.

"She loved her body," said Alice Wong, an activist and author who was a member of the National Council on Disability during the Obama administration and who looked to Fiduccia as a role model. "She was an unapologetically sexual disabled woman—unapologetic about her politics and the way she lived her life."

Fiduccia was among the first to campaign openly for reproductive rights for people with disabilities. In trenchant essays and policy papers, she challenged a dominant culture that viewed them as asexual beings, with no feelings of intimacy or desire to have children.

These attitudes, she said, were translated into public policies that discouraged disabled couples from marrying and having families, and that prevented them from enjoying sexually fulfilling lives.

In her fifteen years as a sexual health educator and counselor in Los Angeles, Fiduccia regularly saw clients who experienced self-loathing and sexual loneliness—a consequence, she said, of internalized cultural notions.

She pushed to broaden the disability rights movement beyond physical access to transportation, public buildings, schools, and places of employment. Disabled people, she wrote in a 1991 essay, are "concerned with being loved and finding sexual fulfillment."

"Why hasn't our movement politicized our sexual oppression as we do transportation and attendant services?" she wrote in the essay, which was published in *The Disability Rag,* a magazine devoted to disability issues. "I believe we don't speak out because we believe we are ultimately to blame for not getting laid—that it is somehow a personal inferiority."

Her message was empowering.

"She believed that denying your sexuality was denying your personhood," Corbett Joan O'Toole, a disability rights activist and owner of Reclamation Press, a publisher of books by authors with disabilities, said in a phone interview. "She came from the place of a woman in an electric wheelchair, speaking for people who were taught to be ashamed of who they are."

Fiduccia pushed for increased access to reproductive services, including mammograms and pelvic exams. She and others successfully lobbied to expand the national

Hate Crime Statistics Act to include violence against people with disabilities. She also served on the California attorney general's Civil Rights Commission on Hate Crimes.

With her future husband, Daniel Fiduccia, a legal affairs consultant she met at a 1992 training session for disability advocates, she fought to raise the income limit for federal health benefits, which stood in the way of marriage for disabled couples. Daniel Fiduccia was a survivor of childhood cancer, and his mobility was limited from radiation treatments that had weakened his bones.

Under federal health limits, Barbara Fiduccia's salary as a single woman was low enough for Medicare and Medicaid to cover the cost of her personal attendants and ventilator. But the couple's combined income was over the limit, forcing them to choose between marriage and the health benefits that helped keep Barbara Fiduccia alive. Her dilemma, she told the *San Jose Mercury News* in 1995, felt "like a dirty joke."

"I was told in so many ways as a girl that I'd always be alone," she told the newspaper. Instead, she said, she found "tremendous love and passion" with a man who wanted to spend his life with her.

"I got over the stigma," she said, "and now I can't get married."

Her ventilator strapped to the back of her wheelchair, Barbara Fiduccia made the rounds on Capitol Hill, advocating alongside other disability activists, while Daniel Fiduccia helped map out a legal strategy. Although Congress did not eliminate the so-called marriage penalty, the rules were changed in the mid-1990s to allow states to grant waivers to individual couples.

"They wanted to be married, and this was their one shot," Marsha Saxton, director of research and training at the World Institute on Disability in Oakland, California, and a friend of Barbara Fiduccia, said in a phone interview. "But they also wanted to change policy."

The couple married in July 1996 in a small Roman Catholic service near their home in Cupertino, California, said Rick Santina, a family friend who attended. They were fond of children, though they had none of their own.

Santina said his children came to know Barbara Fiduccia as "Aunt Beep" because she let them blast the horn on her wheelchair as she gave them rides on her lap.

Barbara Faye Waxman was born in Los Angeles on April 1, 1955, the younger of two children of Sol Waxman, owner of a commercial photography lab, and Toby (Lowsky) Waxman. She and her brother, Michael, had spinal muscular atrophy, an inherited disorder that causes progressive muscle weakness. Her parents were told she would not live past thirty.

Because she could walk as a child, albeit with difficulty, her parents wrestled with whether to enroll her in special education classes, where she was more likely to make friends, or in regular public school classes, where she would receive a better education. They chose the latter, an environment Fiduccia described years later as "psychologically damaging."

During recess in grade school, a teacher routinely admonished her to run, though young Barbara was incapable of doing so. In high school, she tripped almost daily on an uneven carpet as her math teacher walked past her, staring.

"In those twelve years, though they never spoke of it, I believe it was my disability they saw, while forgetting it was a child who possessed it," she said.

After receiving her bachelor's degree in psychology from California State University, Northridge, in 1978, Fiduccia went to work at Planned Parenthood in Los Angeles as a health educator and disability project coordinator. Clients told her that gynecologists, like her former teachers, often focused on their disabilities instead of on their reproductive health needs.

"I know of many times when a woman has been sent back to her orthopedist for a Pap smear," she said in her 1985 testimony before a congressional committee exploring changes to Title IX, which bars gender discrimination at institutions receiving federal funding.

But Fiduccia eventually left Planned Parenthood, pained by what she called a "strong eugenics mentality that established disdain, discomfort and ignorance toward disabled babies."

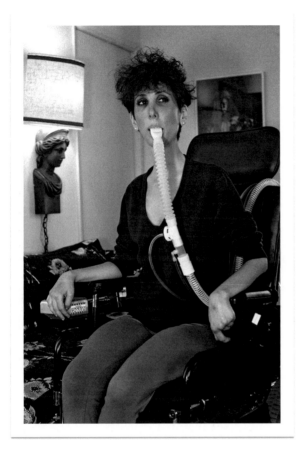

Fiduccia was among the first to campaign openly for reproductive rights for people with disabilities.

She cringed whenever her coworkers discussed prenatal testing and the need to abort a disabled fetus. "There was a feeling that there were bad babies," she told *The New York Times* in 1991.

Fiduccia then worked at the Los Angeles Regional Family Planning Council, an umbrella organization for more than one hundred clinics, where she continued her focus on reproductive health for women with disabilities. After that, she served as a senior associate at the Center for Women Policy Studies, a feminist policy research organization.

Her husband, an advocate for childhood cancer survivors, died after a recurrence of cancer in 2001. Fiduccia herself died eighteen days later, on April 24, when her ventilator equipment failed. She was forty-six.

A year after their marriage, the Fiduccias renewed their vows in a Jewish service in Los Angeles. Surrounded by hundreds of guests, the couple made their way, hand in hand, across a terrace toward a chuppah, he in his scooter and she in her wheelchair, which she rode, her friend Marsha Saxton said, "like a queen on a steed." Under the wedding canopy, in keeping with Jewish tradition, she circled the groom seven times.

Fiduccia's dress, Saxton said, was "full of life," a statement of triumph in bronze and teal.

After the dinner, the Fiduccias took to the dance floor, which was covered in bubble wrap that joyously popped as their wheels rolled over it. Soon guests in wheelchairs joined them on the floor; others looked on, waving light sticks. The celebration ended with fireworks, an explosion of color against the night sky.

**DENISE GELLENE** is a freelance journalist and former staff writer for the *Los Angeles Times*.

## Dancer, Actress, and Storyteller

# Molly Nelson

## 1903–1977

BY WILL DUDDING

IN 1931, when the Penobscot dancer Molly Nelson arrived in Paris to perform at the International Colonial Exposition, she was pleasantly surprised. To gain audiences in North America, she had to resort to ridiculing stereotypes, like wearing a floor-length feathered headdress—and not much else. But in Paris, she found an enthusiastic reception for her traditional Native American dances.

After the expo ended and the other members of her group, the United States Indian Band, returned home, she decided to stay.

"Maybe I am foolish, with no money, but hopes galore," she wrote in her diary. "But I DO want to do something with my Indian dancing here in a serious artistic way. And I'm willing to take a great chance to accomplish it."

Nelson, whose stage name at the height of her career was Molly Spotted Elk, was a Penobscot dancer from Maine who spent much of her young adult life performing both traditional and popular dances in vaudeville troupes, chorus lines, Wild West shows, and nightclubs.

She was also a prolific writer who, over forty years, kept diaries that give rare insight into the hardships faced by Indigenous women in the early twentieth century. During the expo, she also worked as a journalist,

publishing a lengthy account in *The Portland Telegram*.

"She played a dual role," Bunny McBride, the author of *Molly Spotted Elk: A Penobscot in Paris* (1995), said in an interview. "She was on exhibition with other colonized people, yet she was also an observer who chronicled the event for a major newspaper back home."

By several accounts, Nelson was a remarkable dancer and a bridge between Indigenous America and Western audiences. One journalist noted that she could perform traditional dances and popular ones with "equal grace." In Paris, her audiences demanded encores.

Nelson mingled with artists and intellectuals, gave lecture-recitals at salons and museums, and fell in love with a French journalist, Jean Archambaud.

In July 1939, the publishing house Paul Geuthner gave Nelson an opportunity she had long pursued: to publish her collection of Penobscot folktales.

But that September—when promotional materials were set to circulate—the Nazi invasion of Poland threw France into war, setting off a series of events that would end Nelson's book deal and upend her life.

She married Archambaud soon after Poland's surrender and, aided by the philanthropist Anne Morgan, made plans to leave Europe. But she could not secure papers for her husband, and the next year she left with their

Nelson had to resort to stereotypes, like wearing a feathered headdress, to gain American audiences.

six-year-old daughter, also named Jean, to flee German-occupied France across the Pyrenees, largely on foot.

Mary Alice Nelson was born on November 17, 1903, in Old Town, Maine, on Indian Island, the heart of the Penobscot Nation. The oldest of eight siblings, she was called "Molliedellis" or "Molliedell" in the local accent. (The Penobscot language has no hard *R* or *Y* sounds.)

The Nelsons sustained themselves mostly by selling baskets, with her mother, Philomene, weaving and her father, Horace, collecting raw materials. Horace would go on to serve as the nonvoting Penobscot representative in the state legislature and also become tribal chief.

As a young girl, Molly showed an interest in tribal traditions, asking adults to tell her legends in exchange for doing chores. In-house revues and musical events were popular on the island and allowed opportunities for children like her to perform; her first public performance was an Irish jig at a local contest. By the time she was a young teenager, this interest was buoyed by the dimes that she earned by dancing for tourists. To make even more money for her family, she left home at fifteen to travel with a vaudeville act under the name Princess Neeburban and picked up different Indigenous dances along the way. She was often torn between a love for her home and an insatiable curiosity about the larger world.

In 1924, on a tour of colleges with a company of Indigenous dancers, she was reacquainted with an anthropologist she knew from her childhood and audited anthropology and literature classes at the University of Pennsylvania for three semesters. But she ran out of money and joined her sister in a Wild West show headquartered on an Oklahoma ranch, where she worked as a waitress, danced, and learned to perform on horseback.

She moved to New York the next year and started using the stage name Molly Spotted Elk. She modeled for artists between auditions and eventually joined the Foster Girls, a chorus line that traveled to San Antonio for a prolonged tour.

When the tour ended, she returned to New York and made a name for herself performing at nightclubs. The screenwriter W. Douglas Burden, when looking for an "Indian girl," heard about her and cast her in the starring role in *The Silent Enemy* (1930), a critically acclaimed docudrama about a harsh winter faced by pre-Columbian Ojibwe in what is now Canada. Burden sought to cast only Indigenous actors and make a film without stereotypes. In addition to playing a lead role, Nelson also advised on the set, on hunting scenes and canoe building.

A silent film in an increasingly talkie-dominated era, *The Silent Enemy* flopped at the box office but was lauded for its relative realism and stunning scenes of animals in nature.

While Nelson aspired to act in other films, she would only play a few bit parts. But it set her on the road to Paris.

Sometime after returning to the United States, she learned that her husband had died in a refugee camp in 1941, and she spent a year in a mental hospital. She lived

Nelson in 1921 paddling with her sister. As a young girl, she was interested in tribal legends.

the rest of her life on Indian Island, where she contributed to Penobscot research, made dolls and baskets, and told stories to her community.

She died on February 21, 1977, after a fall. She was seventy-three.

Her collected legends were finally published in 2009 by the University of Maine, four miles from Indian Island. The collection, *Katahdin: Wigwam's Tales of the Abnaki Tribe,* was the culmination of years of work, which included a dictionary of terms with French and English translations. At the time, most Indigenous stories were passed orally from a storyteller to a white historian or anthropologist, making Molly Nelson a rare example of an Indigenous documentarian.

"There's a real difference in the voice, and there's a real difference in certain emphases that she put on certain aspects of the stories," John Bear Mitchell, a Penobscot storyteller and educator who knew Nelson, said in an interview.

"To hear them in her words," he added, "is to hear them in her elders' words."

———

**WILL DUDDING** is a staff editor at *The New York Times.* He has a master's degree in theater with a focus on American and European performance in the early twentieth century.

Dorothy Andersen pored over autopsy reports of children who had been misdiagnosed.

## Doctor Who Discovered Cystic Fibrosis

# Dorothy Andersen

## 1901–1963

BY KATIE HAFNER

DOROTHY ANDERSEN stood at a stainless steel table in the basement of Columbia University's Babies Hospital in Upper Manhattan looking over the body of a three-year-old child. Andersen, a thirty-four-year-old pediatric pathologist, was performing an autopsy, and the presumed cause of death was celiac disease.

But in the course of her pathological exam, Andersen encountered something startling: the pancreas was half its normal size and was filled with fibrous cysts, the pancreatic duct a shriveled mass of tough scar tissue. Then another unexpected finding: the lungs were plugged, the bronchial airways cemented with thick mucus.

Her curiosity piqued, Andersen spent two years poring over dozens of autopsy reports from hospitals around the world of children who had been classified as celiac patients. Her conclusion: children who for years had been misdiagnosed as having severe celiac disease were dying of something else that was far more danger-ous, and incurable.

In 1938, three years after that first autopsy, Andersen published a fifty-page paper naming the disease: "Cystic Fibrosis of the Pancreas."

When she first alerted the US medical world to cystic fibrosis, it was a disease that killed children in their first or second year. She also was the first to diagnose the disease in a living patient, the first to recognize it as hereditary, the first to develop effective treatment, and the first to suggest a connection between cystic fibrosis and sweat.

"I hold Dorothy Andersen up to medical students as an exemplar of someone who was brilliant but took the time to really think about what she was looking at, seeing it in a different light and interpreting what she was seeing," Brian O'Sullivan, a pediatric pulmonologist who teaches at the Geisel School of Medicine at Dartmouth, said in an interview.

Andersen's focus on cystic fibrosis remained steady throughout her career. In the 1940s and '50s, the disease was so new to the medical community that parents had trouble finding physicians who knew much about it or who were willing to take on a new cystic fibrosis patient, especially when the prognosis was so grim and death so swift.

Word began to spread that there was a doctor in New York City who knew all about the disease. Desperate parents began bringing their children to Andersen from all over the country.

Andersen's treatment focused on nutrition, pancre-atic enzyme replacement, and antibiotics for pulmonary infection. By the end of the 1940s, some infants she treated were surviving well into childhood.

In 1953, Doris Tulcin took her daughter to see Andersen "after taking her to many, many different doctors who could not figure out what was wrong," she said in a 2021 interview for the podcast *Lost Women of Science*.

"She was a dowdy-looking thing, with a bun in the back of her head, no makeup," Tulcin said. "You could tell she was a big smoker because she smelled of cigarettes, but she was very kind. And you knew that she really, really cared about what she was doing for these kids."

When lecturing to first-year medical students, O'Sullivan makes a point of paying tribute to Andersen. Yet O'Sullivan is an exception. Despite her importance to the history of modern medicine and the recognition she received when she was alive, Andersen's legacy has been largely lost, and she remains relatively unknown, even to many in her field.

Andersen worked at Columbia for more than thirty years, yet her papers fill no more than a single box at the Columbia University Irving Medical Center's Archives & Special Collections. Among the contents are letters and cards from grateful parents and a valentine from one young patient that reads, "To Dr. Andersen who has pulled me through many a tough year."

Dorothy Hansine Andersen was born on May 15, 1901, in Asheville, North Carolina, the only child of Mary Louise (Mason) Andersen and Hans Peter Andersen, who worked as a field secretary for the YMCA. In 1904, the family moved to Summit, New Jersey.

Dorothy's parents died when she was a teenager, leaving her to navigate life largely on her own; she even once called herself a "rugged individualist."

In 1918, she entered Mount Holyoke College in South Hadley, Massachusetts, a women's college with a strong reputation in science education, where her majors were zoology and physiology, and her minor was chemistry.

She graduated in 1922 and was one of five women in her class four years later when she received her medical degree from Johns Hopkins School of Medicine.

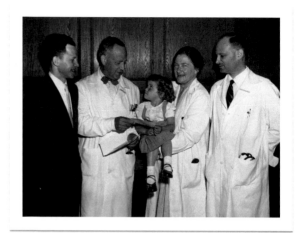

Andersen with one of her patients in 1961.

She took a position as an assistant in anatomy at the University of Rochester School of Medicine in New York and soon thereafter began a surgery internship, only to be denied further training as a surgery resident by "hospital policy." The problem: she was a woman.

"There were very few, if any, women surgeons back then," said O'Sullivan. "There's no question that she was not allowed into that fraternity."

Moreover, patients often objected to being seen by a female physician, which led many women to pathology, where doctors rarely interact with patients.

In 1929, Andersen began work as an assistant in pathology at Presbyterian Hospital at Columbia University Medical Center. After her discovery in the 1930s, she devoted most of her career to studying cystic fibrosis.

During a heat wave in 1948, doctors noticed that an abnormally high percentage of children coming to the hospital with heatstroke had cystic fibrosis. And in 1951, Andersen published a paper suggesting a connection between the body's chloride channels and cystic fibrosis. The connection led to the sweat test, a simple yet reliable diagnostic tool.

"The sweat test became the gold standard of diagnosis," O'Sullivan said. "And even today, in the era of genetic analysis, we still use the sweat test to confirm a diagnosis of cystic fibrosis."

"As a woman, she was working against very strong and unfriendly headwinds," Francis S. Collins, a former National Institutes of Health director, said in an interview. "But undaunted by that, she found a different pathway and ultimately gained the respect of all of her colleagues with her accomplishments, which were truly groundbreaking."

But her contributions did not end with cystic fibrosis.

"She made contributions to the emerging field of pediatric cardiology," John Scott Baird, a pediatric intensive care physician at Columbia University, wrote in a 2021 biography, *Dorothy Hansine Andersen: The Life and Times of the Pioneering Physician-Scientist Who Identified Cystic Fibrosis*. "She identified a novel form of glycogen storage disease, and she was involved in some of the first randomized, controlled trials of medical therapies in pediatrics. She was widely recognized as an expert in nutrition, a respected pediatrician, a renowned pathologist, a popular teacher and a brilliant researcher."

Despite her achievements, Andersen's climb up the hospital hierarchy was painstakingly slow. She didn't become an assistant professor until she was in her forties, and it took another decade for her to become a full professor.

Yet Andersen's value to Babies Hospital was clear. In 1949, when hospital officials announced plans to move the pediatric pathology lab—and thus Andersen—out of Babies Hospital to make room for a new orthopedic unit, Rustin McIntosh, the chair of pediatrics, submitted his resignation in protest to Dwight D. Eisenhower, who was then president of Columbia University. The plans for the move were promptly canceled.

A skilled carpenter, Andersen built a house on land she owned in the Kittatinny Mountains in New Jersey. According to an unfinished biography of Andersen from the 1970s, she built a constant-temperature water bath, years before such a thing was a standard piece of lab equipment.

"Colleagues were divided in their reactions," Libby Machol, the biographer, wrote. "Her admirers praised her originality and daring," while her detractors "considered her undignified. They believed she did a disservice to her profession and particularly to women doctors by lowering herself to work with her hands 'like a common laborer.'"

Yet no one took issue with her work. It was foundational. "Cystic fibrosis became known to virtually all pediatricians," Collins said.

Collins, the former NIH director who, in 1989, was part of a group of scientists who isolated the cystic fibrosis gene, said that in recent years treatments for the disease have extended survival well into adulthood, whereas decades ago "very few kids with cystic fibrosis would make it into adulthood."

Andersen never married, had no children, and lived alone for much of her life, a circumstance underscored by her answer on a Mount Holyoke alumnae questionnaire she filled out in 1944, when she was forty-three. On the back page was this question: "Name and address of person most likely always to know your whereabouts." Andersen responded with a question mark.

Andersen died on March 3, 1963, of lung cancer. She was sixty-one.

That year, a portrait of Andersen was commissioned and hung in the old entrance to Babies Hospital (now New York-Presbyterian Morgan Stanley Children's Hospital). At some point, it disappeared from the institution's walls. In 2021, Baird went on a hunt for the missing portrait, inquiring at departments throughout the Columbia Presbyterian medical complex. No one he spoke with was able to find it.

———

**KATIE HAFNER,** a journalist and author, is the host and co–executive producer of the *Lost Women of Science* podcast. In 2021, the podcast's first season, "The Pathologist in the Basement," focused on the life and work of Dorothy Andersen.

# Sinclair Clark

## 1902–1999

BY GORDON K. HURD

HIS WORK CAN BE SEEN in the preservation of the world-famous racehorse Phar Lap, whose mounted hide is on display at the Melbourne Museum in Australia; in the majestic herd of elephants in the Hall of African Mammals at New York's American Museum of Natural History; and in the lifelike Henry, an eleven-ton massive elephant demanding respect in the rotunda of the Smithsonian National Museum of Natural History in Washington, DC.

Yet few know of the taxidermist Sinclair Clark, whose handiwork of these and other creatures made him one of the industry's first African American practitioners.

Clark was a tanner who worked tirelessly to maintain the appearance of life, making tough, heavy, thick skins workable for taxidermists, who then placed the skins on a mount.

Tanning is a crucial part of taxidermy. Without pliant, clean, well-preserved skin to work with, taxidermists would not be able to create the exhibits seen in institutions around the world. While tanning is a skill better known for turning an animal into shoes or a handbag, Clark's labor-intensive practice focused on preserving the memory of the animal—history frozen for the future.

"The way he handled every knife, tool and machine was masterful," Victoria Lee, an exhibition developer, wrote in a 2022 article for the Field Museum in Chicago.

Taxidermy is sometimes a maligned practice, often associated with poachers and the morbid, but experts in the field describe it more as a nearly alchemical combination of art and science, a visceral practice whose goal is to help people feel closer to animals, to tell a story and resonate with a viewer emotionally in a way that even digital technology cannot achieve.

It requires, said Thomas Holloway, the media and communications officer of the Museums Victoria in Australia, a "knowledge of anatomy, form, and function to complete a scientifically accurate and compelling pose" that is combined with "artistic skills in sculpting, painting and finishing to bring lifelike expression and color to the mount."

"When both disciplines are employed well," he added in an email, "it is hard not to be drawn into the piece and want to know more about it."

Clark's knowledge of his work process has garnered admiration and respect across the industry—from his skill with blades to his uncanny control over the chemical mixtures used in tanning his hides. One of his protégés, John Janelli, would often say that Clark would know when his concoctions were complete after dipping a hand in the vat and tasting them, much like a wine connoisseur.

Sinclair Clark circa 1985. His taxidermy work can be seen in museums around the world.

Clark, working in the belly of a whale, went unnamed in this *LIFE* magazine photo published in 1954.

Though Clark spent most of his career as a freelancer, he achieved a spot in the taxidermy pantheon, his work standing all over the world for millions of people to view. He helped build tanning facilities and trained generations of younger practitioners. Each year, the National Taxidermists Association gives out an award in his name.

Sinclair Nathaniel Clarke (he would later omit the *e* in his last name) was born on January 31, 1902, in the Saint Andrew parish of Barbados to Lita and Grant Clarke.

He moved to the United States in 1924, as many from Barbados did in those times, looking for work opportunities. He soon landed employment as an assistant in the prep and exhibits department at the American Museum of Natural History. There he began to learn the tanning trade and met Carl Akeley, a pioneer in American naturalism and taxidermy, who invited Clark to accompany him on an African safari. (Akeley never returned, and his death, in 1926, made front-page news.)

For the rest of his career, Clark carried forward the so-called Akeley method, emphasizing the mounting of exhibits in natural environments and using lifelike effects, a practice still used industry-wide.

Clark's prominence in his field has recently resurfaced thanks to the efforts of his granddaughter Diane Patrick. Patrick, a journalist who documented Clark's legacy for PBS, found that as a Black man, his brushes with fame were brief and unsurprisingly tenuous.

A handful of newspapers mentioned him in the 1950s and '60s, and he appeared in a photo in the April 26, 1954, issue of *Life* magazine, unnamed, working in the belly of a whale.

"To the taxidermy industry he was totally well-known, because it was all about your work," she said by phone. But "as a Black person," she added, "to the regular public . . . he was just seen as a laborer."

Patrick eventually tracked down her estranged grandfather after navigating a maze of lost family connections from Harlem to the Bronx. She first connected with a paternal uncle, who told her that her grandfather was alive and wanted to meet her. She made her way to his home in the Bronx in the late 1990s.

"I interview people for a living," Patrick said. "So I had all these questions I wanted to ask him. But when I met him, he was in his nineties and he wasn't one of those conversational guys. So we took a picture and that was kind of it."

He died on May 14, 1999, in the Bronx. He was ninety-seven.

Today, Clark's name and work still carry the weight of legend. When Divya Anantharaman, who operates Gotham Taxidermy in New York, was studying the trade, she was inspired to learn that Clark was Black.

"As a woman of color," she said by phone, "I'm clinging to any representation in this field."

Anantharaman reached out to Clark's granddaughter and the two met by the elephants at the American Museum of Natural History, exploring Clark's handiwork. These were two people who would never have met if it hadn't been for Clark's preservation work.

"It's incredible to feel seen and feel the connection to something exciting and bigger," Anantharaman said. "To see the living links of history—it was really electric."

Clark's work includes Henry, an 11-ton elephant in the Smithsonian National Museum of Natural History.

**GORDON K. HURD** is a senior editor at *The New York Times*. He makes every effort to visit the African mammals display at the American Museum of Natural History at least once a year.

## Composer Who Championed Women

# Sorrel Hays

## 1941–2020

BY ALLYSON MCCABE

IN 1983, the composer and artist Sorrel Hays released a hauntingly powerful audio piece called "Celebration of NO," a collage of twenty-one women's voices speaking the word *no* in different languages. It was captured on three multispeed reel-to-reel recorders and manipulated, then spliced together to form an anti-patriarchal chorus of resistance.

The piece came on the heels of another of Hays's successes as a proponent of gender equality: the year before, her "Tunings for String Quartet" was performed in the first concert of women's music at the Library of Congress.

Hays started her career in the early 1970s as a noted concert pianist specializing in new music but was drawn to a less familiar path, one of new sounds that she produced while touring the United States and Europe with a Buchla synthesizer, patch cords, and assorted gadgets.

"I performed concerts with sound from transducer mikes on audience throats and Barcus Berry transducers on the piano soundboard processed through the Buchla synth and mixed with tape," Hays once recalled. "I remember the huge grin on a little girl's face—it was in Albany, Georgia, in 1975—when she heard her voice transformed into a giant's as she held the contact mike to her throat."

Aside from creating electroacoustic works, radio operas, short films, film scores, video artworks, and live intermedia performances, Hays set out to amplify the achievements of other trailblazers. In 1976, she co-curated, with the composer Beth Anderson, a groundbreaking concert series, *Meet the Woman Composer,* at the New School for Social Research. It featured future luminaries such as Annea Lockwood, Laurie Anderson, Laurie Spiegel, and Suzanne Ciani.

As an assistant chair of the International League of Women Composers, she fought for the inclusion of women on the awards panel of ASCAP, the music licensing agency, and for the addition of women to the Rockefeller Foundation's competition for the performance of American music. In an interview, the pianist Loretta Goldberg described Hays as a fierce advocate for gender parity and an innovator who excelled across genres—which may have hampered her name recognition in any single field.

Doris Ernestine Hays was born on August 6, 1941, in Memphis, Tennessee, and grew up outside Chattanooga. Her father, John Walter Ernest Hays, was a residential real estate builder. Her mother, Christina (Fair) Hays, was a homemaker.

The Hayses were active in church life; Doris's grandfather was a preacher, her grandmother an organist.

Hays was described as a fierce advocate for gender parity and an innovator across musical genres.

A desire to elevate women composers led her to trade "financial security for creative freedom."

Though Doris took some inspiration from the church's music and its rituals, she was less enamored with its parochial doctrine. "I took religion very seriously, and so did everyone else I knew," she said in a 1985 documentary. "The nonbelievers took it seriously, too, for the church was a political factor determining many elements in our lives."

She was the valedictorian of her class at Central High School and graduated from the University of Chattanooga in 1963. A Maclellan Foundation scholarship then took her to Munich, where she studied piano before returning to the United States to pursue a master's degree in music from the University of Wisconsin under the mentorship of the pianist Paul Badura-Skoda and the violinist Rudolf Kolisch. She then moved to New York City, where she studied contemporary repertoire with the pianist Hilde Somer.

Hays won first prize in the prestigious International Gaudeamus Competition for Interpreters of Contemporary Music in the Dutch city of Rotterdam in 1971. The next year, she was invited to play *Concerto for Prepared Piano and Orchestra* at the Hague for the composer John Cage's sixtieth birthday. She also became a noted interpreter of Henry Cowell, mastering unconventional techniques that required her to reach inside the piano and pluck, strum, or otherwise manipulate the strings.

Hays's imagination took her even farther into the vanguard. For one piece, she would arrange balloons around her piano and, at some point during a performance, withdraw a BB gun and shoot them. In one of her first electroacoustic works, "Hands and Lights" (1972),

she struck piano keys that set off photocell-activated lights, illuminating the inside of the instrument. In another, "SensEvents," robots were set in motion by the movements of dancers and audience members, which in turn activated musicians.

Just as the composer Charles Ives's New England upbringing was deeply infused in his music, Hays's Southern roots were an enduring touchstone in her work. When the Chattanooga Symphony commissioned her to produce an orchestral work commemorating its fiftieth anniversary, Hays recorded hundreds of interviews, identifying the melodic and rhythmic qualities of Southern speech, which she filtered through her own recollections and emotions. Her conceptual process, and the music it spawned, became the subject of the 1985 documentary *Southern Voices: A Composer's Exploration with Doris Hays,* directed by George C. Stoney.

That same year she adopted the name Sorrel—which belonged to her maternal grandmother's family—for its pleasing sound. It was also when she met Marilyn Ruth Ries, a prominent recording engineer with hundreds of works to her credit, including albums by Sweet Honey in the Rock, Kate Clinton, and Malvina Reynolds. After a long partnership, Hays and Ries married on August 6, 2015—the date of their mutual birthdays.

One of their earliest collaborations was *Disarming the World—Pulling Its Leg,* a 1986 documentary play about the women's peace movement, which Ries engineered and coproduced for the radio station WNYC. Hays's

Hays's album *Voicings for Tape / Soprano / Piano* included one of her seminal pieces, "Celebration of NO."

1995 experimental opera, *Dream in Her Mind,* conjured the saint Hildegard of Bingen and the writers Gertrude Stein and Jessamyn West as cartographers exploring the landscapes of personal consciousness. It was one of eight commissions for the German public broadcaster Westdeutscher Rundfunk.

Hays's "Something (to Do) Doing," a satire about toil featuring fifteen chanting actors and a scat singer, debuted at the Whitney Museum's first exhibition of audio art, in 1990. That same year, the pianist Loretta Goldberg commissioned her to write *90s—A Calendar Bracelet,* a suite for Yamaha's prototype MIDI grand piano celebrating the birthdays of outstanding women. "She went where the commissions were," Goldberg said, "trading financial security for creative freedom."

Hays held teaching appointments at Queens College, Cornell College, the University of Wisconsin, and Yildiz Technical University in Turkey, where she served as consulting designer of the graduate program in electronic music. Her artist residencies included Rhode Island College, the Georgia Council for the Arts, and the New York Foundation for the Arts.

In 2008, Hays and Ries moved to rural Haralson County, Georgia, where they built studios near their cabin. In 2012, Hays published *Touching Sound: Living Lullabies,* the culmination of decades exploring the effect of sound on the body, which involved recording and analyzing traditional lullabies and contemporary lull songs from around the globe.

Hays died at her home on February 9, 2020, of pancreatic cancer. She was seventy-eight.

Though her music had taken her around the world, in her final years, Hays wrote to Lockwood about the elation she experienced playing the organ at her local church, her hands at the helm of a time machine that brought her back to where she first experienced the spark of wanderlust—a feeling she once described in the liner notes for her 1996 album *Dreaming the World.*

"After church and chicken dinner we'd hop into the Chevy. My dad liked to drive the roads he didn't know, unfamiliar dusty roads past falling-down houses and old graveyards. Getting lost was part of the adventure, and in fact that was the point, to get so lost that we always wound up finding something surprising and new. In the fall we picked black walnuts, in June and July, blackberries. Sometimes we caught fish, and poison ivy and chigger bites as well. To this day if I can take a back road, particularly one I have never been on before, that's my preference and my delight."

———

**ALLYSON MCCABE** is a music journalist whose work often airs on NPR, and her book, *Why Sinéad O'Connor Matters,* was published in May 2023 by the University of Texas Press. She owns two turntables and several microphones.

## A Look Inside the Morgue

**BY AMISHA PADNANI**

No, we're not talking about the place where bodies are kept while waiting to be identified. The morgue is also a newspaper's archival room of old clippings, photographs, and books that are stored, in the *Times*'s case, deep in a basement three levels under Times Square. Jeff Roth, the newspaper's archivist, in describing why it's called the Morgue, once said: "It's kind of the reporter's parlance for where all the dead stories lie or lay."

According to Roth—the only person who truly knows how to navigate the maze of rusty file cabinets and their contents—the *Times*'s morgue was created around 1905. The clippings collection, which consists of articles from about two dozen publications, dates back to the 1870s. There are around six million photographs (that the paper only started digitizing recently) of historical moments: the first subway ever built in New York City, the bombing of Hiroshima, a young Muhammad Ali in his prime boxing days, and so many more.

Those yellowing clips and images are gold for the Obituaries desk. Every morning, Roth checks the morgue for anything useful as our team compiles information for obits. Some of the images in this very book are from that labyrinthine room.

The morgue, which sits three levels below ground, is where *The New York Times* stores millions of old photographs and newspaper clippings.

# Creating Art
# That Endures

---

Their dance moves have been copied, their music has been rerecorded, their paintings still hang on the walls of museums. Here you'll read about people who have influenced art through the ages, even if they didn't always get the credit they deserved.

Dancer Known as "Snakehips"

# Earl Tucker

## Circa 1906–1937

BY BRIAN SEIBERT

THERE ARE MANY MYSTERIES about the dancer Earl Tucker, but the meaning of his stage name isn't one of them. To understand why he was called Snakehips, you have only to watch him move.

Take his solo routine in the 1930 short film *Crazy House*. About thirty seconds in, Tucker rolls his hips to one side. He rolls them so far that his torso tilts in counterbalance, his ankles sickle over, and his whole body bends into an S-curve of improbable depth.

He reverses the shape—first churning slowly, then at twice and four times the speed, the smaller, quicker undulations making him slither sideways on one foot. His trailing leg embroiders the glide with lariat-like curlicues, but what draws a viewer's eye, hypnotically, is the motor: the spiraling, snaking motion of those hips.

By the time he appeared in the film, Snakehips Tucker was already a name attraction in Harlem nightclubs like the Cotton Club and Connie's Inn, and he had appeared to acclaim on Broadway and in Paris. He died on May 14, 1937, when he was about thirty-one.

The cause, as described in his obituary in the *Baltimore Afro-American,* was a "mysterious illness." Neither that obituary nor those in other African American newspapers—the mainstream press did not report the death—included many biographical facts about Tucker.

Back then, obscurity wasn't unusual for Black entertainers, but the articles praised him as one of the most imitated artists of the day.

Tucker's influence didn't end with his death. Elvis Presley, who was born two years before Tucker died, probably never saw him dance, yet he scandalized 1950s America with a more timid version of Tucker's below-the-waist action, making girls in the audience scream. Elvis the Pelvis also took on the moniker "Ol' Snakehips."

Later, Tucker's loose kicks and unwinding spins found an echo in the signature moves of Michael Jackson. Some hip-hop dancers who came across video footage of Tucker were said to have experienced a shock of recognition: this guy was doing some of their steps decades before they were.

Even if these dancers didn't imitate Tucker directly, they drew on a style that he had heightened and popularized. He could also tap-dance and do the Charleston, but it was the hip rotations and the shaking that distinguished him from Black male dancers of his day, in part because the moves were associated with the sexually charged ones of female dancers; "shake" dancers were known to shimmy and grind.

(This gender distinction still held when Elvis came on the scene, prompting hostile journalists to liken him

Earl Tucker in the 1930s. His dance moves were echoed by Elvis Presley and Michael Jackson.

The Cotton Club, one of several venues in Harlem where "Snakehips" Tucker became a well-known attraction.

disparagingly to burlesque ladies doing the hoochie coochie.)

Duke Ellington, who hired Tucker to dance with his band at the Cotton Club and elsewhere, once speculated that Tucker had come from "tidewater Maryland, one of those primitive lost colonies where they practice pagan rituals and their dancing style evolved from religious seizures."

Tucker was, in fact, discovered in Maryland, dancing in the streets of Baltimore, and Ellington's claim is probably accurate in other ways: what Ellington called "pagan rituals," scholars would identify as African spiritual practices that informed African American culture. Tucker's trembling was most likely related to dances of spiritual possession, which became part of Pentecostal, Sanctified, and Holiness traditions.

In the film *Crazy House,* Tucker does his shaking while rubbing his hands together, as if he were shivering in the cold while skating on ice. The addition of sleigh bells to the bouncy music underlined the idea.

Whatever its source, his dancing was entertainment that played to the illicit appeal of Harlem nightclubs. (Ellington's art was promoted as "jungle music.") When Tucker appeared on Broadway in the all-Black revue *Blackbirds of 1928,* the program described his act as his "conception of the low down dance."

That low-down quality was in contrast to the upright tapping of the show's star, Bill Robinson. Zora Neale Hurston, in her now-canonical 1934 essay "Characteristics of Negro Expression," cited only two dancers by name: Robinson and Tucker. She used both as exemplars of the "lack of symmetry that makes Negro dancing so difficult for white dancers to learn."

But it's easy to imagine that Hurston was still thinking of Tucker when she wrote: "Negro dancing is dynamic suggestion. No matter how violent it may appear to the beholder, every posture gives the impression that the dancer will do much more."

Reviewers tended to describe Tucker's "double-jointed" dancing with euphemisms or expressions of disbelief. (His death may have been shrouded in euphemisms, too; "mysterious illness" was sometimes code for syphilis.) It took a French critic—who was less squeamish about sex and had different attitudes about race—to hail Tucker as "a marvelous artist who knows all the dances of the universe."

The best information about Tucker comes from the interviews with Black entertainers that Marshall and Jean Stearns conducted in the 1960s for their seminal book *Jazz Dance* (1968). Marshall Stearns himself could remember his embarrassment when, as a white college student in the late 1920s, he took a date to hear Ellington's band at the Cotton Club and encountered the "murderously naughty" Tucker. He spent most of his energy "trying not to look shocked," he said.

Writing in the more freewheeling cultural context of the 1960s, Stearns mocked that response as puritanical; citing the mambo and rock 'n' roll dances, he judged that Tucker's pelvic skill had come "too early."

Today, Tucker's dancing would be considered less disturbing than other aspects of his behavior. The entertainers interviewed by the Stearnses remembered Snakehips as a heavy gambler and "a mean guy" with a violent temper who was nevertheless popular with women. Newspaper reports about the "bad boy of Harlem" covered his arrests as often as his performances.

In one instance he was charged with stabbing a fellow gambler in the abdomen with a penknife. Another time, the charge was "forcing his attentions" on a fifteen-year-old girl. Yet another time, it was rape. All these charges seem to have been dropped, as was the assault charge filed by his dance partner, Bessie Dudley. A few years later, newspapers reported that he had stabbed the performer Lavinia Mack, and that she had stabbed him back.

A gossip columnist for the *Pittsburgh Courier* wrote—falsely—that Tucker died from that stabbing. It must have seemed true to Tucker's character that he would meet his end in such a violent manner. Whatever the cause, when he died, he left behind his wife and a ten-year-old son.

What remains, beyond these fragmented memories, is a few seconds of him at the end of the 1935 musical short

Though Tucker, shown here in 1929, died mysteriously in 1937, his influence lasted for decades.

*Symphony in Black* and his two-minute routine in *Crazy House,* a comedy set in the Lame Brain Sanitarium. He doesn't look so menacing there. His snaps and claps draw attention to a musicality that runs through all his hip rolling, through his every sinking to the ground and miraculously rubbery recovery. He wasn't a contortionist. He was a dancer, one of a kind.

——

**BRIAN SEIBERT** is the author of *What the Eye Hears: A History of Tap Dancing.* Like Tucker, he can tap, but Tucker's contortions are beyond him.

# Esquerita

## 1938–1986

### BY TIM WEINER

LATE ONE EVENING around 1953, a tall, thin, queer Black teenager cruised into an all-night diner at the Greyhound bus station in Macon, Georgia.

His daytime hustle was playing gospel music with a preacher named Sister Rosa. By night, he was becoming another creature entirely: an outrageous diva named Esquerita, playing primeval rock 'n' roll in rough roadhouses.

In the diner, he caught the eye of the off-duty dishwasher, a would-be singer who had performed in drag as Princess Lavonne in a traveling minstrel show. His name was Richard Penniman. They recognized each other, though they had never met.

"So, Esquerita and me went to my house," the man, who later became Little Richard, recounted in Charles White's 1984 biography, *The Life and Times of Little Richard.* That night, or soon thereafter, the visitor played the piano for his host. His huge hands spanned four octaves. With the left, he pumped out propulsive bass rhythms commingling swing, gospel, and rhumba. With the right, he played leaping tremolos of melodies he had heard on the radio—pop, blues, and country. He sang in a soaring operatic falsetto.

"It sounded so pretty," Little Richard remembered. He asked Esquerita: "Hey, how do you do that?"

"'I'll teach you,'" he recalled Esquerita replying.

"And that's when I really started playing," Little Richard said.

Historians of rock 'n' roll—a genre so new back then it barely had a name—liken this moment to the discovery of fire.

From that night on, the two performers became friends, collaborators, and occasional rivals. They traded tips on makeup and costumes as well as music. Each had one foot planted on the platform of gospel music and one foot aboard the about-to-depart rock 'n' roll railroad. Little Richard was older and wiser and more ambitious; Esquerita was a gayer, more gifted musician—and a good deal wilder.

In September 1955, at the Dew Drop Inn in New Orleans, Little Richard picked up a ditty about the pleasures of anal sex, cleaned up the lyrics, and recorded it by distilling all he had learned from Esquerita's playing, singing, and style. "I think Little Richard copied off him a lot, but Little Richard got to the studio first," Guitar Lightnin' Lee, a New Orleans guitarist, told the journalist Baynard Woods for a rare profile of Esquerita, published by the *Oxford American* in 2019.

Little Richard's "Tutti Frutti" was the wildest song ever to reach American airwaves. The crazy cadenzas and

Esquerita in the 1970s. His lively style on the piano inspired musicians like Little Richard.

Esquerita signing autographs in 1958. By nine years old, he was singing in his mother's church.

# If Richard Penniman sometimes struck his fans as being from another planet, Esquerita was from another galaxy.

octave-vaulting vocals owed a fair part of their power and flow to Esquerita's influence. It came screaming into the lives of millions of teenagers and soared to number two on the rhythm-and-blues charts in February 1956. When it hit, Esquerita, not yet eighteen, got off the gospel train in New York and returned to his hometown in South Carolina in search of rock 'n' roll stardom.

Esquerita—also known as S. Q. Reeder, Estrelita, Escorita, the Magnificent Malochi, and Fabulash—was born Eskew Reeder Jr. in Greenville, South Carolina, on November 20, 1938, Social Security records show. ("Eskew Reeder" spoken in a deep South Carolina accent melts easily into "Esquerita.")

Greenville was entirely segregated; he grew up in a Black neighborhood called Greasy Corner. Nothing is known for sure about his father. His mother, Othie (Wilson) Reeder, was the choir director at the Black Tabernacle Baptist Church. A neighbor woman taught young Eskew piano when he was five; her daughters played 78 rpm records of opera divas for him.

By the time he was nine, he was playing and singing in his mother's church. In his early teens, he worked with the gospel guitarist Sister O. M. Terrell and the Sanctified singer Brother Joe May; their work was deeply rooted in the blues. Upon returning to Greenville in 1956, he began

honing his own act at the Owl Club, Greasy Corner's leading nightspot, performing boogie-woogie and rock 'n' roll tunes, billing himself as Professor Eskew Reeder.

Then, in October 1957, Little Richard said he had a vision from God while performing before 72,000 fans in Sydney, Australia, and he gave up rock 'n' roll for religion. His glittering wardrobe wound up with Esquerita in Greenville. And with that plumage, Esquerita emerged full-fledged into the world, in silk and satin, rhinestone sunglasses, and pomaded hair as high as a top hat.

A producer at Capitol Records had the idea that he could be the next Little Richard. So did Esquerita. But if Richard Penniman sometimes struck his fans as being from another planet, Esquerita was from another galaxy.

In 1958, Capitol recorded and released Esquerita's first singles. Among them was "Esquerita and the Voola," *voola* being his word for the spirit, the juju, the animating force. The record was two minutes and ten seconds of otherworldly shape-shifting piano and voodoo drums and Esquerita's wordless keening, the primordial howl of a shaman. Other records of the era, like "Rip It Up" or "Great Balls of Fire," might have hinted at danger. This music was dangerous, like rough sex or hard drugs.

"The violence that was normally only a promise (or threat) in rock 'n' roll was realized in Esquerita's sound,"

# Without Esquerita, there might have been no Little Richard, nor Prince, nor Lil Nas X.

the British music journalist and DJ Charlie Gillett wrote in his 1970 book *The Sound of the City: The Rise of Rock and Roll.*

*Esquerita!* came out in 1959. The LP's raucous tracks comprised "a chaotic symphony," Gillett wrote. The album's label proclaimed it "truly the farthest out man has ever gone." But radio stations deemed it too far out, and it fell stillborn from the presses. Its creator moved on.

He spent much of the early 1960s in New Orleans, a place where he could be someone: Esquerita by day, on the street, as well as onstage by night. His hangout was the Dew Drop Inn, the Black-owned nightclub and hotel where musical luminaries performed, drag queens emceed, and the annual New Orleans Gay Ball convened.

"Anyone who was someone came to the Dew Drop when they were in New Orleans: Duke Ellington, Jackie Wilson, Charles Brown, Esquerita and Ray Charles," said the renowned New Orleans composer and producer Allen Toussaint in a 1991 *Washington Post* article; he placed the outsider's singular sound in that pantheon.

In the mid to late 1960s, Esquerita was in New York, part of the ever-changing ensemble of musicians surrounding Little Richard, who had returned to the fold after the Beatles had a number one hit with his "Long Tall Sally." They wrote two songs together—"Freedom Blues"

and "Dew Drop Inn." The latter was a revival of their musical roots; the former became Little Richard's biggest hit in thirteen years. "Freedom Blues" was a liberation anthem, with the opening lyrics "I hope that I should live to see / When every man should know he's free."

In 1966, Esquerita recorded with the avant-garde drummer Idris Muhammad, freely melding jazz, blues, pop, gospel, soaring vocals, and a strong dose of the voola. The tracks, including a nearly nine-minute rendition of the African American spiritual "Sinner Man," remained unreleased for forty-six years until Norton Records put them out on vinyl in 2012.

He saw royalties from "Freedom Blues," which went to number forty-seven on the charts in 1970, but spent much of the next decade adrift, with a cocaine habit and without a recording contract. On occasion he played less-than-elegant gay clubs in full drag as Fabulash. On occasion he landed in jail.

He pulled himself together in 1983 and put together a string of appearances at Tramps, a popular 150-seat venue in Manhattan, dressed in a plain suit and tie, with close-cropped hair. In a three-paragraph review in *The New York Times,* the music critic Jon Pareles wrote that Esquerita's falsetto holler had vanished, but his piano playing was strong, moving through gospel and rhumba and boogie-woogie to the call-and-response of New Orleans rhythm and blues.

"He would sometimes stand and dance as the spirit took him," Pareles noted.

Esquerita closed the set with "Amazing Grace"—*how sweet the sound that saved a wretch like me.* But he was soon lost, crushed first by crack and then by AIDS.

He died alone on October 23, 1986, at Harlem Hospital in Manhattan. He was forty-eight.

He is buried in an unmarked grave on the far edge of New York City's potter's field on Hart Island, though he cannot be found in the Hart Island database under any of his names. In those days, funeral directors would not embalm AIDS victims. The prison guards commanding the Rikers Island inmates who buried the dead did not want to handle them. So the gravediggers wore hazmat suits and the corpses rested in body bags, not caskets, while a backhoe dug trenches fourteen feet deep, and the dead were dumped there, without ceremony.

"He taught me how to play piano," Little Richard said of Esquerita in David Kirby's *Little Richard: The Birth of Rock 'n' Roll* (2009). "He was one of the greatest pianists, and that's including Jerry Lee Lewis, Stevie Wonder, or anybody I've ever heard." Without Esquerita, there might have been no Little Richard, nor Prince, nor Lil Nas X, and the radical, rebellious, quintessentially queer qualities at the heart of American popular music might be less loud.

The tracks on the album *Sinner Man: The Lost Session* remained unreleased for forty-six years.

**TIM WEINER** worked for *The New York Times* in Washington, Afghanistan, Pakistan, Sudan, Liberia, Haiti, Mexico, and Cuba, among other garden spots. His obituary about Little Richard led him to write an "Overlooked" for Esquerita.

Madhubala, shown here in 1951, often portrayed modern young women testing the limits of traditions.

## Bollywood Legend Whose Tragic Life Mirrored Marilyn Monroe's
# Madhubala
## 1933–1969

BY AISHA KHAN

IT WAS PROBABLY THE FIRST ghost story in Indian cinema. A bewildered young man in a mansion chasing glimpses of an ethereal, veiled beauty. The movie, *Mahal,* was a huge success, making the lead actress, Madhubala, who was barely sixteen, a superstar overnight.

Nearly seven decades later, strains of the film's signature song, "Aayega aane wala" (He will come), are instantly recognizable to most Indians, evoking the suspenseful tale of lost love and reincarnation.

Madhubala's tragic turn in the film as an enigmatic young woman in search of love seemed to foreshadow her own glittering but short life. She died twenty years later as an icon of beauty and tragedy—her dazzling career, unhappy love life, and fatal illness more dramatic than any movie she starred in.

Asked once to describe herself, Madhubala said she was so young when she entered the "maze" of the film industry—she made her debut at nine—that she had lost herself.

"When you have forgotten yourself, what can you tell people about yourself?" she once said.

Besotted poets called her "a living Taj Mahal," but Madhubala's radiant beauty was not cold or forbidding. Her dreamy eyes, vivacious smile, and mischievous laughter gave her a girl-next-door appeal.

She has been compared to Marilyn Monroe: the smoldering looks, the short career, the tragic end. "There was a remarkable similarity in the soft vulnerability of their faces," writes Khatija Akbar in her biography of Madhubala. "The same abandon to their laughter, head thrown back, that same incandescent glow."

Starting in the late 1940s—in a newly independent India finding its place in the world—Madhubala often portrayed modern young women testing the limits of traditions. Her roles "embodied the optimism of a new generation which was rather consciously moving away from its colonial past," write Nupur Sharma and Inam Abidi Amrohvi, independent journalists researching Hindi cinema.

Unlike other actresses of her time, she wasn't typecast. Her natural, understated acting style brought her equal success in serious social dramas like *Amar* (Eternal) and in lighthearted comedies and period pieces.

She could play with equal ease a spoiled heiress in *Mr. and Mrs. '55* (1955), a reporter investigating a murder in *Kala pani* (Exile; 1958), and a rebellious woman whose car breaks down in the comedy *Chalti ka naam gaadi* (If it ain't broke; 1958).

Younger Indians may not have seen all her films, but in Bollywood, an industry that churns out musicals,

Madhubala is associated with dozens of iconic songs: a flirty number in *Howrah Bridge* (1958), a folk song in *Phagun* (1958), and an ode to love in *Barsaat ki raat* (A rainy night; 1960). Though like most Indian actors, she was only lip-syncing.

Madhubala's movies were also hits abroad, even in faraway places like Greece. *Theatre Arts,* a New York magazine published from 1916 to 1964, called her "the biggest star in the world." *Life* sent a photographer to profile her.

Frank Capra Jr., visiting Bombay for a film festival in 1952, was said to have offered her a job in Hollywood. But Madhubala's father, who controlled her career, forbade it.

Despite her success and the breadth of her work, Madhubala's acting skills were still underappreciated. She never won any awards, even for her biggest hits.

"Everyone went on about how beautiful she was, but she really held her own against some acclaimed actors," said Tejaswini Ganti, an associate professor of anthropology at New York University who studies Bollywood.

Madhubala (Muh-DHOO-baa-laa) was born Mumtaz Begum on February 14, 1933, in Delhi to a poor Pashtun family. Her father moved the family to Bombay, where they lived in a shantytown that happened to be near the Bombay Talkies film studio. Mumtaz caught the eye of the studio's cofounder, Devika Rani, who later gave her the name Madhubala, or "Honeybelle."

Madhubala was soon known for her fastidious work ethic—on set at six a.m., no matter what. She took on as many films as possible, to support her family. She had already appeared in seventeen films by the time she starred in *Mahal* (Mansion), one of ten movies she made in 1949.

She was born with a ventricular septal defect, a hole in her heart, diagnosed after she began working. There was no treatment for her condition, and she continued her punishing pace, completing more than seventy films in her short career. She told a friend: "No sooner had I learned what I was doing, God said, 'Enough.'"

Madhubala was uninhibited for an Indian actress of that time. She was playful and flirtatious, and made news for her dalliances. *Tarana* (Anthem; 1951) paired her with the star Dilip Kumar, who played a doctor who fell for Madhubala's feisty village girl. She was immediately smitten with Kumar, ten years her senior, and reportedly sent him a rose, the beginning of a long romance.

The two were the talk of film magazines, and fans loved their pairing. "She lived a far more liberal lifestyle than most Indian women, with romance itself an act of subversion in a conservative society," Sharma said.

Kumar recommended Madhubala as his costar for *Mughal-e-Azam* (The Great Mughal), based on the legend of a romance between the Mughal prince Salim and a dancer, Anarkali.

The director was K. Asif, whose painstaking vision made it the most expensive Indian movie of its time, and for years, the most successful.

One of its most memorable sequences, the only one originally filmed in color, is a dance in a hall of mirrors, faithfully re-created from a Mughal palace. A defiant Anarkali declares her love before the disapproving Emperor Akbar with a daring refrain: "I have only fallen in love, I have nothing to fear."

In keeping with the era, the two lovers barely embrace, let alone kiss. Yet, a scene when Salim caresses Anarkali's face with a feather is considered one of the most erotic in Indian cinema. But by the time the scene was filmed (the movie took about a decade to make), the two were long estranged, according to Kumar.

They had been eager to marry, but Madhubala's father had set conditions, including that they star in movies he would produce. Kumar demanded that she choose between him and her father. She chose her family. An ugly lawsuit over another movie hastened their breakup.

"The romance that wasn't realized was the big story of her life, which added to her legend," Ganti said.

Once asked her thoughts on love, Madhubala said: "No peace or happiness is possible in life without true love."

In 1960, the year *Mughal-e-Azam* was finally released, she married her frequent costar Kishore

Madhubala and Dilip Kumar in a scene from the 1960 film *Mughal-E-Azam* (The Great Mughal).

Kumar, a talented singer. While their pairing in a string of comedies was cinema gold, offscreen the two were quickly estranged.

Madhubala made a few more hit movies, but her health deteriorated rapidly, and she spent her last years at home, out of the public eye. In her final days, according to her sister, Madhubala would say: "I want to live. Please, God, let me live." She died on February 23, 1969, nine days after her thirty-sixth birthday.

———

**AISHA KHAN** is an assistant editor at *The New York Times*. The first Indian movie she ever saw was *Mother India*. Her capsule review: "Heartbreaking."

Ana Mendieta found refuge in painting after being uprooted from her Cuban homeland as a girl.

# Ana Mendieta

## 1948–1985

BY MONICA CASTILLO

ANA MENDIETA'S ART was sometimes violent, often unapologetically feminist, and usually raw.

She incorporated unusual natural materials like blood, dirt, water, and fire, and displayed her work through photography, film, and live performances.

"Nothing that she did ever surprised me," Mendieta's sister, Raquelín, told *The New York Times* in 2016. "She was always very dramatic, even as a child—and liked to push the envelope, to give people a start, to shock them a little bit. It was who she was, and she enjoyed it very much. And she laughed about it sometimes when people got freaked out."

In the 1973 short film *Moffitt Building Piece,* Mendieta and her sister captured the reactions of strangers who walked by a puddle of pig's blood that Mendieta had spilled outside her apartment. Some stared and most walked around the mess. Eventually someone washed it off the sidewalk. To Mendieta, the recording offered a thought-provoking experiment on people's indifference to violence.

Mendieta's stature as an artist was never fully recognized in her lifetime. She died in 1985 at thirty-six; her husband, the sculptor Carl Andre, was accused of pushing her out of a window of their thirty-fourth-floor apartment in Greenwich Village but was acquitted of murder charges.

As an immigrant, Mendieta felt a disconnect in the United States. The trauma of being uprooted from her Cuban homeland as a girl would leave her with questions about her identity and make her more conscious of being a woman of color.

These questions would echo in her work, which explored themes that pushed ethnic, sexual, moral, religious, and political boundaries. She urged viewers to disregard their gender, race, or other defining societal factors and instead connect with the humanity they shared with others.

In this way she gained footing as an ambitious and audacious artist. Writing about a retrospective of her work at the Whitney Museum of American Art in New York in 2004, the *New York Times* critic Holland Cotter wrote that "if not naturally fearless," Mendieta "used fear well, transmuting a profound sense of psychological and cultural displacement into an experience of merging with the natural world and its history through art."

Ana Maria Mendieta was born into a middle-class family in Havana on November 18, 1948. Her father, Ignacio, was a prominent political figure who ran afoul of Fidel Castro's government; her mother, Raquel, was a chemistry teacher.

She and her sister attended a Roman Catholic school on the island before their parents sent them to the United

An untitled photograph from the *Silueta Series*,
which included around two hundred works, from 1976.

under the German artist Hans Breder, who made video and performance art and encouraged students to move back and forth across artistic frontiers. Mendieta adopted those forms and added her own style, mixing elements of performance, body, and land art into one work, then capturing it through photography or Super 8 film.

In 1973, while she was in college, Mendieta learned about the on-campus rape and murder of a nursing student named Sarah Ann Ottens. Her outrage over the incident drove her to stage one of her most confrontational and violent pieces, *Rape Scene.*

For the piece, Mendieta upended her apartment, covered herself with blood, and tied herself to a table to re-create the aftermath of brutal sexual assault. She invited an audience to the made-up crime scene, where she remained bent over the table with blood dripping down her legs and pooling at her feet as they discussed the incident. Photographs of the scene are still displayed in museum exhibits around the world, including at the Brooklyn Museum in 2018.

"There's a way in which her work is about performance," Catherine Morris, a senior curator for the Elizabeth A. Sackler Center for Feminist Art at the museum, said in a telephone interview. "It's about theater. It's about kind of capturing moments through various forms of documentation. And she takes all of these things to the world at large that might not be considered fine arts. She turns them into something intelligent, harrowing, and emotional."

Mendieta exemplified this best through a series called Siluetas, or "Silhouettes," which focused on sculptured figures made out of earthy materials like grass, flowers, branches, and mud and incorporated themes like creation, faith, and womanhood.

In one of her best-known *siluetas, Imagen de Yagul* (Image from Yagul) from 1973, Mendieta incorporated her body into the piece by lying down nude in an old neglected stone tomb in Mexico. She then strategically placed white flowers over her, as if they were growing out of her body.

In all, about two hundred pieces make up the series, which she worked on throughout the 1970s and early '80s.

States through Operation Pedro Pan, a secret program run by the church with the aid of the State Department to smuggle thousands of children out of Cuba in the early days of Castro's regime. The experience would leave Ana, who was twelve at the time, and Raquelín, who was fourteen, with a feeling of loss as they moved through group and foster homes in Florida and then in Iowa. Mendieta would not see her mother for five years, her father for eighteen.

She found refuge in painting and pursued her interest in the arts at the University of Iowa, where she studied

*Isla*, from 1981, references the island nation of Cuba.

"The making of my 'Silueta' in nature keeps the transition between my homeland and my new home," she once said. "It is a way of reclaiming my roots and becoming one with nature. Although the culture in which I live is part of me, my roots and cultural identity are a result of my Cuban heritage."

Moving to New York City in the late 1970s, Mendieta quickly found a community of fellow artists, including Andre, a sculptor who, like Mendieta, often worked with natural materials. She married him in 1985 despite a tempestuous relationship.

The circumstances of Mendieta's death later that year remain a mystery. What is certain is that she plunged from her apartment window in the early hours of September 8, and that her husband was charged with her murder.

Over three years of court proceedings, Andre denied the charges. He said that he and Mendieta had argued about his recognition in the art world as surpassing hers. When he walked into their bedroom, he said, she was gone and the window was open. But a passerby who testified said he had heard cries of a struggle. Andre was acquitted for lack of evidence.

To this day, Andre's shows draw protesters, who blame him for Mendieta's death.

In recent years, awareness of Mendieta's work has grown considerably, a sign that "the world has caught up," said Morris, the Brooklyn Museum curator.

"They understand her as a pioneer, a maverick, and as a great artist," she said.

———

**MONICA CASTILLO** is a critic, journalist, and curator. She's lived in New York City, the place Ana Mendieta called home, three times.

Postwar Poet Unafraid to Confront Her Own Despair

# Sylvia Plath

## 1932–1963

BY ANEMONA HARTOCOLLIS

SHE MADE SURE TO SPARE THE CHILDREN, leaving milk and bread for the two toddlers to find when they woke up. She stuffed the cracks of the doors and windows with cloths and tea towels. Then she turned on the gas.

On the morning of February 11, 1963, a Monday, a nurse found the poet Sylvia Plath in her flat on Fitzroy Road in London, an address where W. B. Yeats had once lived. She was "lying on the floor of the kitchen with her head resting on the oven," according to a local paper, the *St. Pancras Chronicle.*

Plath had killed herself. She was thirty.

Because the death was a suicide, Plath's family did not much advertise it, said Peter K. Steinberg, an editor, with Karen V. Kukil, of *The Letters of Sylvia Plath.* And although she was a published poet who had received good reviews and had determinedly made her way in a literary world dominated by men, the press did not pay much attention.

There were eight-line death notices in tiny print in *The Boston Globe* and the *Boston Herald.* To find them, a sharp-eyed reader had to look under *H* for Plath's married name, Hughes. The notices were almost as terse as a headstone: of London, England, formerly of Wellesley, Massachusetts, wife of Ted Hughes, mother of Frieda and Nicolas (her son's given name mysteriously missing its *H*), daughter of Aurelia, older sister of Warren.

Plath's hometown paper, *The Townsman* of Wellesley, falsely reported that she had died of "virus pneumonia." It nodded toward her literary career "as poet and author." But it did not name her poetry collection, *The Colossus,* first published in 1960 to positive reviews in the British press, or say that her poems had been printed in prestigious magazines like *The New Yorker.*

In its Fleet Street sensationalism, the *St. Pancras Chronicle*'s report was more satisfying, and more truthful.

"Tragic Death of Young Authoress," the headline blared, before subordinating her reputation to that of her husband. "Found with her head in the gas oven in the kitchen of their home in Fitzroy-road, N.W. 1, last week was 30-year-old authoress Mrs. Sylvia Plath Hughes, wife of one of Britain's best-known modern poets, Ted Hughes," the article said. It went on to say that her doctor had arranged for her to see a psychiatrist, "but the letter was delivered to the wrong address." It ended with the coroner's verdict that Plath had died of carbon monoxide poisoning and, to leave no doubt in the matter, "that she killed herself."

Sylvia Plath in 1953. One critic said shortly after her death that she could be "the most gifted woman poet of our time."

Leading up to her death, Plath grappled with the rejection
of editors and her husband.

# In death, Plath found her literary due.

At that moment in time, it was easy to see why she might have wanted to. She was estranged from Hughes after discovering that he was having an affair with another woman, Assia Wevill.

On December 28, 1962, just weeks before her death, Alfred A. Knopf, which had published her poetry, had rejected her novel *The Bell Jar*. Judith B. Jones, the editor who sent Plath the rejection notice, did not try to soft-pedal it.

"To be quite honest with you, we didn't feel that you had managed to use your materials successfully in a novelistic way," wrote Jones, who has been credited with rescuing the diary of Anne Frank from the reject pile and with discovering Julia Child. Jones said she had found the attitude expressed in the first half of *The Bell Jar*, about the young heroine's adventures as a magazine intern in New York, "perfectly normal," and had liked it well enough. As for the second half, Jones wrote, "I was not at all prepared as a reader to accept the extent of her illness and the suicide attempt."

An editor at Harper & Row concurred with Jones's assessment. In a letter addressed to "Mrs. Ted Hughes," this editor wrote, a little more charitably, that the first part of the novel was "arresting, a fresh and bright recreation of a girl's encounter with the big city—universal and individual." But she added, "With her breakdown, however, the story for us ceases to be a novel and becomes more a case history."

As she grappled with the rejection of editors and her husband, Plath spent her last months writing the poems that would secure her literary reputation.

Six days after she died, her friend the literary critic A. Alvarez predicted in *The Observer* that those poems, many of which were later published in her collection, *Ariel*, would establish her as "the most gifted woman poet of our time."

Thus it was in death that Plath found her literary due.

The public fascination with her death has hovered over her family. One of Warren Plath's two daughters, Susan Plath Winston, recalled the surprise that she and her sister would feel when their aunt's name appeared, for instance, in a snippet of *The Simpsons*.

Worse was when Plath's son, Nicholas, a fisheries biologist in Alaska, hanged himself in 2009, at forty-seven. Because of who his mother was, his death received front-page treatment. "Your family pain being literary/celebrity news is a bizarre place to be," said Winston, a lawyer in Oklahoma City who represents victims of domestic violence.

Sylvia Plath was born in Boston on October 27, 1932. Her father, Otto Emil Plath, a German-born professor at Boston University, died when she was eight, and her mother, born Aurelia Schober, made ends meet teaching in a university secretarial program. Biographers have linked Plath's bouts of depression to the childhood trauma of losing her father, as well as to her own perfectionism and her mother's smothering nature.

As a student at Smith College, Plath won a "guest editorship" at *Mademoiselle* magazine in New York in 1953, an experience that became the basis of *The Bell Jar*. Later that summer, she had a breakdown after being rejected from a writing course at Harvard. She received shock treatment and then swallowed most of a bottle of sleeping pills.

She met Hughes, a future British poet laureate, at a party in 1956 while studying at Cambridge University on a Fulbright grant. (In describing the encounter in her journal, she wrote of biting his cheek so hard she drew blood; he pocketed her earrings.) They married within four months, a romantic union that was also a literary partnership.

It was after their separation in fall 1962 that Plath—jealous, feverish, addicted to sleeping pills, and writing at dawn while her children slept—produced poems like "Lady Lazarus" and "Daddy" that helped make *Ariel* an exemplar of confessional poetry.

*The Bell Jar* was not published in the United States until 1971. (It had been published in England a month before Plath died, under the pseudonym Victoria Lucas, for fear, said Kukil, the associate curator of special collections at Smith, that its resemblances to real life would attract libel suits.) In 1982, she was awarded a posthumous Pulitzer Prize.

Gloria Steinem, who was a year behind Plath at Smith College, published Plath's BBC radio play, *Three Women,* in an early edition of *Ms.* magazine—"probably one of the reasons she was taken up by second-wave feminism," said Kukil. *The Bell Jar* has risen from the ashes of rejection to become a perennial favorite of high school and college students. It spent twenty-four weeks on the *New York Times* bestseller list in 1971 and had sold nearly three million paperback copies by the twenty-fifth anniversary of its publication in 1996.

"I like to think she somehow helped to open up and legitimate female anger," said Gail Crowther, author of *The Haunted Reader and Sylvia Plath,* among other books about the writer.

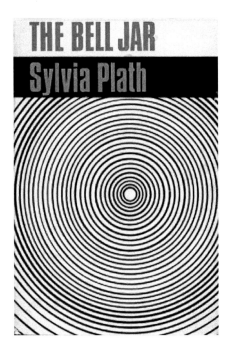

*The Bell Jar* was initially published under a pseudonym, one month before Plath's death.

Plath made the object of much of that anger clear elsewhere in "Lady Lazarus."

*Out of the ash*
*I rise with my red hair*
*And I eat men like air.*

**ANEMONA HARTOCOLLIS** is a national correspondent for *The New York Times,* covering higher education. Her paperback copy of *The Bell Jar* was so old and brittle—but still precious—she had to tape it back together while writing this obit.

# Beyond the Obit: Important Lives Forgotten

## BY AMISHA PADNANI

"Sylvia Plath never got a *New York Times* obituary?!"

I've been asked that question so many times when describing "Overlooked" to people since the series began in 2018. It's hard to imagine that Plath—someone so accomplished, someone whose work is read in classrooms across the United States— was not recognized by the paper of record at the time of her death in 1963.

In fact, she wasn't the only surprising omission. The newspaper failed to note the deaths of Ida B. Wells, the pioneering investigative journalist who started a campaign against lynching—even though her wedding notice made the front page; Diane Arbus, the photographer whose evocative portraits have compelled viewers for decades; Alan Turing, the British mathematician whose decoding of German messages helped end World War II; Robert Johnson, the bluesman whose complex guitar work inspired musicians for generations; and Gertrude Chandler Warner, the schoolteacher who penned the famous Boxcar Children series.

We can speculate about why these remarkable people were overlooked, but more important, we can use this as an opportunity to add them to the record now and ensure that such oversights never happen again.

Plath's unassuming grave in West Yorkshire, England, has become a pilgrimage site for her admirers.

# Jobriath

## 1946–1983

BY DAVID CHIU

ON MARCH 8, 1974, American TV viewers got their first glimpse of the American glam rocker Jobriath on the popular NBC music program *The Midnight Special.* Jobriath, who was introduced by the singer Gladys Knight as "the act of tomorrow," made a striking debut, wearing a futuristic silver-gray, hoop-shaped costume and singing a baroque-sounding number titled "I'maman."

For his second song, the electrifying "Rock of Ages," he wore a tight-fitting, one-piece purplish suit and a large bubble helmet that, with the touch of his fingers, broke apart into petals that surrounded his head. His space-alien persona and theatrical rock music drew comparisons to David Bowie's Ziggy Stardust character, and his swaggering sound was likened to that of Mick Jagger. Onstage he moved like a ballet dancer.

"We were so excited," the actress Ann Magnuson, then a teenager, said in a phone interview. "'Oh, did you see that helmet?' You would talk about that in school the next day."

But Billy Cross, who played the guitar alongside Jobriath, remembered the performance, and the audience, differently. "It was horrible," he said in a phone interview. "They hated us, and that wasn't fun."

Such was the complicated existence of Jobriath, who is generally regarded as the first openly gay rock star. His image came with risks: he released just two albums,

and both were poorly received by an audience that was largely unwilling to accept his effeminate persona. His short-lived career became a footnote to rock 'n' roll history, and he ultimately died alone, his body discovered by the police sometime later.

He was born Bruce Wayne Campbell on December 14, 1946, in Pennsylvania (accounts differ on precisely where), the second of three children of James and Marion (Salisbury) Campbell. His father came from a military background, and his mother was a homemaker who later worked as an insurance secretary. (The full name he used, Jobriath Salisbury, was "an amalgam of his teenage obsession with religion and his mother's maiden name," Robert Cochrane wrote in the liner notes of a 2004 Jobriath compilation.)

Bruce Campbell was a musical prodigy who could sight-read any composition at the piano, said Peter Batchelder, who met him in 1964 when they were music students at Temple University.

"He could play pretty much the whole first movement of the Prokofiev second piano concerto," he said by phone. "He could handle musical data like nobody I ever met before or since."

Finding Temple's music courses elementary, Bruce dropped out after one semester and joined the military.

Jobriath was admired by some, but unaccepted by others who objected to his effeminate persona.

Jobriath on *The Midnight Special* in 1974. His onstage persona
drew comparisons to David Bowie's Ziggy Stardust.

# "He could write, he could sing, he could dance. I bought it. I mean, he seduced me, period."

"He wanted to impress his father," said Willie Fogle, his half brother. "Of course he hated it, so he ran away."

Relocating to California under the name of Jobriath Salisbury, he agreed to play the piano accompaniment for a friend who was auditioning for the 1968 Los Angeles production of *Hair*. The musical's director, seeing Jobriath as a good fit for a production celebrating the counterculture, gave him a role.

"We were all dumbfounded," said Oatis Stephens, a friend who also acted in *Hair*. "It was like, 'Why aren't you playing concerts with the Philharmonic?'"

Jobriath later joined the New York City company of *Hair* but was fired, by his account, for upstaging the other actors. He then found himself lost and bingeing on alcohol. "I was floating down in the gutter," he told *Interview* magazine in 1973.

He was rescued, however, by the music entrepreneur and club owner Jerry Brandt, who heard a demo tape that Jobriath had sent to CBS Records. Brandt asked to become his manager.

"He could write, he could sing, he could dance," Brandt said in the 2012 documentary *Jobriath A.D.* "I bought it. I mean, he seduced me, period." (Brandt died in 2021.)

At Brandt's direction, Jobriath transformed himself from a 1960s hippie to a glittering rock star, and in interviews he took aim at musicians like Bowie and Marc Bolan, the front man for the band T. Rex, whose personas only hinted at sexual ambiguity.

"I'm a true fairy," he would say. He told NBC Los Angeles: "There's a lot of people running around, putting makeup on and stuff, just because it's chic. I just want to say that I'm no pretender."

Brandt brought Jobriath to the attention of Elektra Records, which signed him for a reported $500,000, a huge sum at the time for an unknown musician, equal to almost $3 million today. (In Mick Houghton's 2010 book *Becoming Elektra*, Jac Holzman, the label's founder, said that the actual figure was closer to $50,000.)

Jobriath's debut album, titled simply *Jobriath* and released in October 1973, was a mix of glam rock, cabaret, and funk, all given sophisticated arrangements at the Electric Lady recording studios in Manhattan. His lyrics could be risqué ("I'd do anything for you or to you," he sang in "Take Me I'm Yours"), tender ("I know the child that I am has hurt you / And I was a woman when I made you cry," in "Be Still"), or witty ("With you on my arm Betty Grable lost her charm," in "Movie Queen").

"The material just impressed me by its complexity, sensitivity, breadth, and quirkiness," Eddie Kramer, who

Today, those who knew Jobriath in his various guises—classical music wunderkind, glam rocker, interpreter of the Great American Songbook—remember his talent.

coproduced the record with Jobriath, said in a phone interview. "He was a genius."

Before the album was released, Brandt mounted a heavy promotional campaign, including full-page advertisements in *Rolling Stone* and *Vogue,* posters on the sides of buses, and a gigantic billboard in Times Square depicting Jobriath as a nude statue. Coinciding with the album's release, Jobriath had planned to make his live performance debut with three shows at the Palais Garnier, where he would emerge in a King Kong costume climbing a mini replica of the Empire State Building. The production cost was estimated at an exorbitant $200,000.

The ad campaign is one reason Jobriath is considered to this day to have been among the music industry's most overhyped acts.

With the gay liberation movement growing in the early 1970s, Brandt assumed that Jobriath would be readily embraced. "The kids will emulate Jobriath," he told *Rolling Stone* in 1973, "because he cares about his body, his mind, his responsibility to the public as a leader, as a force, as a manipulator of beauty and art."

The album earned some positive reviews, including one from *Rolling Stone*, which said it "exhibits honest, personal magnetism and talent to burn." Other publications were more mixed. In his review for *The New York*

*Times,* Henry Edwards made the inevitable comparison to Bowie. "Jobriath, too, writes about 'space clowns,' 'earthlings' and 'morning starships,'" he wrote. "The results can only be described as dismal."

Sales of the album were poor, and the Palais Garnier shows were scrapped.

"When it started out," said Cross, Jobriath's guitarist, "it was all about the music. After Jerry Brandt got involved, it was all about the career. Then after that started to take hold, it was all about Jobriath's sexuality. America was not ready for that."

"Any time you tell the public what they should be listening to, or when you claim something is great, there's going to be a backlash," Kieran Turner, who directed *Jobriath A.D.*, the documentary film, said in an interview. "That was the biggest mistake that Jerry made."

Jobriath put out a second album, *Creatures of the Street*, in 1974 and embarked on a national tour, only to encounter homophobic slurs during a performance at Nassau Coliseum on Long Island. By the next year, even after his appearance on *The Midnight Special*, Elektra had dropped Jobriath from its roster, and he and Brandt had parted ways.

"He didn't sell any records," Brandt said in the documentary. "What gets a record company going is the smell of money. And there was no money. He didn't generate fifty cents."

From the late 1970s onward, Jobriath performed pop standards as a cabaret musician, calling himself Cole Berlin, and lived at the Chelsea Hotel in Manhattan. In a 1979 interview, he spoke of his former alter ego in the past tense: "Jobriath committed suicide in a drug, alcohol and publicity overdose."

He was found dead at the Chelsea Hotel in the summer of 1983. He was thirty-six. AIDS, which had reached epidemic dimensions by then, was given as the cause.

In the decades since his death, Jobriath's music has been reissued, and a number of musicians have expressed admiration for him, including Morrissey, Jake Shears of Scissor Sisters, and Def Leppard's Joe Elliott.

Jobriath's impact on LGBTQ music history also went through a reappraisal. "He was a sexual hero," the British singer Marc Almond wrote in *The Guardian* in 2012. "For all the derision and marginalization he faced, Jobriath did touch lives."

Today, those who knew Jobriath in his various guises—classical music wunderkind, glam rocker, interpreter of the Great American Songbook—remember his talent. "Whether he was composing epic symphonic music of searing intensity (and orchestrating it at sixteen) or brazenly appropriating the Rolling Stones's idiom," Batchelder, his former classmate, said in an email, "there was always beauty in his work."

Jobriath's second album, *Creatures of the Street*, was released by Elektra Records in 1974.

**DAVID CHIU** is a writer and editor based in Brooklyn, New York. He doesn't own a jumpsuit or platform boots, but he does have a bass guitar that is collecting dust in his closet.

A photo booth portrait taken in the 1930s, one of the only confirmed photographs of Robert Johnson.

## Bluesman Whose Life Was a Riddle

# Robert Johnson

## 1911–1938

---

### BY REGGIE UGWU

LITTLE ABOUT THE LIFE Robert Leroy Johnson lived in his brief twenty-seven years, from approximately May 1911 until he died mysteriously in 1938, was documented. A birth certificate, if he had one, has never been found.

What is known can be summarized on a postcard: He is thought to have been born out of wedlock in May 1911 in Mississippi and raised there. School and census records indicate he lived for stretches in Tennessee and Arkansas. He took up guitar at a young age and became a traveling musician, eventually glimpsing the bustle of New York City. But he died in Mississippi, with just over two dozen little-noticed recorded songs to his name.

And yet, in the late twentieth century, the advent of rock 'n' roll would turn Johnson into a figure of legend. Decades after his death, he became one of the most famous guitarists who had ever lived, hailed as a lost prophet who, as the dubious story goes, sold his soul to the devil and epitomized Mississippi Delta blues in the bargain.

In the late 1960s, the Rolling Stones, Eric Clapton, and Led Zeppelin covered or adapted Johnson's songs in tribute. Bob Dylan, who, in the memoir *Chronicles: Volume One*, attributed "hundreds of lines" of his songwriting to Johnson's influence, included a Johnson album as one of the items on the cover of *Bringing It All Back Home*.

In the 1990s, a lightning-in-a-bottle compilation of Johnson's music—*The Complete Recordings*, released by Columbia Records in 1990—revived interest in the blues for yet another generation, selling more than two million copies and winning a Grammy for best historical album. In 1994, a United States postage stamp in Johnson's likeness memorialized him as a national hero.

The chasm between the man Johnson was and the myth he became—between mortal reach and posthumous grip—has marooned historians and conscientious listeners for more than a half century. It would have made fertile terrain for one of Johnson's own songs, many of which frankly and masterfully tilled the everyday hopelessness and implausibility of segregated African American life.

Indeed, his story is no more or less than the handiwork of the country in which it was written, a country where the legacy of African Americans has often been shaped by others.

Johnson was born in Hazlehurst, Mississippi, in the wake of the Redemption era, a period following Reconstruction when white supremacists across the South reversed many of the freedoms and rights granted to Black people after the Civil War.

His mother was Julia Major Dodds, the daughter of slaves, who had ten children with her husband, Charles

Dodds, before conceiving another with a field hand named Noah Johnson.

When Robert was around seven, his mother married another man, and he moved with them to Robinsonville, Mississippi. It was there, in the town's popular juke joints—segregated stores or private houses that doubled, after hours, as recreational places—that his now legendary music career began.

As recounted in Barry Lee Pearson and Bill McCulloch's biography, *Robert Johnson: Lost and Found* (2003), Johnson, perhaps as a teenager, attended juke joint performances by the early Delta blues pioneer Son House. The young musician had trained on a diddley bow—one or more strings nailed taut to the side of a barn—and wasn't much of a guitar player. But a surplus of ambition outweighed his lack of skill.

In a 1965 interview with the writer and academic Julius Lester, cited by Pearson and McCulloch, House recalled Johnson's habit of commandeering the stage during intermissions in order to play songs of his own. Chastened by House—and the howls of his audience—Johnson reportedly left town. But he returned six months later eager to perform again, this time asking for House's permission.

"He was so good!" House said of the new and improved playing style Johnson exhibited on the night of his reemergence. "When he finished all our mouths were standing open. I said, 'Well, ain't that fast! He's gone now!'"

Variations on House's story—a mysterious sojourn, sudden virtuosity—are the source of the myth that Johnson, like Faust, sold his soul in exchange for his genius.

But friends of Johnson have given conflicting testimonies as to whether the singer himself ever endorsed the tale. And the two of his songs most often associated with the story, "Cross Road Blues" and "Hellhound on My Trail," make no mention of an unholy encounter. Historians now suggest that Johnson's real benefactor may have been a guitarist in the Hazlehurst area named Ike Zinnerman (sometimes spelled Zimmerman).

The album *King of the Delta Blues Singers* was posthumously released in 1961.

214

As Johnson's music began to find an audience in the years after his death, however, critics—many of them white and mystified by Black culture in the South—leaned into the legend.

The music historian Elijah Wald wrote in *Escaping the Delta: Robert Johnson and the Invention of the Blues* (2004): "As white urbanites discovered the 'race records' of the 1920s and '30s, they reshaped the music to fit their own tastes and desires, creating a rich mythology that often bears little resemblance to the reality of the musicians they admired."

What is true is that the guitar playing on Johnson's recordings was unusually complex for its time. Most early Delta blues musicians played simple guitar figures that harmonized with their voices. But Johnson, imitating the boogie-woogie style of piano playing, used his guitar to play rhythm, bass, and slide simultaneously, all while singing.

Another innovation associated with Johnson, as noted by the critic Tony Scherman in 2009 in *The New York Times,* is the boogie bass. Appearing on the Johnson songs "Ramblin' on My Mind" and "I Believe I'll Dust My Broom," the boogie bass—a low, ambling rhythm that evokes a swaggering strut—became a building block of both Chicago blues and rock 'n' roll in the hands of the Johnson apostles Muddy Waters and Elmore James.

Like many bluesmen who lived in the shadow of Jim Crow, Johnson was a wanderer for most of his adult life and performed in juke joints—often traveling with his fellow blues artist Johnny Shines—as far as New York City. He married twice—first to Virginia Travis, who died while giving birth to their child, who also died, then to Caletta Craft. In 2000, a court ruled that Claud Johnson, the child of a girlfriend of Johnson's named Virgie Jane Smith, was legally his son.

What survives of Johnson's short career is based on his only two recording sessions, arranged by the American Record Company executive Don Law in 1936 and 1937 in Texas. One song from the first session, the vibrant "Terraplane Blues," sold a respectable five thousand copies, giving the singer the only real taste of fame he would know in his life.

Another record executive, John Hammond of Columbia Records, championed Johnson's music decades after his death. Hammond, who launched the recording careers of Billie Holiday, Aretha Franklin, Bob Dylan, and Bruce Springsteen, issued a posthumous Johnson album in 1961, *King of the Delta Blues Singers,* which compiled most of the American Record Company recordings.

The album captivated a fledgling generation of musicians at the dawn of rock's golden age. Eric Clapton wrote in 2007 in *Clapton: The Autobiography,* describing his first encounter with *King of the Delta Blues,* "I realized that, on some level, I had found the master."

The story of how Johnson died, like so many facts of his life, is contested.

A death certificate recovered by the researcher Gayle Dean Wardlow showed that he died on August 16, 1938, at a plantation near Greenwood, Mississippi. The cause was complications of syphilis, according to a note on the back of the certificate that was attributed to the plantation's owner.

But David "Honeyboy" Edwards, a contemporary of Johnson's who is believed to have performed with him just days before his death, said that Johnson had been poisoned, and that he was probably targeted by the vengeful husband of one of his mistresses.

The location of Johnson's grave has never been confirmed. Headstones at three different churches in the Greenwood area claim to mark his resting place—the final riddle of a man whose brief, turbulent life became a cipher nearly as sensational as his songs.

———

**REGGIE UGWU** is a culture reporter at *The New York Times*. Black music is always playing at the juke joint in his heart.

For Mr and Mrs James Weldon Johnson with sincere admiration for you both

— Nella Larsen Imes
March 30, 1930

Nella Larsen in 1930. Her novels are read today in American literature and Black studies courses

## Author Who Wrestled with Race

# Nella Larsen

## 1891–1964

BY BONNIE WERTHEIM

WHEN NELLA LARSEN DIED, in 1964, she left little behind: a ground-floor apartment, two published novels, some short stories, a few letters. She was divorced, had no children, and was estranged from her half sister, who, in some accounts, upon learning she was to inherit $35,000 of Larsen's savings, denied knowing the writer existed.

It was a fitting end for a woman whose entire life had been a story of swift erasure.

Larsen's immigrant parents—Mary Hanson, from Denmark, and Peter Walker, from the Danish West Indies—had settled in a mostly white, working-class neighborhood in Chicago, a city that was rapidly growing and segregating by the time Larsen was born on April 13, 1891.

Two years later, Walker disappeared, leaving Hanson alone with the couple's young daughter. In his absence, Hanson married a fellow Dane, Peter Larsen, with whom she had another daughter, Anna.

By all appearances, the family was white. But Nella Larsen was different, something that would come to inspire her fiction—celebrated during the Harlem Renaissance, forgotten by midcentury, and rediscovered to be read today in American literature and Black studies courses.

The public schools that Larsen attended in Chicago drew students from mostly German and Scandinavian backgrounds. So it wasn't until she left Chicago for Nashville in 1907 to attend the Fisk Normal School, a teacher-training program affiliated with the historically Black Fisk University, that she was surrounded by faces that weren't white.

Larsen later enrolled at the Lincoln School for Nurses in the Bronx, which was founded to recruit Black women into the field. After graduating with the equivalent of a registered nurse's degree in 1915, she was hired as a superintendent of nurses at the Tuskegee Institute in Alabama.

The next year, she moved back to New York to join the staff at Lincoln. She met Elmer Imes, the second African American to receive a PhD in physics, whom she married in 1919. As the Harlem Renaissance began to take shape in the 1920s, Larsen and Imes took up with a circle of Black intellectuals that included W. E. B. Du Bois and Langston Hughes.

Larsen first expressed a professional interest in literature and art as a volunteer helping to prepare the New York Public Library's first exhibition of African American artists. She later enrolled in the library's teaching program, eventually becoming its first Black female graduate.

Her initial placement was on the Lower East Side of Manhattan, but she transferred to the library's 135th

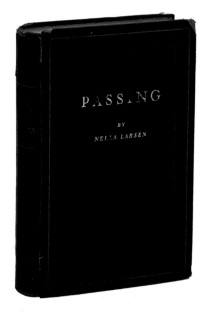

*Passing* is about two mixed-race women who grew up together and reunited after years of separation.

Street location to be closer to home and to the heart of the Harlem Renaissance. Today the branch is the Countee Cullen Library (named for a poet who contributed to Harlem's artistic prosperity) and is near the Schomburg Center for Research in Black Culture, where the archive includes two of Larsen's letters.

In one of the letters, from 1928, in a looping scrawl, Larsen addresses Edward Wasserman, a wealthy bohemian whose social circle included the novelist Zora Neale Hurston and the publishing matron Blanche Knopf. After years in which she had written stories under a pseudonym, her first novel, *Quicksand*, had just been published by Alfred A. Knopf, and she was eager to get Wasserman's opinion:

"I do want to see your review," she wrote. "Will you have a copy? I'm too poor to subscribe to a clipping bureau. Besides, what's the use? It seems that your review will be the only notice I'll have."

But that was not the case. Thadious M. Davis, one of Larsen's biographers and a professor of English at the University of Pennsylvania, said that *Quicksand* was widely and positively reviewed, including in *The New York Times, The Times Literary Supplement,* and *The Nation.*

The novel follows Helga Crane, a teacher at Naxos, a Black boarding school in the South where excellence is measured by its proximity to whiteness. Helga, whose mixed-race background mirrors Larsen's, is unsettled by Naxos's rigid and racially fraught standards. So she leaves in search of financial stability and her own identity. When she connects with her mother's white relatives, they treat her with a mix of contempt (in Chicago, her remarried uncle's wife rejects her) and fascination (her aunt in Copenhagen parades her around the predominantly white city as an exotic).

According to Davis, Larsen was remarkable in approaching the subject of race as a modernist, rather than drawing on Southern tropes or vernacular to convey her characters' Blackness.

Larsen followed *Quicksand* the next year with *Passing*, which tells the story of Irene Redfield and Clare Kendry, two mixed-race women who grew up together and reunite at a Chicago hotel after years of separation. Clare, Irene discovers, has been living as a white woman married to a racist who is none the wiser about his wife's background. The relationship between the two women flirts with the sensual as each becomes obsessed with the other's chosen path.

In its review of *Passing, The New York Times* noted that "Larsen is quite adroit at tracing the involved processes of a mind that is divided against itself, that fights between the dictates of reason and desire."

When *Passing* was reissued in 2001, the *Times's* book critic Richard Bernstein wrote that "reading it and knowing that its author wrote very little after it imparts a sense of loss, giving as it does a glimpse of an original and hugely insightful writer whose literary talent developed no further." (*Passing* was adapted for a film of the same name in 2021 starring Ruth Negga as Clare and Tessa Thompson as Irene.)

In 1930, one of Larsen's short stories became the subject of plagiarism accusations. She had riffed on a story by a British contemporary, Sheila Kaye-Smith, infusing its arc with racial tension.

"I think she was much too smart an individual to bold-face plagiarize that story," Davis said.

Despite the controversy, that same year she became the first African American woman to receive a Guggenheim fellowship. She used the grant, worth roughly $2,500 at the time, to pay for a period as an artistic expatriate in Europe.

When Larsen returned to New York, she was forced to confront the realities of her marriage. She knew that Imes, who had moved to Nashville for a post at Fisk University, was having an affair, and it led to their divorce in 1933. Supported by alimony, she continued as a fiction writer, producing at least one novel and a number of short stories that were not published. After Imes died in 1941, she moved downtown from West 135th Street to Second Avenue and returned to nursing to support herself.

Having cut her ties to Harlem's circle of artists and intellectuals, and with no connection to her last living relatives, Larsen had, wittingly or not, created the conditions necessary to disappear quietly. She died of a heart attack in her apartment on March 30, 1964. She was seventy-two.

Larsen approached race as a modernist, rather than drawing on Southern tropes to convey characters' Blackness.

**BONNIE WERTHEIM** is a deputy editor on *The Wall Street Journal*'s Style News desk and a former editor at *The New York Times*. She first read Nella Larsen in an undergraduate class on literary modernism.

Eccentric Chicago Street Artist

# Lee Godie

## 1908–1994

BY JEREMY LYBARGER

ANYONE WHO PASSED THROUGH downtown Chicago in the 1970s or '80s might have encountered a weathered blond woman wearing a rabbit-fur coat and men's orthopedic slip-ons as she hawked her art on Michigan Avenue. If you looked like a prospective buyer, she would slowly, seductively, unfurl her latest canvas as you approached.

Sometimes she would recite an old tune in her lilting voice; "Oh! Frenchy," a racy hit from World War I, was her favorite. If you were exceptionally lucky, she would treat you to hors d'oeuvres: Oreo cookies whose cream filling had been replaced with cheese; instant iced tea made with water from a civic fountain. The eccentric "bag lady," as she was often called, was Lee Godie, one of the city's most iconoclastic artists.

For nearly twenty-five years, Godie lived mostly outdoors and slept on park benches, even in subzero temperatures. She stashed her possessions in rented lockers around the city. Her studio was wherever she happened to be—an alley, a bridge, atop a deli counter.

She was prolific, producing paintings, drawings, and watercolors on materials that included canvas, discarded window shades, cardboard, pillowcases, and paper. In the 1970s, she took hundreds of self-portraits in photo booths at the Greyhound bus terminal and in the train station. In these black-and-white snapshots—which she often embellished with paint or a ballpoint pen—she portrayed her many sides: a coquette; a Katharine Hepburn lookalike; a rich lady flashing a wad of cash; and above all, an uncompromising artist whose work can be found today in American museums.

She was born Jamot Emily Godee in Chicago on September 1, 1908, one of eleven children raised in a Christian Scientist family on the Northwest side. The Godee house was small, and the sisters slept in the attic.

Because Godie was intensely private and a fabulist regarding her own life, it can be difficult to distinguish truth from self-invention. She claimed to have once worked as a telephone operator, although her real ambition was to be a nightclub singer. In 1933, she married George Hathaway, a steamfitter with whom she had three children; a son died of pneumonia at eighteen months, and a daughter died of diphtheria at age seven.

Godie married again in 1948 and moved to Tacoma, Washington, under the impression that her new husband, Austin Benson, would champion her singing career. Instead, she found herself marooned on his chicken farm, pregnant yet again. She ran away shortly after, abandoning her family for good.

Godie disappeared for some time after that. Kapra Fleming, who in 2021 released a documentary film, *Lee*

*The Gibson Girl,* undated. Godie's images often have a deliberately exaggerated expressiveness.

*Godie: Chicago French Impressionist,* said in an interview that she couldn't find any record of the artist between 1952 and 1968. Then Godie, at sixty, suddenly appeared on the steps of the majestic Art Institute of Chicago, declaring herself a French Impressionist who was "much better than Cézanne."

In a 1982 profile of her in the *Chicago Reader,* Alex Wald, an early collector, recalled for the writer Michael Bonesteel the first time he saw Godie: "She had big orange balls painted on each cheek, painted eye shadow and eyebrows painted above her actual eyebrows, all from the same paint box she was making her pictures with."

It's unclear when Godie began painting or what inspired her to sell her art in public. She liked to claim that a red bird had told her to pick up a brush. Her clientele was initially made up of students from the nearby School of the Art Institute of Chicago, who purchased her works for bargain rates of $5 to $20 apiece. (Godie would write the "real" value of her art—usually $2,500 or more—on

the reverse.) She occasionally included cheap brooches or live carnations as bonuses to sweeten a sale. She also sometimes sewed her photo-booth portraits to a canvas as a kind of advertisement for herself.

"She lived in a fantasy world," Marianne Burt, one of her student customers, said by phone. "In her mind she was a world-famous artist. And everything was about France."

Godie even pronounced her name with a French accent, as in "go-DAY." In a 2008 exhibition catalog for Intuit: The Center for Intuitive and Outsider Art in Chicago, where Godie's art has been shown, the curator Jessica Moss conveyed Godie's rapture over a French Impressionist show at the Art Institute. "To save herself from passing out in such a revered institution," Moss wrote, "she devoured a small piece of cheese that she had been saving in her armpit in case of an emergency."

At first glance, Godie's work can appear childlike, her figures rendered in a cartoonish style that verges on grotesque. She was primarily a portraitist, although one less interested in capturing a subject's likeness than in evoking moods, like wariness or anxiety, as evidenced by the clenched teeth she depicted in work such as *Tidle— Gay Artist Lee Godie a French Impressionist.* Her images have a deliberately exaggerated expressiveness, as in *Sweet Sixteen* (1973–74) or the undated *Smiling Girl.* Both her men and women sport garish red lips, wide eyes that are lusciously over-lashed, and hair that can be unnaturally blond or orange.

"The uncanny nature of her people is arresting, sometimes disturbing and even alarming, but as authentic as the artist herself," Bonesteel wrote in a 1993 exhibition catalog. "In the course of making her work, she psychically imprints her emotional state upon it."

There were recurrent figures, including a woman in left profile with a topknot and bared teeth, the so-called Gibson Girl inspired by Charles Dana Gibson's turn-of-the-century illustration of idealized feminine beauty; Prince Charming, or Prince of the City, a patrician figure with a bow tie and parted hair, often portrayed in front of Chicago's John Hancock Center; and a waiter, a mustachioed man with sideburns, based on a real waiter whom Godie found handsome.

Some of her female figures resembled the actress Joan Crawford. Other common motifs were birds, leaves, insects, grape clusters, and hands playing piano. Godie sometimes wrote on her canvases, too: "Staying Alive" and "Chicago—we own it!" appear with the frequency of personal mottos.

Godie hosted themed parties to showcase new work. The "red party," for example, was held around dawn in Grant Park and featured red appetizers and art with a red palette. In the 1980s, she streamlined her enterprise by tracing compositions she had made and selling the copies, essentially mass-producing her greatest hits. She reportedly earned as much as a thousand dollars a day, which she squirreled away in her shoes, underwear, and hidden pockets of her coat. On brutally cold nights, she splurged for a $10 room at a flophouse.

As word of Godie spread, so did reports of her combative behavior. She was notorious for refusing to sell to buyers who ran afoul of her mood or who otherwise displeased her; women who wore pants rather than dresses were blacklisted.

Frank Zirbel, a bike messenger at the time, recalled Godie throwing pizza at police officers. Marga Shubart, who developed a friendship with her, once saw Godie smash a stranger's camera in front of a Bonwit Teller department store. "It was a windy day," Shubart said by phone, "and Lee said, 'Pictures don't turn out on windy days.'"

But Godie had a soft side. She was known to dispense quirky advice, like telling people to eat crunchy peanut butter so that they would "possess the refreshing breath of peanut aroma at all times," according to Bonesteel.

In the mid-1980s, Godie befriended the Chicago gallerist Carl Hammer, who gave her her first solo exhibition, in 1991.

"I had a love affair with her work," Hammer said in an interview. "She was one of the most special people in my life. She was the epitome of what I was doing in the gallery."

A retrospective at the Chicago Cultural Center followed in 1993.

Godie was also the subject of articles in *People* magazine and *The Wall Street Journal*. The *Journal* piece caught the eye of Bonnie Blank, Godie's estranged daughter by her first husband; she hadn't known of her mother's career on the streets of Chicago. Blank lived in Plato Center, Illinois, and reunited with her mother, who by then showed signs of dementia. Blank was granted legal guardianship in 1991. (She says she is now writing a book about her mother.)

Shortly afterward, Godie was moved to a nursing home, where she died on March 2, 1994. She was eighty-five.

Today her work is in the permanent collections of the American Folk Art Museum in New York, the Smithsonian, the Philadelphia Museum of Art, and others.

Godie was a tangle of contradictions: a flâneuse in patchwork clothes and safety pins who considered herself a fashion plate; a short-tempered bohemian who insisted on decorum; a camera-shy woman who ruthlessly dramatized her interior states. She was an artist who savored beauty even in her harsh concrete environment.

"I always try to paint beauty," she wrote in her journals, "but some people say my paintings aren't beautiful. Well, I have beauty in mind, but it isn't always easy to make paintings beautiful."

———

**JEREMY LYBARGER** is the features editor at the Poetry Foundation. One of Lee Godie's Prince Charming paintings hangs in his bedroom and is the first face he sees every day.

## Blues Performer Who Became 1920s Harlem Royalty

# Gladys Bentley

## 1907–1960

BY GIOVANNI RUSSONELLO

WHEN IT COMES to loosening social mores, progress that isn't made in private has often taken place onstage.

That was certainly the case at the Clam House, a Prohibition-era speakeasy in Harlem, where Gladys Bentley, one of the boldest performers of her era, held court.

In her top hat and tuxedo, Bentley belted gender-bending original blues numbers and lewd parodies of popular songs, eventually becoming Harlem royalty. When not accompanying herself with a dazzling piano, the mightily built singer often swept through the audience, flirting with women in the crowd and soliciting dirty lyrics from them as she sang.

By the early 1930s, Bentley was Harlem's most famous lesbian figure—a significant distinction, given that gay, lesbian, and gender-defying writers and performers were flourishing during the Harlem Renaissance. For a time, she was among the best-known Black entertainers in the United States.

Bentley sang her bawdy, bossy songs in a thunderous voice, dipping down into a froglike growl or curling upward into a wail. In his 1940 autobiography, Langston Hughes called her "an amazing exhibition of musical energy—a large, dark, masculine lady, whose feet pounded the floor while her fingers pounded the keyboard—a perfect piece of African sculpture, animated by her own rhythm."

In a letter to Countee Cullen, the Harlem socialite, Harold Jackman wrote: "When Gladys sings 'St. James Infirmary,' it makes you weep your heart out."

Indeed, Bentley knew her success was built on talent as much as notoriety. "The world has tramped to the doors of the places where I have performed to applaud my piano playing and song styling," she wrote in a 1952 essay for *Ebony*. "Even though they knew me as a male impersonator, they still could appreciate my artistry as a performer."

Bentley's rise to fame demonstrated how liberated the Prohibition culture of the Harlem Renaissance had become, and how welcoming the blues tradition could be to gay expression. She often confronted male entitlement and sexual abuse in her lyrics and declared her own sexual independence. This was, in fact, the continuation of a tradition begun by other singers of the early twentieth century, particularly Bessie Smith, Ma Rainey, and Lucille Bogan, who were some of the most vocal musician critics of patriarchy of their time.

But Bentley was the first prominent performer of her era to embrace a trans identity, implicating her body differently in these acts of musical defiance. (Throughout her life, Bentley used female pronouns to describe herself—at least in public.)

Gladys Bentley was among the boldest and best-known Black entertainers in the United States.

On a 1928 recording of her "Worried Blues," for OKeh Records, Bentley sang: "What made you men folk treat us women like you do? / I don't want no man that I got to give my money to."

Between lines, she improvises vocal fills, uncannily mimicking a trumpet and hitting the notes spot-on. On "How Much Can I Stand?," from later that year, she depicted an abusive relationship with a sense of wry humanity:

*Said I was an angel, he was bound to treat me right*
*Who in the devil ever heard of angels that get beat up*
  *every night?*
*How much of that dog can I stand?*

Gladys Bentley was born on August 12, 1907, to Mary Bentley, who was from Trinidad, and George Bentley, an American, and she was raised in Philadelphia. (While most sources list Philadelphia as Bentley's birthplace, during a rare TV appearance in 1958, she told Groucho Marx that she was originally from Port of Spain, Trinidad.)

The eldest of four siblings, Bentley remembered her childhood as an unhappy one, and from an early age her parents worried about her attraction to women. But she poured her frustrations and self-interrogations into music, and her talents as a pianist and songwriter showed themselves quickly. In 1923, at sixteen, she left home for New York City, where the Harlem Renaissance was already in high gear.

Bentley immediately began performing at house parties and at so-called buffet flats. These were illicit clubs, usually in brownstones, that offered music, alcohol, gambling, and often prostitution. But it was at the Clam House—Harlem's most popular gay-friendly speakeasy, on 133rd Street, nicknamed Swing Street for its countless underground clubs—that Bentley established herself as the main attraction.

Her reputation took off. The house became the talk of Harlem, attracting uptown bigwigs as well as celebrities from all over the city. Bentley's performances there inspired characters in at least three novels based on Harlem's nightlife, including Carl Van Vechten's voyeuristic *Parties*.

The Clam House appears prominently on the cartoonist Elmer Simms Campbell's *Night-Club Map of Harlem*. In the center of the image, just off Seventh Avenue, Campbell drew a sketch of Bentley at the piano, writing, "Gladys' Clam House: Gladys Bentley wears a tuxedo and high hat."

Bentley recorded intermittently in the twenties and thirties, but none of the recordings capture the licentious immersion of her live performances, and she was not widely played on the radio.

Instead, Bentley became a fixture of clubs across the city and eventually toured nationally. At the height of her fame, she said in the *Ebony* essay, she was living on Park Avenue with a team of servants, paying $300 a month in rent (over $5,000 in today's dollars), and driving a luxury car. She told reporters that she had married a white woman at a ceremony in New Jersey, though the woman's identity does not appear to have become public.

In the mid-thirties, Bentley was the headliner at the Ubangi Club, running a stage show that featured flamboyantly dressed men dancing in a chorus line behind her. Advertisements for the show stated that she was in charge of a "cast of 30." She sometimes appeared at the Apollo Theater and the Cotton Club, and held a residency at a club on Park Avenue in midtown.

During Prohibition, lines blurred between mainstream nightlife and more illicit forms of entertainment. But over the course of the thirties, after the Eighteenth Amendment was repealed and the country found itself in the Depression, tolerance waned. Even as Bentley grew more popular, her celebrity became less acceptable—and performing south of Harlem became difficult. In 1934, a run at the King's Terrace on Fifty-Second Street was cut short under pressure from the police.

In 1937, Bentley left New York for Los Angeles. She became a leading entertainer there and in the Bay Area, though she sometimes had to wear skirts onstage to appease club owners. She was less restricted at Mona's 440 Club, the first lesbian bar in San Francisco, which became her home base for a time.

The Red Scare brought a new wave of repressive social politics, and McCarthyite attacks on artists placed a particular target on homosexuals. Bentley never stopped touring, but she began to appear consistently in women's clothing, and in the 1950s she claimed to have gotten married twice to men. (One of them, the journalist J. T. Gibson, denied it.) In 1952, the same year she signed a recording contract with the Swing Time label, she wrote in the *Ebony* essay (titled "I Am a Woman Again") that she had undergone hormone treatments to help her identify as heterosexual.

By 1958, she said she had completed an autobiography, *If This Be Sin*, but it was never published. Bentley died in 1960, from complications of the flu, at fifty-two, while studying to become a Christian minister.

For a time, she had been a monarch of the New York night: the simple mention of her name was enough to clue readers in. In October 1936, a *New York Times* entertainment columnist wrote: "The Ubangi Club, Harlem's reigning hot spot, will offer a brand new revue tomorrow evening, featuring (of course) Gladys Bentley."

In another article that month, the *Times* described the scene she cultivated: "The Ubangi still draws a mixed crowd, is noisy and intimate and gay—altogether Harlem."

At the height of her fame, Bentley, shown here in 1937, was living on Park Avenue.

**GIOVANNI RUSSONELLO** is the jazz critic for *The New York Times*, where he also covered the last two presidential campaigns for the Politics desk. He's seen his fair share of concerts in unmarked Harlem brownstones, but he doubts that any would have rivaled Gladys Bentley's revue.

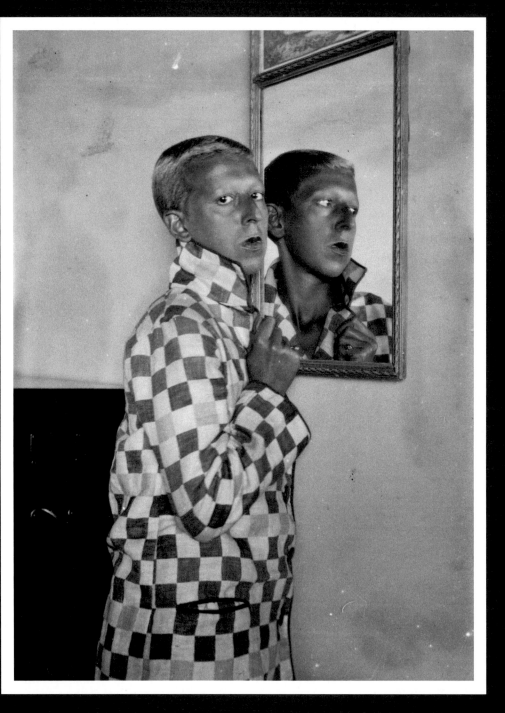

A 1928 portrait of Claude Cahun, whose work protested gender and sexual norms.

Photographer Who Explored Gender and Sexuality

# Claude Cahun

## 1894–1954

BY JOSEPH B. TREASTER

IN EARLY-TWENTIETH-CENTURY France, when society generally considered women to be women and men to be men, Lucy Schwob decided she would rather be called Claude Cahun.

It was her way of protesting gender and sexual norms. She thrived on ambiguity and she chose a name, Claude, that in French could refer to either a man or a woman. She took the last name from her grandmother Mathilda Cahun.

Cahun (ca-AH) made ambiguity a theme in a lifelong exploration of gender and sexual identity as a writer and photographer. Decades after her death, she has a growing following among art historians, feminists, and people in the lesbian, gay, bisexual, transgender, and queer community.

Working in Paris in the racy 1920s and '30s alongside Surrealist artists and writers, long before the rise of the gender-neutral *they* as a third-person singular pronoun and the advent of terms like *transgender* and *queer theory*, Cahun created stark, sometimes playful, but deliberately equivocal photos of herself.

Here she's a man. There she's a woman. Sometimes she's a little of both. Sometimes her head is shaved. In one photograph, Cahun brings together two silhouette portraits of herself, bald and austere, sizing each other up. "What do you want from me?" her caption reads.

"Masculine? Feminine?" she wrote in her book *Aveux non avenus,* published in English as *Disavowals.* "It depends on the situation. Neuter is the only gender that always suits me."

As a writer and photographer, Cahun worked at upending convention. "My role," she wrote in an essay published after her death, "was to embody my own revolt and to accept, at the proper moment, my destiny, whatever it may be."

Cahun's writing is complex and often difficult to follow, scholars say. But it provides context for the photographs and the weave of her life.

The photographs are by far her most compelling work. At first, scholars thought of them as self-portraits. But the gathering consensus is that Cahun choreographed and posed for the photos, and that her romantic partner, Marcel Moore, who was born Suzanne Malherbe, often pressed the button. It was a collaboration.

Cahun died on December 8, 1954, at age sixty, on the tiny Channel Island of Jersey off the Normandy coast of France. Hardly anyone noticed. *Disavowals,* her most heartfelt book, had not been well received. And she had never exhibited her photographs.

In the 1990s, however, she received a rush of attention as gender issues were gathering steam around the world.

Cahun created deliberately equivocal photos of herself, including this one from the late 1920s.

"Suddenly," said Vince Aletti, a New York photography critic and curator, "she seemed incredibly of the moment."

A French writer, François Leperlier, published a book on Cahun and helped organize the first exhibition of her work, at a museum in Paris. An English edition was published as *Claude Cahun: Masks and Metamorphoses*.

Professors and graduate students in art history and in feminist and gender studies began writing about her. Art museums wanted her work.

Cahun's photographs have been displayed in group shows in nearly a dozen museums in London, Paris, Washington, Melbourne, Warsaw, and elsewhere. Tellingly, many middle and high school students attended an exhibit at the Contemporary Jewish Museum in San Francisco, said Lori Starr, the museum's director.

"In Cahun you've got an artist who turns the camera on themselves to see who else they can become," said David J. Getsy, a professor at the School of the Art Institute of Chicago who specializes in gender and sexuality in art. "Isn't that what we're all doing now with cell phone photos? This is one reason young people might see themselves in Cahun."

Paris named a street for Cahun and Moore in 2018. That same year, Christian Dior brought out an androgynous collection inspired by Cahun.

**JOSEPH B. TREASTER** is a professor at the University of Miami and a contributor to *The New York Times* after working there for more than thirty years as a reporter and foreign correspondent. After writing about Claude Cahun, he visited her grave on the Channel Island of Jersey in the church cemetery next to the granite house she shared for years with her life partner, Marcel Moore.

Though she was also a writer, Cahun's photographs, like this one from 1929, are her most compelling work.

Elis Regina in 1968 in Paris. She performed and recorded music internationally throughout the 1960s.

# The "Greatest Singer in Brazil"

# Elis Regina

## 1945–1982

BY JON PARELES

EARLY IN HER CAREER, the Brazilian singer Elis Regina earned a nickname from the poet and bossa nova lyricist Vinicius de Moraes. It was "Pimentinha"—"little pepper." The singer Maria Rita Camargo Mariano, Elis Regina's daughter, said it was better translated as "hot pepper" to match a fierce, strong-willed, creative personality.

"She was short and she was thin and she was loud and she was all over the place," Maria Rita said in an interview. "She was fabulous, she was curious and she had this drive towards justice. It was a very feisty and fiery combination."

Regina was not conventionally glamorous: she was just five feet tall and slightly cross-eyed, and she kept her hair cut short. Yet in the 1950s, when she was barely into her teens, she became a regional pop star, conquering radio and later television. Throughout the 1960s and '70s, as she took charge of her own repertoire and expanded her artistic ambitions, she was widely acclaimed as Brazil's greatest singer.

Her voice, a tangy alto, held passion, playfulness, strength, and finesse, earning comparisons to Edith Piaf, Janis Joplin, Billie Holiday, and Ella Fitzgerald. She could caress a ballad, rasp with anger, ricochet off Afro-Brazilian rhythms, cackle with irony, sparkle with girlish laughter, or scat-sing with acrobatic precision.

"She was such a musician, but she had such emotion as well," Maria Rita said. "How could she do it? She would cry and scream and yell—and all at the right time, at the perfect pitch."

Regina created hybrids of samba, jazz, blues, rock, funk, and regional styles from across Brazil and Latin America. Even as advancing technology offered flexibility and easy fixes, Regina recorded live with her musicians in the studio, delivering now-or-never real-time performances.

In a 1981 interview, she said, "Perfection is a goal. I was looking for it. I keep looking. I don't know if I'll ever get there."

Throughout her career, Regina sought out new songwriters. She was among the first to record such major Brazilian figures as Milton Nascimento, Gilberto Gil, Caetano Veloso, and João Bosco.

"All the songs I made from the moment I met Elis were made for her," Nascimento said in 2012. "Whenever I go to do something, I think of her singing."

Regina chose material that held both musical and literary intricacies, singing not only about love but also about folklore, aspirations, feminism, and, during an increasingly harsh Brazilian dictatorship, a spirit of perseverance and resistance.

"Music is my bow, my arrow, my engine, my fuel, and my solitude," Regina said in a Brazilian television interview. "Singing is an act that is done absolutely alone, and I love it."

Regina's stage shows merged concert and musical theater in startling ways—particularly her groundbreaking 1975 production *Falso brilhante* (Fake diamond), which included dancers, costumed musicians, actors, and puppets. Regina also started a production company and record label, Trama, and in 1978 she was a founder of the Association of Interpreters and Musicians, which sought to create an alternative to Brazil's official musicians' union.

She was married and divorced twice: from 1967 to 1972 to the songwriter, producer, director, and journalist Ronaldo Bôscoli, and from 1973 to 1981 to the keyboardist César Camargo Mariano, whose adventurous, intricate arrangements supported her definitive albums in the 1970s. She had three children: João Marcello Bôscoli, Pedro Mariano, and Maria Rita.

Her influence reached far beyond Brazil. In a 1996 interview with *Folha de São Paulo,* the avant-garde artist Björk said she wrote the song "Isobel" with Regina in mind.

"It has something to do with the energy with which she sings," Björk said. "She also has a clarity in her voice, which is full of spirit. What I like about Elis is that she covers a whole spectrum of emotions. In one moment, she is very happy, seems to be in heaven. In another, she may be very sad and become suicidal."

Elis Regina Carvalho Costa was born on March 17, 1945, in Porto Alegre in southern Brazil. Her father, Romeu de Oliveira Costa, had assorted jobs, including factory work and running a butcher shop; her mother, Ercy Carvalho, was a washerwoman and homemaker. As a child, Elis was eager to take piano lessons, and she progressed so fast that her teacher insisted that she needed a piano at home to practice. The family couldn't afford one, so Elis turned to singing instead.

At eleven, she auditioned for a weekly radio show, *Clube do guri,* that presented children singing pop hits.

Stage fright made her so nervous that she had a nosebleed, staining her white dress. She thought she had failed. But she was invited back, and over the next two years she emerged as the show's standout performer.

In 1958, while Regina was still in school, she became her family's breadwinner when she signed a contract to perform regularly on Rádio Gaúcha in Porto Alegre. She recorded her first albums, aimed at a teen pop market, during school vacations.

Just days before the 1964 military coup that would plunge Brazil into dictatorship, she moved to Rio de Janeiro to sign with a larger record label. She joined the show *Noite de gala* on Rio TV, while also working with forward-looking, jazz-loving musicians at Beco das Garrafas, a renowned cluster of clubs.

Regina won the first Festival de Música Popular Brasileira, a televised competition in 1965, singing "Arrastão" (Fishing net) by Edu Lobo and Vinicius de Moraes, about a fisherman who captures the Afro-Brazilian sea goddess, Yemanjá. Her robust, full-throated style was a sharp contrast to the fashionable cool of the era's bossa nova.

She began hosting *O fino da bossa* (The best of bossa), a music-and-talk television show, with Jair Rodrigues, and the two recorded three albums together. Their *Dois na bossa* became the first Brazilian album to sell a million copies. By 1966, Regina was the highest-paid singer on Brazilian television. She also released a 1965 solo album, *Samba—Eu canto assim* (Samba—I sing like this), which signaled her adult identity with a selection of virtuosic, poetic songs. She followed it with a 1966 album, *Elis*—the first of many albums, all superb, with the same title—that featured songs from Gil, Veloso, and Nascimento.

Through the late 1960s, Regina performed and toured internationally, with recording sessions in Brazil, London, and Sweden. Brazilian music was in ferment; a new movement, Tropicália, was embracing rock guitars and using psychedelia, parody, and absurdism to call for freedom. At the end of 1968, two of Tropicália's leading songwriters, Gil and Veloso, were arrested, jailed, and

*Samba—Eu canto assim* (Samba—I sing like this),
a solo album released in 1965.

exiled to England. Regina's 1970 album . . . *Em pleno verão* ( . . . In full summer) pointedly included songs they sent from London: Gil's "Closed for Balance" and Veloso's "Do Not Be Afraid."

In a 1969 newspaper interview in the Netherlands, Regina described Brazil's ruling military junta as "gorillas." Three years later, the dictatorship took revenge; under threat of imprisonment, Regina led the singing of the national anthem at the televised Army Olympics. Brazil's leftists criticized her as a collaborator.

In a 1973 televised concert showcase, Arthur de Faria recounted in *Elis: Uma biografia musical* (2015), a heckler shouted at Regina, "Go sing for the army!" and Veloso, who had returned from exile, responded, "Respect the greatest singer in Brazil!"

For the rest of her career, Regina's albums and performances made clear that she did not support the dictatorship. João Marcello Bôscoli, her son, recalled in his memoir, *Elis e Eu* (Elis and I), that his family had its phone tapped and was often surveilled by government agents.

While overt protest songs were prohibited in Brazil, metaphors, allusions, irony, and vocal inflections could not be suppressed, and Regina's 1970s albums held clear undercurrents of struggle and discontent with the dictatorship. She also toured universities to reach a younger, more politically minded audience.

"Cartomante" (Fortune teller), by Ivan Lins and Vítor Martins, from the 1977 album *Elis*, warns, "These days, it's good to protect yourself." In 1979, Regina released "O bêbado e a equilibrista" (The drunk and the tightrope walker) by João Bosco and Aldir Blanc. The song became an anthem for Brazil's amnesty movement, which called for the return of political exiles. "Our gentle mother country is crying," Regina sang. "Marias and Clarices are crying on Brazil's soil / But I know that pain this sharp won't be in vain."

In 1974, Regina visited Los Angeles to record with the bossa nova pioneer Antônio Carlos Jobim. There was friction during the sessions; Regina later recalled, "These were moments lived by two very tense people, who can only relax through music." Yet the album, *Elis & Tom*, has often been considered a pinnacle of Brazilian music, a collection of songs that encompasses both airborne whimsy and profound melancholy. It sounds simultaneously casual and immaculately poised.

Regina's stage production *Falso brilhante* was a massive undertaking. It took shape over seven months of rehearsals and ran from December 1975 to February 1977 at the Bandeirantes Theater in São Paulo, the city where she had settled. The show's first act turned Regina's autobiography into a fable, tracing the story of a girl who achieves stardom only to be swallowed by a monster. The second act offered reflections on continuity and change between generations. *Falso brilhante* sold 280,000 tickets; its run ended when Regina was pregnant with Maria Rita.

Two months after Maria Rita was born, Regina opened another show: *Transversal do tempo* (Transversal of time). Presented at a theater in Porto Alegre and then on a European tour, it had a starkly industrial set and dressed its performers as workers, while the songs hinted at the dictatorship's growing clampdown. "The show intends to be journalistic," Regina told a Brazilian TV station.

"Essa mulher" (This woman), the title song of her 1979 album and show, *Elis, essa mulher*, was written for her by Joyce Moreno and Ana Terra. Regina told a radio interviewer, "She is a person who thinks, a person who suffers, a person who is mocking, who is ironic, who is playful, who is naughty, who is a kid. I mean, this record is me. This whole mess, there, is the mess that I am."

Regina was invited to perform at the 1979 Montreux Jazz Festival, where an impromptu encore—three unrehearsed duets with Hermeto Pascoal, the Brazilian keyboardist and composer sharing the bill—was a tour de force of daredevil improvisation, each of them pushing the other toward rhythmic and harmonic feats.

Her 1980 stage production, *Saudade do Brasil* (Longing for Brazil), was a search for and tribute to Brazil's resilient spirit. "It's not about longing for something that ended or a person who died," Regina said. "It is nostalgia for what is there alive, loose, and has never ceased to exist." It included the ballad "Aos nossos filhos" (To our children) by Lins and Martins, a plea for forgiveness from a younger generation: "Forgive the lack of choice / The days were like this," she sang.

Censors prevented her from wearing a T-shirt that showed the Brazilian flag with her name in place of the national motto, "Ordem e Progresso," in performances of *Saudade do Brasil*. She would be buried in it.

In Los Angeles, and then at her home, she worked on a prospective album with the jazz composer and saxophonist Wayne Shorter, a longtime admirer of Brazilian music. But the project fell apart. Her marriage was also ending. She assembled a 1981 show, *Trem azul* (Blue train), featuring songs from her 1980 *Elis* album, but broke up with Mariano just days before its premiere; the show went on. A rough cassette recording of the performance would become one of her bestselling albums after her death.

On January 19, 1982, with a new recording contract and some songs already chosen for her next album, Regina died of an accidental overdose of cocaine and alcohol. She was thirty-six.

Her death was mourned across Brazil. A memorial concert at Morumbi Stadium in São Paulo brought together top Brazilian musicians and drew a hundred thousand people, all singing along when the performers gathered to share "O bêbado e a equilibrista." The words *Elis Vive* appeared as graffiti around her hometown, Porto Alegre, and beyond. There were tribute concerts, radio series, and podcasts; Porto Alegre erected a statue of her in 2015. Live and archive recordings were released; DVDs collected her television performances and rare stage footage. *Elis: A Musical* was staged in Rio de Janeiro in 2013; a movie biography, *Elis*, appeared in 2016.

Gil, who would later become Brazil's minister of culture, was visiting the United States and unable to attend Regina's funeral in 1982. He sent a wreath inscribed: "Your voice will belong to all songs, your soul to all hearts."

———

**JON PARELES** is the chief pop music critic of *The New York Times*. He once marched in Rio de Janeiro's Carnaval, dressed as the rain forest.

Regina's songs were about love, feminism, and, during a Brazilian dictatorship, a spirit of perseverance.

# Master Juba

## Circa 1825–1852

BY COREY KILGANNON

IT IS 1842 in an alehouse in the gritty Five Points section of Manhattan. A lithe Black teenager boldly steps up before a raucous crowd of white drinkers and proceeds to dance.

He ties his limber legs into knots, twirls wildly on one foot, and flings himself about, all while brandishing his signature gregarious laugh.

Among those in the pub was Charles Dickens, who wrote about the performance that year in his travelogue *American Notes*. After "spinning about on his toes and heels like nothing but the man's fingers on the tambourine," Dickens wrote, the boy finished to thundering applause by "leaping gloriously on the bar-counter, and calling for something to drink."

The writer went on to use surreal language in recounting the performer's unique style—"dancing with two left legs, two right legs, two wooden legs, two wire legs, two spring legs—all sorts of legs and no legs."

The performer was Juba—or Master Juba—an upstart in New York's vibrant street and tavern dancing scene.

Juba, helped by Dickens's account, would go on to achieve international fame. Today he is hailed by some dance historians as the most influential American dancer of the nineteenth century; his unique blending of Irish and Black dance styles helped form the foundations of modern tap, step, and jazz dance.

"Juba's extraordinary ability to synthesize rhythmic and aesthetic elements from the African diaspora with English and Irish influences—along with his unusual fame as a Black artist—helped make him foundational not just to tap dancing but to all of American popular dance," said Brian Seibert, a *New York Times* dance critic and tap historian, who wrote about Juba in his 2015 book *What the Eye Hears: A History of Tap Dancing*.

His career evolved from sleazy Five Points saloons to being managed by the showman P. T. Barnum to performing on London's most vaunted stages for high society.

Given Juba's race and his lower-class status as a street performer, his personal life was poorly chronicled. The scant biographical details that exist come mainly from articles written well after his lifetime that are likely infused with lore.

An 1876 newspaper article identified him as William Henry Lane, which has now become widely accepted as his given name. He is believed to have been born to free parents around 1825, perhaps in Providence, Rhode Island.

By Juba's youth, slavery had been legally abolished in parts of the North, but Black people still faced extreme racism and segregation. Black artists, unwelcome on the

Master Juba's blending of Irish and Black dance styles made him an upstart in New York.

"Dancing with two left legs, two right legs, two wooden legs, two wire legs, two spring legs—all sorts of legs and no legs."

stage, were relegated to performing on the street and in taverns.

But in Five Points, Black people often intermingled with Irish immigrants, another underclass. In particular, racial mixing occurred in dancing cellars like the one where Dickens may have seen Juba.

Juba likely managed to win the favor of the roughest white crowds in the roughest of taverns by using both his dance and diplomatic skills to sidestep racial clashes, said Lenwood Sloan, a choreographer and historian.

"If you're a fifteen-year-old Black boy dancing in the Irish taverns in Five Points, you better be good or you won't make it out the door," Sloan said in a telephone interview. "You have to be so good that your Blackness doesn't count. But you better not be so good that you humiliate a white man. You had to be able to dance so brilliantly that a room full of Irishmen could set aside this notion of color."

He would then present his own blending of steps, incorporating Irish and English step dancing with African styles passed down by enslaved people. One such step was juba, the style from which he gained his nickname. It involved stomping and slapping the body rhythmically as well as spinning, often with a raised leg.

In fact, reviewers described Juba's turning his body into a percussive instrument by tapping his arms, legs, and chest.

"Surely he cannot be flesh and blood, but some more subtle substance, or how could he turn, and twine, and twist, and twirl, and hop, and jump, and kick, and throw his feet almost with a velocity that makes one think they are playing hide-and-seek with a flash of lightning!" raved a reviewer in *The Manchester Examiner* in 1848.

Juba came under the management of Barnum, who presented him as a challenge dancer, taking on and defeating the best white dancers of the day.

In the mid-1850s, Juba faced off against John Diamond, an Irish-American performer who was his main rival, for hundreds of dollars in prize money and the title of world champion. More often than not Juba was the victor with his exhaustive series of jigs and reels.

Barnum also placed Juba into the white minstrel troupes Georgia Champion Minstrels and the Ethiopian Minstrels, billing him as "the Wonder of the World." These popular shows featured white performers in blackface makeup imitating Black people in a racist and derisive fashion.

# "You had to be able to dance so brilliantly that a room full of Irishmen could set aside this notion of color."

Since Black people did not appear onstage with white performers, Barnum had Juba blacken his face to blend in with the other white minstrel performers.

In 1848, Juba traveled to London with Pell's Ethiopian Serenaders and became a sensation as the first Black man believed to perform on England's most renowned stages.

Though he was often objectified as an exotic spectacle for white audiences, he also enjoyed more acceptance in England, where viewers marveled at his ability. He was eventually able to perform openly as a Black man, and by some accounts, he married a white woman, which would have caused upheaval in America. He could stay in the same hotels as white people and could "walk on the street with a white woman and not be beaten," said Christine Kinealy, a professor of Irish history at Quinnipiac University.

And as a master of the jig, Juba was also a hit in Ireland, which he toured in 1849 and early 1850, not long after Frederick Douglass visited the country in 1845 to give speeches on abolition. The last known performance of Juba's life was in Dublin around 1851, Kinealy said.

Although his style became a stage staple, he died in poverty and obscurity in England in the early 1850s. He was likely in his late twenties and is believed to have suffered from overwork and malnutrition, his body ravaged by his many grueling performances. One account, from 1858 in a Scottish newspaper, speculated that Juba had "danced himself to death," Kinealy said.

His death was not publicly noted at the time and his legacy was largely forgotten until scholars began writing about it a century later.

The location of his grave remains unknown. His rapid decline from stage star to forgotten figure may reflect that his fame as a showman did not help lift his social status.

"The fact that he could disappear so totally," Kinealy said, "tells you a lot about the world he inhabited."

————

**COREY KILGANNON** has been a staff reporter on the Metro desk at *The New York Times* since 2000, covering news and human interest stories.

## Turkey's First Rock Star

# Zeki Müren

## 1931–1996

BY NAYANIKA GUHA

THE FIRST TIME ZEKI MÜREN performed live on Istanbul Radio, calls started flooding into the station, including from Hamiyet Yüceses, a Turkish classical music singer, who said, "My child, I listened to you and cried. Who are you?"

Müren's radio performances would continue for fifteen years, and he would go on to play at large-scale venues. Over the course of his career, he would record around six hundred cassettes and phonograph records.

The opportunity for that first radio show started with a stroke of luck. It was January 1, 1951, and the original singer slated to perform, Perihan Altındağ Sözeri, had fallen ill, giving Müren a chance to step in.

But some of the phone calls were from listeners expressing confusion: Was Müren a man or a woman? Though his voice, which was often described as androgynous, enthralled one and all, in the decades that followed, his glittery appearance and choice of clothes left his fans and followers wondering about his sexual identity. He was known to dress in miniskirts, capes, and platform boots, often bejeweled, and wear heavy makeup and jewelry. He also gave names to his costumes, many of which he designed himself, such as Mountain Flower, Moon Prince, and Veil of Fortune.

Zeki Müren was born on December 6, 1931, in Bursa, in northwest Turkey, to Kaya Müren, a timber merchant, and Hayriye Müren. Zeki grew up listening to his grandfather Bıçkıcı Mehmet Efendi, a muezzin who called people to prayer at the Şehadet Mosque and who became renowned for his voice. Zeki's grandmother, a Greek immigrant, had an expansive record collection of Turkish and Western tunes, which also had a profound influence on Zeki's upbringing, and he is believed to have started singing when he was just three years old.

Müren spent his early school years in Bursa, then convinced his father to let him study in Istanbul, graduating from high school in 1946 at the top of his class. He then joined the Istanbul State Academy of Fine Arts (now Mimar Sinan Fine Arts University), where he studied until 1953.

While in university, Müren won Turkish Radio and Television's music competition, had his first live performance, and created his first phonograph record with help from the clarinetist Şükrü Tunar.

Müren's first live concert was on May 23, 1955, headlining at a nightclub. From then on, he began to shape his image as a glamorous star. To better engage with audiences, he used a handheld microphone and a T-shaped stage. His shows always sold out.

In 1955, he won an award for his song "Manolyam" (My Magnolia). He also became the first Turkish artist to perform at the Royal Albert Hall in London, in 1976. In

Zeki Müren's voice was one of hope as Turkey struggled to stay true to its culture.

A 2014 exhibit commemorating Müren's life, "İşte Benim Zeki Müren" (Here I am, Zeki Müren), in Istanbul.

1991, the Turkish government named him a state artist for his contributions to Turkish culture. However, these were far from his only claims to fame.

He was also an actor, performing in more than a dozen films throughout his life, many of them hits that earned some of the highest revenue in the industry. One of those films, *Beklenen Şarkı* (The expected song), a musical in which he played the lead role, included ten of his compositions. He also performed the leading role in the play *Çay ve sempati* (Tea and sympathy) in 1955, and he published a poetry book in 1965 called *Bıldırcın yağmuru* (The quail rain), with about one hundred poems.

His rise to fame was an anomaly, as his conservative nation grappled with political turmoil. From the 1960s to the '90s, Müren's voice was one of hope and creative resistance as Turkey struggled to stay true to its culture—a voice that found the balance between the country's Eastern roots and its Western-facing interests. His ability to charm a crowd was unparalleled, and his fans' acceptance of his vibrant, androgynous look was in part driven by their respect for his military service. In a 2016 research paper, "Queerly Turkish: Queer Masculinity and National Belonging in the Image of Zeki Müren," Spencer Hawkins noted, "He was exceptional enough as a patriot and musician to become an exception to normal gender expectations."

In the 1950s, when Turkish people would buy a radio, they were known to ask, "Does this play Zeki Müren?" and there were jokes about people's dressing up to watch Müren on TV, in case Müren was watching them, too.

Müren was also a great equalizer, bringing fans who ranged from newer generations of young people who never got to see him perform live to older people who reminisced about his shows. They included religious people, secular people, and people from the LGBTQ community. There were the urban rich and those who couldn't afford to attend his shows; they crowded outside venues to hear him sing or catch a glimpse of him when he left.

"The General," "Sun of Art," and "Pasha"—a term used to describe an official of high rank—were all nicknames given to him.

Over the course of his career, Müren would record around
six hundred cassettes and phonograph records.

Müren's last concert was on September 24, 1996.
Wearing his bejeweled clothes, he was handed a
microphone—the same one he had used during his first
radio show, nearly fifty years beforehand. "I don't know
whether to laugh or cry," he said.

A few minutes later, he had a heart attack and died.
He was sixty-four.

Müren's money was donated to the Türk Eğitim Vakfı
(Foundation for Turkish Education) and the Mehmetçik
Vakfı, a foundation for disabled veterans, their families,
and the families of soldiers who have died. The Zeki Müren
Art Museum, on a street in Bodrum bearing his name, has
had more than 250,000 visitors since opening in 2000. The
museum houses artworks made by Müren, his personal
belongings, photos, awards, clothes, furniture, and his car.
In 2014, an exhibit in Istanbul, "İşte Benim Zeki Müren"
(Here I am, Zeki Müren), included his costumes, drawings, diaries, and previously unseen photos from throughout his life. The Bardakçı Cove in Bodrum, where Müren
last lived, is now known as Zeki Müren Cove.

Most recently, the Zeki Müren Hotline, an interactive documentary directed by Beyza Boyacıoğlu and Jeff
Soyk, which invites fans to leave phone messages about
his legacy, has revived people's love for Müren.

"Oh, dear General," reads one of the phone messages.
"It's been a long time since you left. You can't imagine how
I long for you."

However, there were still some who could not accept
his style; on one occasion, a conservative mob armed with
sticks appeared at his stage door, protesting his queerness. Müren's response, which has since been widely
repeated, was: "Just have a listen to my songs. If you still
want to beat me up, you can." They put the sticks away
and stayed for the rest of the show.

Müren claimed that his gender-subversive ways were
not all that uncommon. In a 1970 *Hafta Sonu* magazine
article, he confessed that his outfits were meant to retain
the public's attention, and that boxers, Ottoman sultans,
whirling dervishes, monks, and even Caucasian tribesmen
had dressed in ways that society would deem feminine.

But because Müren never came out as gay, he has
been rejected by some in the LGBTQ community. In fact,
he sometimes asserted that he was heterosexual. In one
instance, outlined in "Queerly Turkish," he lost his temper
when a teenage boy shouted, "Hey, sister Zeki!" Müren
responded by yelling a profanity and asking, "Now who
are you calling sister?"

———

**NAYANIKA GUHA** is a freelance journalist who focuses on issues of health and social justice. She is
pursuing her master's in journalism at New York
University.

# How to Write a Good Obituary

BY AMISHA PADNANI

While only a small number of people ever write a formal news obit for a major newspaper like *The New York Times,* many of us must one day capture a life on the page, whether for a local paper, grieving relatives, or another audience. Writing an obit for a loved one (or even, perhaps, for yourself) may seem melancholic and can be challenging in a difficult moment. But remember, usually just one sentence addresses death; the rest of the piece celebrates life. On that note, it would be worth asking what the word count should be if you're planning on having the obit published in a local paper or elsewhere. Here are some tips for creating an effective remembrance:

**1** Gather basic information, like date and place of birth and death, educational or military background, career details, and names of family members and spouses.

**2** Read letters, journals, or social media accounts the person may have left behind, along with interviews the person might have done.

**3** Ask friends or relatives for interesting anecdotes. Ask about favorite hobbies or objects, personality quirks, notable memories, and family stories. Here's how obituary writer Sam Roberts wove in details about David Mintz, the creator of the nondairy ice cream Tofutti:

> *It took several years, and he gained fifty pounds. He began his research by buying a carton of soy milk in Chinatown, and he poured gallons of unappetizing gelatinous white concoctions down the drain of his kitchen in the Bensonhurst section of Brooklyn.*
>
> *"I am personally responsible for clogging the sewers of New York City," he told* Forbes *magazine in 1984.*

**4** Make it real. The more you present a person as a human being, in all of their complexity, the more relatable the story will feel—and the more precisely a person will be remembered. When writing about Frances Gabe, the inventor of the world's only self-cleaning house, obituary writer Margalit Fox found an entertaining way to describe her temperament:

> *"She was very difficult to get along with," Mr. Brown said, warmly. "She had an adversarial relationship with all her neighbors, and she didn't do anything to discourage it."*
>
> *Perhaps it was the cement mixer residing permanently in Ms. Gabe's yard that inflamed the neighbors so. (It was essential to her house-building enterprise.) Perhaps it was the series of snarling Great Danes she kept. Perhaps it was her penchant, at least in her younger days, for doing her yard work in the nude.*

# Facing the Fight

---

What makes a good fighter? The people in this section
exhibited those qualities, never backing down despite,
in some cases, threats to their lives, multiple arrests, and
even physical harassment. They pushed back against
what they saw as blatant injustices to make the world a
different place. However, not all of them lived to see the
impacts they made.

Student Who Fought Segregation on Boblo Boats

# Sarah E. Ray

## Unknown—2006

BY AUDRA D. S. BURCH

ON A JUNE MORNING IN 1945, Sarah E. Ray walked onto a steamship with a group of classmates to celebrate their graduation from secretarial school. The boat ride, which would head downriver to an island amusement park, was a popular one among white Detroiters.

But this was in the thick of the Jim Crow era, a period that legally, economically, and socially restricted nearly every aspect of African American life. Almost always, race trumped rights.

Just after boarding, Ray, then in her early twenties and the only Black student in the class, was approached by representatives of the Bob-Lo Excursion Company, which operated the boats. She had to leave, they told her, and escorted her back onto the dock.

Ray fired back with a phone call to the NAACP, setting in motion an extraordinary, but largely untold, journey to desegregate Boblo steamers. The legal challenge she mounted ascended all the way to the US Supreme Court, with an NAACP lawyer and future Supreme Court justice named Thurgood Marshall filing an amicus brief in the case.

A decade before Rosa Parks refused to give up her seat to a white man on a crowded city bus in 1955, Ray pursued her dogged fight for integration. It ultimately became one of the building blocks of *Brown v. Board of Education*, the 1954 landmark Supreme Court decision outlawing racial segregation in public schools. Ray's case was among several that the NAACP was monitoring and intervening in, in order to build a legal strategy to dismantle segregation. After her story was rediscovered decades later, Ray became known by some as "Detroit's Other Rosa Parks."

Little of Ray's story was known for decades, and it might have been lost to the annals of history had a curious journalist not approached her in 2006.

Desiree Cooper, then a *Detroit Free Press* columnist, knocked on Ray's door that February to interview her about her life and the fight to integrate Boblo rides. Cooper said Ray's retelling of the story six decades later still conjured fresh emotions.

"She was still extremely indignant about what they did to her," Cooper said in a phone interview.

In the months before her death, Ray sat down for two separate interviews, one with Cooper and the other with Clayton Rye, a filmmaker and professor emeritus of television and film production at Ferris State University. In the Rye interview, Ray's own words spoke to her enduring spirit in a lifetime marked by Jim Crow, the civil rights movement, and a week in July 1967 when Detroit burned.

Sarah E. Ray in 1954. She turned a seat denial into a civil rights victory.

The Boblo steamship, pictured in 1946, that Ray
was kicked off a year earlier.

"I was always a free soul," Ray firmly declared in the
video interview with Rye. "I was free."

Ray died on August 10, 2006, without the wider public
recognition she deserved, partly because she so rarely
spoke about that day in 1945. She never again set foot
on a Boblo boat.

Even some family members did not know the story.

Adding to the mystery, she took her husband's last
name after marrying and changed her given name by
choice—adding more distance between her and the
Boblo incident.

Ray spent decades as an outspoken community
activist known as Lizz Haskell, passionately calling out
the need to help the poor, improve race relations, and
stamp out blight in neighborhoods.

About a decade after Cooper's column was published
in 2006, she connected with Aaron Schillinger, a film-
maker who was making a documentary called *Boblo
Boats: A Detroit Ferry Tale*. The two later founded the
Sarah E. Ray Project, an interactive multimedia project
designed to highlight Ray's life and place in American
history.

The pair worked to rescue Ray's story, unearthing
personal letters, journals, and photos from her abandoned home; combing archives; and searching for relatives and friends who might share the tiniest details
about her life. In 2020, Schillinger and Cooper made a
short film called *Detroit's Other Rosa Parks*.

Sarah Elizabeth Cole was born in Wauhatchie,
Tennessee, a rural community outside of Chattanooga
(her year of birth is not certain). She was the elev-
enth of thirteen children of Richard Cole and Malda
Brogden. Like so many African Americans at the time,
she believed that freedom was on the other side of the
Mason-Dixon Line. By the time she was twenty, she had
moved to Detroit, where she married Frank Ray. The
marriage ended in divorce in 1944.

"I ran away with a young man who had relatives in
Detroit," she said in the 2006 *Free Press* interview. "I
thought I would find absolute freedom here. But day
after day, year after year, I discovered it wasn't so."

Perhaps never more so than that summer of 1945.
After studying at Wayne State University for a year, Ray
left and accepted a job at the Detroit Ordinance District.
While there, she took a secretarial course sponsored
by the department that was conducted at a local high
school. There were about forty students in the class,
according to a court transcript.

For the graduation celebration, Ray thought she would
cruise along the Detroit River to Boblo Island and have a
picnic with her class. But when she was ordered to leave
while seated on the top deck with her classmates, she
asked why she had been singled out. Ray was told it was
because she was "colored," she said in court testimony.

"I was so angry. Angry and hurt and humiliated and
embarrassed before all these girls," she said in the 2006
interview with Rye. "To think, I had spent months with
these girls and all of a sudden, I'm different?"

The Bob-Lo Excursion Company owned the amusement park on the island (known locally as Detroit's
Coney Island) and operated two steamships to transport patrons. Company policy banned two classes: the
"disorderly" and "colored people."

In denying Ray a ride, the company violated Michigan's civil rights act. The case eventually reached the US Supreme Court, where Marshall, chief counsel for the NAACP Legal Defense Fund, filed a brief.

The boat company argued that the Michigan law did not apply because the boat operated internationally, cruising to and from Boblo Island, which is part of Ontario. In 1948, the Supreme Court affirmed the lower court rulings, with a 6–2 vote, reasoning that the law applied because the island was essentially an "amusement adjunct of the city of Detroit."

After the ruling, the Boblo operation was shut down and eventually sold. The new owner allowed African Americans to ride the boats and visit the amusement island, which closed in 1993. The case was among a string of early decisions that the highest court would consider in the protection of civil rights, which helped break ground for the *Brown* case.

Public transportation, which was adjacent to Ray's case, was one of the key battlefields of the movement, said Adriane Lentz-Smith, an associate professor of history and African and African American studies at Duke University.

In the early 1960s, Ray married Rafael Haskell, a Jewish community and labor activist. At some point, she stopped using her first name, Sarah, and began going by Lizz, an abbreviation of her middle name, Elizabeth. In a 1974 *Detroit Free Press* interview, she said she added the extra *Z* to her name so she would be unforgettable.

After the 1967 race rebellion, the Haskells founded Action House, a community center whose mission was to promote racial harmony and uplift neighborhood children through enrichment and recreational programs. The center was open for about twenty-five years. A 1974 profile of Ray (referred to as Mrs. Haskell) in the *Detroit Free Press* described her as strong-willed and determined.

"Mrs. Haskell is one of those grass-roots people who have a way—often an uncomfortable one—of calling attention to the needs of her community," the story read, "and she has been doing it with particular vigor since the days of the traumatic riots."

Ray, pictured here in 1974, became a community activist, later going by the name Lizz Haskell.

Kourtney Thompson, a great-nephew of Ray's, remembered hearing her talk about the work of Action House at family gatherings and over meals. She never spoke of the Boblo boats.

About four years after Ray's death, Thompson scattered his great-aunt's ashes in the Detroit River, not far from where she had turned a seat denial into a civil rights victory sixty-five years earlier.

"She was indomitable," Thompson, a social studies teacher in Detroit, said in a phone interview with *The New York Times*. "She confronted racism head-on and was not to be deterred or defeated."

———

**AUDRA D. S. BURCH** is an award-winning National Enterprise correspondent for *The New York Times*.
SUSAN BEACHY contributed research.

## Feminist Beheaded by Imperial Forces

# Qiu Jin

## 1875–1907

BY AMY QIN

WITH HER PASSION FOR WINE, swords, and bomb making, Qiu Jin was unlike most women born in late nineteenth-century China. As a girl, she wrote poetry and studied Chinese martial heroines like Hua Mulan (yes, that Mulan), fantasizing about one day seeing her own name in the history books.

But her ambitions ran up against China's deeply rooted patriarchal society, which held that a woman's place remained in the home. Undeterred, Qiu rose to become an early and fierce advocate for the liberation of Chinese women, defying prevailing Confucian gender and class norms by unbinding her feet, cross-dressing, and leaving her young family to pursue an education abroad.

Her legacy as one of China's pioneering feminists and revolutionaries was cemented on July 15, 1907, when she was beheaded at thirty-one by imperial army forces who charged her with conspiring to overthrow the Manchu-led Qing government. It was her final act of resistance, and it would later earn her a place in the pantheon of China's revolutionary martyrs.

To this day, she is often referred to as "China's Joan of Arc."

"Qiu Jin lived at a time when women in China were not permitted to venture out of their homes, let alone participate in public affairs," said Zhang Lifan, a writer and historian in Beijing. "So Qiu Jin not only participated in politics, her actions alone were a rebellion."

Throughout her life, Qiu wrote often of what she saw as China's stifling gender roles, as seen in this passage from a 1903 poem:

*My body will not allow me*
*To mingle with the men*
*But my heart is far braver*
*Than that of a man.*

At the time of the poem's writing, China was an empire in distress. The Qing government was on its last legs, heaving under the weight of internal bureaucratic decay and external pressure from foreign powers.

With the uncertainty of the period came opportunities for educated Chinese women like Qiu. As a result, Qiu soon found herself at the forefront of an emerging wave of new feminists who believed that women's rights and political revolution naturally went hand in hand.

But scholars say the enduring strength of Qiu's legacy lies not only in her leadership but also—and perhaps more important—in her willingness to ultimately sacrifice her life for the cause.

Qiu Jin defied prevailing gender and class norms in China by experimenting with cross-dressing and swordplay.

# "She believed you had to be willing to put your life on the line. And the fact that she really did put her life on the line is what made her words stick."

"She argued that it wasn't enough for women to just sit around and ask for equality," said Hu Ying, a professor of Chinese literature at the University of California, Irvine. "She believed you had to be willing to put your life on the line. And the fact that she really did put her life on the line is what made her words stick."

As is often the case with any historical martyr, it is difficult to disentangle the facts of Qiu's life from later myth making.

Qiu Guijin (pronounced Cho GWAY-jeen) was born into a respected, albeit declining, gentry family in the southern port city of Xiamen on November 8, 1875 (some scholars say 1877). Her father, Qiu Shounan, was a government official. Her mother, surnamed Shan, also came from a distinguished family.

With her older brother and younger sister, Qiu grew up in Xiamen and her family's ancestral home of Shaoxing in China's eastern Zhejiang Province. By all accounts, she had a comfortable childhood. But she was forced to bind her feet, learn needlework, and—worst of all, in Qiu's eyes—submit to an arranged marriage.

The man Qiu's father chose for her was Wang Tingjun, the son of a wealthy merchant in Hunan Province. In 1903, seven years after marrying, the young couple moved with their two children from Hunan to Beijing.

For Qiu, life in the imperial capital was decidedly less dull. She struck up friendships with like-minded women and took an interest in China's political affairs. She unbound her feet, drank copious amounts of wine, and experimented with cross-dressing and swordplay.

Still, the frustrations of her marriage took a deep toll on her psyche. Her husband, she felt, was uncultivated and had no interest in poetry or learning.

So in the summer of 1904, Qiu, then twenty-eight, acted on a bold decision: She left her husband and two children, sold her jewelry, and sailed for Japan. (For that reason, scholars sometimes call her "China's Nora," after the character in Henrik Ibsen's 1879 play *A Doll's House*.)

She summed up her life in a 1904 poem called "Regrets: Lines Written En Route to Japan":

> *Sun and moon have no light left, earth is dark,*
> *Our women's world is sunk so deep, who can help*
>   *us?*
> *Jewelry sold to pay this trip across the seas,*
> *Cut off from my family I leave my native land.*
> *Unbinding my feet I clean out a thousand years of*
>   *poison,*
> *With heated heart arouse all women's spirits.*
> *Alas, this delicate kerchief here,*
> *Is half stained with blood, and half with tears.*

In Tokyo, Qiu enrolled at Shimoda Utako's Women's Practical School, shortening her name to Qiu Jin. But she

Qiu was beheaded by imperial forces on
July 15, 1907, becoming a revolutionary martyr.

By 1907, Qiu was running the Datong School—a front for a group that recruited and trained young revolutionaries—in Shaoxing when she learned that Xu Xilin, who was her friend and the school's founder, had been executed for assassinating his Manchu superior.

After Xu's death, friends warned Qiu that Qing troops were coming to Shaoxing to find the woman thought to be his co-conspirator. But Qiu refused to run away. In a scene that has since been memorialized and embellished in a multitude of forms, Qiu attempted to fight back but was quickly captured, tortured, and beheaded.

Over the years, critics have accused her of being naïve in her belief—widely shared at the time—that overthrowing the Qing could resolve China's social and political ills. Others said her death was unnecessary since she had ample time to escape from the advancing soldiers.

Perhaps her most notable critic was Lu Xun, one of China's greatest twentieth-century writers, who believed Qiu's reckless behavior in Shaoxing was linked to the enormous adulation she received during her time in Japan. She was "clapped to death," he told a friend.

More than a century after her death, many Chinese still visit her tomb beside West Lake in Hangzhou to pay their respects to the woman now embedded in the national consciousness as a bold feminist heroine.

Some can also still recite the famous words she wrote just before her death: "Autumn wind, autumn rain, fill one's heart with melancholy."

The line was a play on her surname, Qiu, which means "autumn" in Chinese.

focused most of her energy outside the classroom, connecting with other reform-minded Chinese students keen on fomenting revolution back home. She joined influential anti-Manchu secret societies, including the Restoration Society and Sun Yat-sen's Revolutionary Alliance.

She came back to China in 1906 determined to advance women's causes and topple the Qing government. She started the short-lived *Chinese Women's Journal,* which, unlike most feminist magazines at the time, used vernacular language to appeal to a broader audience on topics like the cruelty of foot binding and arranged marriages. She also learned how to make bombs.

—

**AMY QIN** spent more than a decade in Asia, most recently as an international correspondent covering politics, culture, and society in China. Growing up, Mulan was her favorite Disney heroine.

Ida B. Wells, one of the nation's most influential investigative reporters, in 1920.

# Journalist Who Took On Racism in the Deep South

# Ida B. Wells

## 1862–1931

———

BY CAITLIN DICKERSON

IT WAS NOT ALL THAT UNUSUAL when, in 1892, a mob dragged Thomas Moss out of a Memphis jail in his pajamas and shot him to death over a feud that began with a game of marbles. But his lynching changed history because of its effect on one of the nation's most influential journalists, who was also the godmother of his first child: Ida B. Wells.

"It is with no pleasure that I have dipped my hands in the corruption here exposed," Wells wrote in 1892 in the introduction to *Southern Horrors,* one of her seminal works about lynching. "Somebody must show that the Afro-American race is more sinned against than sinning, and it seems to have fallen upon me to do so."

Wells is considered by historians to have been the most famous Black woman in the United States during her lifetime, even as she was dogged by prejudice, a disease infecting Americans from coast to coast.

She pioneered reporting techniques that remain central tenets of modern journalism. And as a former slave who stood less than five feet tall, she took on structural racism more than half a century before her strategies were repurposed, often without crediting her, during the 1960s civil rights movement.

Wells was already a thirty-year-old newspaper editor living in Memphis when she began her anti-lynching campaign, the work for which she is most famous. After

Moss was killed, she set out on a reporting mission, criss-crossing the South over several months as she conducted eyewitness interviews and dug up records on dozens of similar cases.

Her goal was to question a stereotype that was often used to justify lynchings—that Black men were rapists. Instead, she found that in two-thirds of mob murders, rape was never an accusation. And she often found evidence of what had actually been a consensual inter-racial relationship.

She published her findings in a series of fiery editorials in the newspaper she co-owned and edited, the *Memphis Free Speech and Headlight.* The public, it turned out, was starved for her stories and devoured them voraciously. *The Journalist,* a mainstream trade publication that covered the media, named her "the Princess of the Press."

Readers of her work were drawn in by her fine-tooth reporting methods and language that, even by today's standards, was aberrantly bold.

"There has been no word equal to it in convincing power," Frederick Douglass wrote to her in a letter that hatched their friendship. "I have spoken, but my word is feeble in comparison," he added.

He was referring to writing like the kind that she published in the *Free Speech* in May 1892.

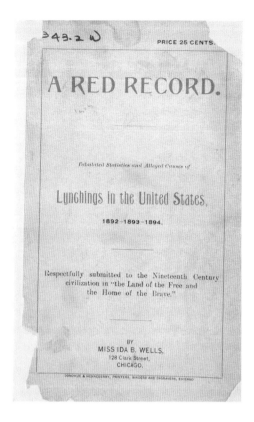

With *A Red Record*, Wells documented a resurgence in lynchings that sought to maintain white supremacy.

"Nobody in this section of the country believes the threadbare old lie that Negro men rape white women," Wells wrote.

Instead, Wells saw lynching as a violent form of subjugation—"an excuse to get rid of Negroes who were acquiring wealth and property and thus keep the race terrorized," she wrote in a journal.

Wells was born into slavery in Holly Springs, Mississippi, in 1862, less than a year before Emancipation. She grew up during Reconstruction, the period when Black men, including her father, were able to vote, ushering Black representatives into state legislatures across the South. One of eight siblings, she often tagged along to Bible school on her mother's hip.

In 1878, her parents both died of yellow fever, along with one of her brothers, and at sixteen, she took on caring for the rest of her siblings. She supported them by working as a teacher after dropping out of high school and lying about her age. She finished her own education at night and on weekends.

Around the same time, the Civil Rights Act of 1875 was largely nullified by the Supreme Court, reversing many of the advancements of Reconstruction. The anti-Black sentiment that grew around her was ultimately codified into Jim Crow.

"It felt like a dramatic whiplash," said Troy Duster, Wells's grandson, who is a sociology professor at the University of California, Berkeley, and New York University. "She cuts her teeth politically in this time of justice, justice, justice, and then injustice."

Observing the changes around her, Wells decided to become a journalist during what was a golden era for Black writers and editors. Her goal was to write about Black people for Black people, in a way that was accessible to those who, like her, were born the property of white owners and had much to defend.

Her articles were often reprinted abroad, as well as in the more than two hundred Black weeklies then in circulation in the United States.

Whenever possible, Wells named the victims of racist violence and told their stories. In her journals, she lamented that her subjects would have otherwise been forgotten by all "save the night wind, no memorial service to bemoan their sad and horrible fate."

Wells also organized economic boycotts long before the tactic was popularized by other, mostly male, civil rights activists, who are often credited with its success.

In 1883, she was forced off a train car reserved for white women. She sued the railroad and lost on appeal before the Tennessee Supreme Court, after which she urged African Americans to avoid the trains, and later, to leave the South entirely. She also traveled to Britain to rally support for her cause, encouraging the British to stop purchasing American cotton and angering many white Southern business owners.

Wells was as fierce in conversation as she was in her writing, which made it difficult for her to maintain close relationships, according to her family. She criticized people, including friends and allies, whom she saw as weak in their commitment to the causes she cared about.

"She didn't suffer fools and she saw fools everywhere," Duster, her grandson, said.

One exception was her husband and closest confidant, Ferdinand L. Barnett, a widower who was a lawyer and civil rights activist in Chicago. After they married in 1895, Barnett's activism took a backseat to his wife's career. Theirs was an atypically modern relationship: he cooked dinner for their children most nights, and he cared for them while she traveled to make speeches and organize.

Later in life, Wells fell from prominence as she was replaced by activists like Booker T. Washington and W. E. B. Du Bois, who were more conservative in their tactics and thus had more support from the white and Black establishments. She helped to found prominent civil rights organizations, including the National Association for the Advancement of Colored People and the National Association of Colored Women's Clubs, only to be edged out of their leadership.

During the final years of her life, living in Chicago, Wells ran for the Illinois state senate but lost abysmally. Despite her ebbing influence, she continued to organize around causes such as mass incarceration, working for several years as a probation officer, until she died of kidney disease on March 25, 1931, at sixty-eight.

Wells was threatened physically and rhetorically constantly throughout her career; she was called a harlot and a courtesan for her frankness about interracial sex. After her anti-lynching editorials were published in the *Free Speech*, she was run out of the South, her newspaper ransacked and her life threatened. But her commitment to chronicling the experience of African Americans in order to demonstrate their humanity remained unflinching.

"If this work can contribute in any way toward proving this, and at the same time arouse the conscience of the

Wells published *Lynch Law* in 1892, even as she herself was dogged by prejudice.

American people to demand for justice to every citizen, and punishment by law for the lawless, I shall feel I have done my race a service," she wrote after fleeing Memphis. "Other considerations are minor."

———

**CAITLIN DICKERSON** is a staff writer for *The Atlantic* and a former *New York Times* reporter. More than a century later, she still uses the reporting techniques that were pioneered by Ida B. Wells.

Marsha P. Johnson in Greenwich Village in 1988. She moved to New York with $15.

# Marsha P. Johnson

## 1945–1992

—————

BY SEWELL CHAN

MARSHA P. JOHNSON WAS AN ACTIVIST, a prostitute, a drag performer, and, for nearly three decades, a fixture of street life in Greenwich Village. She was a central figure in a gay liberation movement energized by the 1969 police raid on the Stonewall Inn. She was a model for Andy Warhol. She battled severe mental illness. She was usually destitute and, for much of her life, effectively homeless.

When she died at forty-six, under murky circumstances, in summer 1992, Johnson was mourned by her many friends, but her death did not attract much notice in the mainstream press.

In the years since, however, interest in her legacy has soared. She has been praised for her insistent calls for social and economic justice; for working on behalf of homeless street youth ostracized by their families for being gay or otherwise not conforming to traditional ideas about gender; and, later, for her advocacy on behalf of AIDS patients. Some have called her a saint.

Many transgender people have also come to hail Johnson, and her longtime friend and colleague Sylvia Rivera, as pioneering heroes. (The term *transgender* was not in wide use in Johnson's lifetime; she usually used female pronouns for herself but also referred to herself as gay, as a transvestite, or simply as a queen.)

"Marsha P. Johnson could be perceived as the most marginalized of people—Black, queer, gender-nonconforming, poor," said Susan Stryker, an associate professor of gender and women's studies at the University of Arizona. "You might expect a person in such a position to be fragile, brutalized, beaten down. Instead, Marsha had this joie de vivre, a capacity to find joy in a world of suffering. She channeled it into political action, and did it with a kind of fierceness, grace, and whimsy, with a loopy, absurdist reaction to it all."

Johnson was born Malcolm Michaels Jr. on August 24, 1945, in Elizabeth, New Jersey, the fifth of seven children in a working-class family. Her father, Malcolm Michaels Sr., worked on the assembly line at a General Motors factory in Linden. Her mother, the former Alberta Claiborne, was a housekeeper.

Johnson was around five when she began to wear dresses, but she felt pressure to stop because of other children's aggression. Later, Johnson said in an interview toward the end of her life, she was sexually assaulted by another boy, who was around thirteen.

She began attending the Mount Teman African Methodist Episcopal Church as a child and practiced her Christian faith throughout her life; later, she was drawn to Catholicism and visited houses of worship of other faiths frequently. She graduated from Thomas A. Edison High School in Elizabeth in 1963 and promptly moved to New York City, she later recalled, with $15 and a bag of clothes.

It was not an easy time to live outside the sexual mainstream. Although New York State downgraded sodomy from a felony to a misdemeanor in 1950, persecution of gay people and criminalization of their activities were still common. Same-sex dancing in public was prohibited. The New York State Liquor Authority banned bars from serving gay people alcoholic beverages. People could be charged with sexual deviancy for cross-dressing. Police enforcement was often arbitrary.

After arriving in New York, Johnson alternated between going by her given name, Malcolm, and a persona she had created, Black Marsha. She engaged in prostitution and was often arrested—she stopped counting after the hundredth time, she later said—and was once, in the late 1970s, even shot. She could often be found in seedy hotels near Times Square, including the Dixie Hotel (now the Hotel Carter) on West Forty-Third Street.

"The ones that used to make the most money was the boys that could wear their own hair, with just a little bit of makeup," she later recalled.

Johnson was a key figure in the disturbances that followed a police raid at the Stonewall Inn, a gay bar on Christopher Street, early in the morning of June 28, 1969. Many legends have grown around the event—often characterized as a riot, but more recently described as a rebellion or uprising—but the evidence suggests that Johnson was among the "vanguard" of those who resisted the police, according to David Carter, the author of *Stonewall: The Riots That Sparked the Gay Revolution.* She was twenty-three at the time.

Stonewall helped to galvanize a more assertive, even militant, gay-rights movement. It prompted the first gay pride parades, in 1970. The same year, Johnson joined Rivera in founding Street Transvestite Action Revolutionaries, or STAR, to advocate for young transgender people—and, for a time, house, clothe, and feed them, from a tenement at 213 East Second Street. STAR grew out of the Gay Liberation Front, which advocated

Johnson's activism work included helping to create Street Transvestite Action Revolutionaries, or STAR.

for sexual liberation and pushed to align gay rights with other social movements.

Her goal, she declared in an interview for a 1972 book, was "to see gay people liberated and free and to have equal rights that other people have in America," with her "gay brothers and sisters out of jail and on the streets again." She added, in a reference to the radical politics of the time, "We believe in picking up the gun, starting a revolution if necessary."

The 1970s were a time of greater visibility for Johnson. Tall and slender, she had a knack for commanding attention. Her outfits—red plastic high heels; slippers and stockings; shimmering robes and dresses; costume jewelry; bright wigs; plastic flowers and even artificial fruit in her hair—were often assembled from scavenged or discarded materials.

"I was no one, nobody, from Nowheresville, until I became a drag queen," she said in a 1992 interview.

Among those who noticed was Warhol. He took Polaroids of Johnson and included her in *Ladies and Gentlemen,* a 1975 portfolio of screen prints depicting drag queens and transgender revelers at the Gilded Grape, a nightclub. Johnson was also part of a drag performance group, Hot Peaches, which began performing in 1972. She told anyone who asked—including, once, a judge—that her middle initial stood for "pay it no mind." The surname came from a Howard Johnson's restaurant where she liked to hang out.

Yet life was never easy for Johnson. She had the first in what she said was a series of breakdowns in 1970, and was in and out of psychiatric institutions after that. ("I may be crazy, but that don't make me wrong," she often said.) She was generally known for her warmth and charisma, but she also could get into physical scraps and be frightening to others.

"She would wander, start off talking about one thing and end up miles away; people would say that drugs had ruined her mind, that she was a permanent space cadet," the historian and author Martin Duberman wrote in *Stonewall,* adding that Johnson's mind had "concentrated wonderfully" when she was organizing STAR.

In 1980, a pivotal year for Johnson, she was invited to ride in the lead car of New York's annual gay pride parade and began living at the home of a close friend, the gay activist Randy Wicker, in Hoboken, New Jersey. She cared for Wicker's lover, David Combs, before he died of AIDS, in 1990. Grieving for friends, she could sometimes be found prostrate before a statue of the Virgin Mary at the Catholic Community of Saints Peter and Paul in Hoboken. She was also an AIDS activist, attending protests by and meetings of ACT UP, the AIDS advocacy organization.

In a June 26, 1992, interview, Johnson said she had been HIV-positive for two years. "They call me a legend in my own time, because there were so many queens gone that I'm one of the few queens left from the '70s and the '80s," she said.

Several days later, she was seen for the last time. On July 6, 1992, her body was pulled from the Hudson River, near the Christopher Street piers. Her death was quickly ruled a suicide, a determination that many of her friends and acquaintances questioned.

Later in 1992, the authorities reclassified the cause of death, to drowning from undetermined causes, and in 2012, they agreed to take a fresh look at the case, which officially remains open.

Johnson has been the subject of several film projects, including work by Reina Gossett and Sasha Wortzel and documentaries in 2012 by Michael Kasino and in 2017 by David France. France's film, *The Death and Life of Marsha P. Johnson,* focused in part on the efforts of Victoria Cruz, a transgender activist and a volunteer with the New York City Anti-Violence Project, to investigate the case.

Johnson's ability to mix flamboyant joy with determined activism is a central part of her legacy.

"As long as gay people don't have their rights all across America," she once said, "there's no reason for celebration."

———

**SEWELL CHAN,** who worked at *The New York Times* from 2004 to 2018, is a lifetime member of NLGJA: The Association of LGBTQ Journalists. He is currently the editor-in-chief at *The Texas Tribune.*

Pioneering Lesbian Writer

# Lisa Ben

## 1921–2015

BY JULIA CARMEL

WHEN LISA BEN was twenty-five and pretending to be hard at work as a secretary for RKO studios in Los Angeles, she began dreaming up a magazine that would critique art and society through a lesbian lens.

Working from her office typewriter, she put together the first edition in June 1947, calling the magazine *Vice Versa* and writing in an introductory essay that it would be "dedicated, in all seriousness, to those of us who will never quite be able to adapt ourselves to the iron-bound rules of Convention."

"There is one kind of publication which would, I am sure, have a great appeal to a definite group," she wrote. "Such a publication has never appeared on the stands."

Though only about ten copies of each issue were created and circulated hand-to-hand, *Vice Versa,* which was a blend of reviews, literary pieces, and editorials, is considered to be the first lesbian magazine in the US.

"For Lisa Ben to be breaking down and showing how an article that's, like, anti-gay is problematic, and calling it out and, like, saying, 'No,'" said Kate Litterer, who did her dissertation on Ben and created a digital archive called LisaBenography, "that was a really big deal."

Her magazine was published nearly a decade before *The Ladder,* another pioneering lesbian magazine that was distributed nationally, setting a precedent at a time when the Comstock Act of 1873 was still being used to arrest and imprison those who sent what it deemed "obscene" publications through the mail, including those about contraception or abortion. (The act was enforced until 1965, when the Supreme Court ruled with *Griswold v. Connecticut* that it was unconstitutional to restrict access to birth control.)

Ben also wrote and performed gay parodies of popular songs, poetry, and short stories and was an early author of science fiction. Though she worked across different realms, much of her work was rooted in an interest in fantasies.

"She could imagine a world where gays and lesbians were just a part of daily life," Loni Shibuyama, the librarian of the ONE Archives at the University of Southern California, said by phone.

"She was kind of a queer nerd," Shibuyama added. "That's what makes her remarkable in my head, because she was creating a lot of conversation about pop culture and LGBT representation and—not intentionally, but perhaps sort of in her own way—looking at things with an LGBTQ lens when people didn't think to look at it that way."

Ben was born Edythe DeVinney Eyde on November 7, 1921, in San Francisco to Olive (Colegrove) Eyde, a homemaker, and Oscar E. Eyde, an insurance salesman.

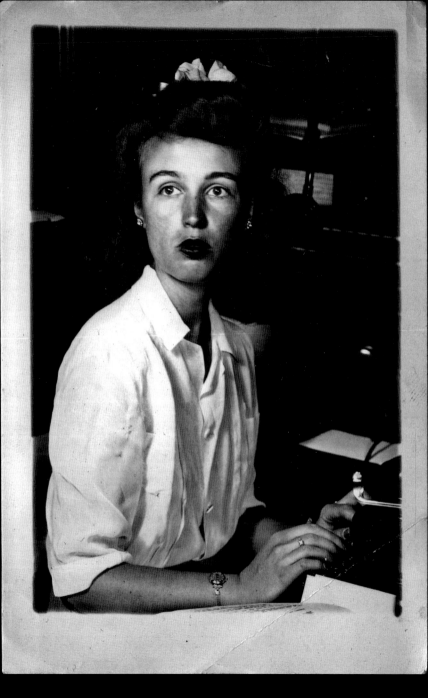

Lisa Ben in the 1940s, around the time she put together the first edition of *Vice Versa*.

Ben, shown here in the 1950s, was also a
science fiction author under the name Tigrina.

When Edythe was about three, her family moved to a thirty-three-acre apricot farm in Los Altos, California.

"It was kind of a lonely life because I was an only child," she said in a 1988 interview for the Lesbian Herstory Archives. "But there were plenty of animals around to play with—a dog and a cat and then later on we added a goat for the goat milk. And at ten years of age my parents bought me my own riding pony."

She went to high school in Palo Alto, where she developed her first crush on a girl, in her orchestra.

"Gradually, as our acquaintance grew, we found out how pleasant it was to kiss one another and hug one another," she said in the 1988 interview, adding, "I just loved her."

But by the next school year, the girl started spending time with someone new. Ben said she would go home and cry that her friend didn't love her anymore.

"Finally, one day, Mother said, 'You and she never did anything wrong together, did you?'" Ben said. "And I looked at her and I said, 'Wrong? What do you mean?' And only then did I realize that was probably unusual and I should cool it talking to my mother about such things."

After graduating, her parents kept her at home for two years to study violin until her mother enrolled her at Mills College in Oakland, California.

"Frankly I don't think I had the brains to go to college," Ben said, adding, "I didn't give a hoot for history and tennis and all the rest of it."

There she started exchanging letters with a young man in Los Angeles who had come across her writing in a science fiction magazine under a pen name—Tigrina, a character in an obscure French novel. After a while, he asked if she was a lesbian.

"I wrote to him and I said, 'What exactly do you mean?' And he wrote back to me and explained what it was," she said in the interview. "And I wrote back to him and I said, 'Yeah, that's exactly how I feel!'"

After her sophomore year, her father announced that he was enrolling her in secretarial school.

After working and saving up for two years, Ben moved to Los Angeles in 1945. For nine months she wrote monthly issues of *Vice Versa,* making each copy using carbon paper at RKO.

"I wrote *Vice Versa* mainly to keep myself company," she told Eric Marcus in a 1989 interview that eventually aired on his podcast *Making Gay History.* "Because I thought, 'Although I don't know any gay gals now, by the time I finish a couple of these magazines, I'm sure I will.' I was such a little optimist."

She stopped writing *Vice Versa* when she left RKO but continued working as a secretary elsewhere. In the late 1950s, she joined the lesbian organization Daughters of Bilitis and started writing for *The Ladder*, which was edited by Phyllis Lyon and her partner Del Martin. They didn't let her use her first choice for a pen name—Ima Spinster—so she settled on Lisa Ben, an anagram of *lesbian*.

Throughout the 1940s and '50s, Ben also wrote folk songs, poems, and science fiction stories that she shared with friends.

She performed gay parodies of popular music (for instance, "I'm Gonna Sit Right Down and Write Myself a Letter" became "I'm Gonna Sit Right Down and Write My Butch a Letter") at gay and lesbian clubs like the Flamingo, as well as at private parties in Los Angeles.

Some of Ben's songs were formally released, like the ones she performed for the 1960 Daughters of Bilitis record, *The Gayest Songs on Wax*. But many of her lesser-known songs have since been archived on Lisa Ben's Songbook, a website created by Lydia Légaré, who transcribed Ben's songs and released an EP called *Fondly, Lisa Ben* (2022).

Through her sci-fi writing she befriended author Forrest J. Ackerman, who wrote of Ben in his stories, once describing her as a Scorpio and a violin virtuosa who had a strong connection to the number thirteen.

"When they were young, they were totally thick as thieves," Litterer said. "I have photos from the archives of these hearts that said 'Forrest' and 'Tigrina' overlapping."

In 1960, Ben bought a bungalow in Burbank, California, that she called her "hEyde away." She often rescued animals and housed more than a dozen cats at a time.

She became more reclusive after she retired in the 1970s. After learning she had breast cancer and undergoing a mastectomy in 1974, Ben wrote in letters of feeling unappealing and uninterested in dating.

She occasionally invited queer historians into her home for interviews but quietly struggled with depression.

Around 2013, Ben moved into a retirement home, which forced her to give up her thirteen cats.

Ben in 1996. She often rescued animals at her "hEyde away" bungalow in Burbank, California.

She died on December 22, 2015. She was ninety-four.

Though she shied away from many of her friends toward the end of her life, Ben always remained confident and candid about the way she lived.

"As far as being gay I never felt guilty about it," she said in 1988. "I never felt remorseful or had a single regret about it."

---

**JULIA CARMEL** writes about West Coast experiences for the *Los Angeles Times* and previously worked at *The New York Times* covering nightlife, culture, and queer communities. If they had to use an anagram à la Lisa Ben, it would probably be Garvy Ye (very gay).

## India's Warrior Queen

# Rani of Jhansi

## Circa 1827–1858

———

### BY ALISHA HARIDASANI GUPTA

BY THE TIME LAXMIBAI was a teenager, she had already violated many of the expectations for women in India's patriarchal society. She could read and write. She had learned to ride a horse and wield a sword. She talked back to anyone who tried to tell her to live her life differently.

But where those spirited ways might have been scorned in another young Indian woman, they would prove to serve her well as she went on to leave an indelible mark on Indian history.

In the mid-nineteenth century, what became the modern nation of India was dotted with hundreds of princely states, one of which, Jhansi, in the north, was ruled by Queen Laxmibai. Her reign came at a pivotal time: the British, who were expanding their presence in India, had annexed her realm and stripped her of power.

Laxmibai tried to regain control of Jhansi through negotiations, but when her efforts failed, she joined the Indian Rebellion of 1857, an uprising of soldiers, landowners, townspeople, and others against the British in what is now known as India's first battle for independence. It would be ninety years before the country would finally uproot the British, in 1947.

The queen, or rani, went on to train and lead her own army, composed of both men and women, only to perish on the battlefield in June 1858.

In the decades that followed, her life became a subject of competing narratives. Indians hailed her as a heroine, the British as a wicked, Jezebel-like figure. But somewhere between these portrayals she emerged as a symbol not just of resistance but of the complexities associated with being a powerful woman in India.

"Her story has come to us less as history and more as mythology," Harleen Singh, an associate professor of literature and women's studies at Brandeis University, said in a phone interview. "It's female heroism that is bound to the family and the nation."

She added, "In a way, she's considered singular—and she is singular—because she fought for the nation, for something larger than herself."

Laxmibai wasn't of royal blood. Manikarnika, as she was named at birth, is widely believed to have been born in 1827 in Varanasi, a city in northeast India on the banks of the Ganges River. She was raised among the Brahmin priests and scholars who sat atop India's caste system. Her father worked in royal courts as an adviser, giving her access to an education, as well as horses.

In 1842, Manakarnika married Maharaja Gangadhar Rao, the ruler of Jhansi, and took on the name Laxmibai. (It was—and, in some parts of the country, still is—a common practice for women to change their name after marriage.)

A painting depicting the Rani of Jhansi on horseback.
She trained and led her own army.

By most accounts she was an unconventional queen. She refused to abide by the norms of the purdah system, under which women were concealed from public view by veils or curtains. She insisted on speaking with her advisers and British officials face-to-face. She wore a turban, an accessory more common among men. And she is said to have trained women in her circle to ride and fight. She was also compassionate, attending to the poor, regardless of their caste, a practice that even today would be considered bold in parts of India.

While she was queen, the powerful British East India Company was beginning to seize more land and resources. In 1848, Lord Dalhousie, India's governor general, declared that princely states with leaders lacking natural-born heirs would be annexed by the British under a policy called the Doctrine of Lapse.

Laxmibai's only child had died, and her husband's health was deteriorating. The couple decided to adopt a five-year-old boy to groom as successor to the throne and hoped that the British would recognize his authority.

"I trust that in consideration of the fidelity I have evinced toward government, favor may be shown to this child and that my widow during her lifetime may be considered the Regent," her husband, the maharaja, wrote in a letter, as quoted in *The Rani of Jhansi, Rebel Against Will* (2007).

His pleas were ignored. Soon after he died, in 1853, the East India Company offered the queen a pension if she agreed to cede control. She refused, exclaiming: *"Meri Jhansi nahin dungee"* ("I will not give up my Jhansi")—a Hindi phrase that to this day is etched into India's memory, stirring up feelings of pride and patriotism.

Beyond Jhansi's borders, a rebellion was brewing as the British imposed their social and Christian practices and banned Indian customs.

The uprising spread from town to town, reaching Jhansi in June 1857. Dozens of British were killed in the ensuing massacre by the rebels. The British turned on Laxmibai, accusing her of conspiring with the rebels to seek revenge over their refusal to recognize her heir. Whether or not she did remains disputed. Some accounts insist that she was wary of the rebels and that she had even offered to protect British women and children during the violence.

Tensions escalated, and in early 1858 the British stormed Jhansi's fortress.

"Street fighting was going on in every quarter," Dr. Thomas Lowe, the army's field surgeon, wrote in *Central India During the Rebellion of 1857 and 1858* (1860). "Heaps of dead lay all along the rampart and in the streets below.

"Those who could not escape," he added, "threw their women and babies down wells and then jumped down themselves."

As the town burned, the queen escaped on horseback with her son, Damodar, tied to her back. Historians have not reached a consensus on how she managed to pull this off. Some contend that her closest aide, Jhalkaribai, disguised herself as the queen to distract the British and buy time for her to get away.

In the end, the British took the town, leaving three to five thousand people dead, and hoisted the British flag atop the palace.

The fortress at Jhansi in the 1880s. The British stormed the fort in 1858.

Left with no other options, Laxmibai decided to join the rebel forces and began training an army in the nearby state of Gwalior.

The British troops, close on her heels, attacked Gwalior on a scorching summer morning in June 1858. She led a countercharge—"clad in the attire of a man and mounted on horseback," the British historians John Kaye and George Malleson wrote in *History of the Indian Mutiny* (1890)—and was killed. (Accounts differ on whether she was stabbed with a saber or struck by a bullet.) It was the last battle in the Indian Rebellion.

"The Indian mutiny had produced but one man," Sir Hugh Rose, the leader of the British troops, reportedly said when fighting ended, "and that man was a woman."

The violence left thousands dead on both sides. The British government dissolved the East India Company over concerns about its aggressive rule and brought India under the control of the crown. It then reversed Lord Dalhousie's policy of annexing kingdoms without heirs.

Today, Queen Laxmibai of Jhansi has been immortalized in India's nationalist narrative. There are movies, TV shows, books, and even nursery rhymes about her.

Streets, colleges, and universities are named after her. Young girls dress up in her likeness, wearing pants, turbans, and swords. Statues of her on horseback, with her son tied to her back, have been erected in many cities throughout India. And nearly a century after her death, the Indian National Army formed an all-female unit that aided the country in its battle for independence in the 1940s.

It was called the Rani of Jhansi Regiment.

———

**ALISHA HARIDASANI GUPTA** is a reporter at *The New York Times*. When she was growing up, her parents would respond to her short temper (jokingly and out of exasperation) with "Who do you think you are? The rani of Jhansi?"

Rosa May Billinghurst, center, in 1908. She used a tricycle wheelchair, which she was known to ram into police officers.

## Militant Suffragette Who Fought for Women's Rights

# Rosa May Billinghurst

## 1875–1953

BY SARAH FIELDING

THE INSIDE OF A PRISON was certainly not an ideal place to campaign for a national cause, but in Rosa May Billinghurst's case it would have to do. It was March 1912, and Billinghurst, a British suffragette, had been sentenced to one month of hard labor for her role in a window-smashing campaign in which demonstrators destroyed property in popular neighborhoods of London to make a statement: Let women vote!

Even as she toiled in the prison yard, Billinghurst worked her cause, enlarging the movement by recruiting inmates to join her in the fight for women's suffrage.

This wasn't Billinghurst's first time in jail, and it wouldn't be her last. For many years she clashed with the police, joining riots and using other militant protest tactics, dressed in the colors of the movement: purple for royalty, white for purity, and green for hope.

Billinghurst, who went by her middle name, May, was born on May 31, 1875, in Lewisham, in southeast London, the second of nine children of Henry and Rosa Ann Billinghurst. She contracted polio as a child and used a tricycle wheelchair for most of her life. As a young woman she took up social work, assisting women at a workhouse, an institution for people who could not support themselves. She also taught Sunday school.

She joined the Women's Social and Political Union, a group that endorsed militant tactics to further the cause of women's rights, in 1907. By then the suffrage movement was in full force in Britain.

It had started in 1792, with the publication of Mary Wollstonecraft's book *A Vindication of the Rights of Women,* which argued for men and women to be treated equally, a revolutionary concept at the time. The movement took on steam in the 1840s, when Chartists, members of a working-class movement, called for the passage of voting rights legislation.

Committees began to form across the region, and petitions with millions of signatures were submitted to Parliament. It wasn't until 1869 that taxpaying women were granted the right to vote in municipal elections, but not in parliamentary elections.

By the end of the century, the committees had merged into the National Union of Women's Suffrage Societies. Emmeline Pankhurst founded the Women's Social and Political Union in 1903, calling on its members to eschew peaceful protests (which were more common in the United States, where the activists were more often called suffragists) in favor of hunger strikes and even violence. Billinghurst started the organization's Greenwich chapter. At protests, she was known to ram into police officers with her tricycle.

The women's union suspended militant campaigning, however, in 1910 in anticipation of a vote on legislation known as the Conciliation Bill, which, if passed, would have allowed about a million women, mostly wealthy property owners, to vote in parliamentary elections.

But for Prime Minister Herbert Henry Asquith, giving women the vote was a low priority. He was focused on passing another bill, the People's Budget, which would impose a higher tax on the wealthy.

On what became known as Black Friday, Billinghurst, along with about three hundred other suffragettes, gathered outside government buildings and demanded to speak with Asquith. When he refused, they tried to storm the buildings but were driven back by the police. Billinghurst was forcibly removed from her tricycle.

"At first, the police threw me out of the machine onto the ground in a very brutal manner," she said in a police statement on November 18, 1910. "Secondly, when on the machine again, they tried to push me along with my arms twisted behind me in a very painful position, with one of my fingers bent right back, which caused me great agony. Thirdly, they took me down a side road and left me in the middle of a hooligan crowd, first taking all the valves out of the wheels and pocketing them, so that I could not move the machine, and left me to the crowd of roughs, who, luckily, proved my friends."

This was not the last time Billinghurst clashed with law enforcement. In November 1911, she was among 220 women arrested for smashing windows with hammers and stones in a protest in Parliament Square against a bill that would give all men, not just property owners, the right to vote but would continue to exclude women. She was arrested again in March 1912 during a coordinated protest in which 150 women smashed windows across London.

From jail, she continued to push for women's suffrage.

"Miss Billinghurst is here with her tricycle," wrote Alice Ker, another imprisoned suffragette, in a letter to her daughter. "She has irons on each leg, and can only walk with crutches, her tricycle works with handles. She drives it round the yard at exercise time. It is painted in the colors, with a placard, Votes for Women, on the back of it."

Billinghurst was arrested again in December 1912, this time on charges of damaging mailboxes in the Blackheath neighborhood of London. Pankhurst encouraged Billinghurst to represent herself in court, an opportunity she used to plead the case for women's suffrage once again.

In 1913, the newspaper *The Suffragette* published the entire defense that Billinghurst had delivered to an all-male jury, titling it "The Guilt Lies on the Shoulders of the Government."

"This is a women's war," she told the jurors, "in which we hold human life dear and property cheap, and if one has to be sacrificed for the other, then we say let property be destroyed and human life be preserved.

"We are not hooligans seeking to destroy," she added, "but we mean to wake the public mind from its apathy."

She was convicted and sentenced to eight months in prison. She responded by going on a hunger strike, and in a letter to her mother wrote of being force-fed. When her health declined, Pankhurst and others secured her release.

But Billinghurst immediately returned to the cause. In May 1914, *The Suffragette* reported that the police had again attacked her and destroyed her tricycle after she chained herself to the gates of Buckingham Palace.

While her bodily weaknesses had been exploited, Billinghurst said, her inner strength would never be shaken.

"The government may further maim my crippled body by the torture of forcible feeding, as they are torturing weak women in prison today," she said in her trial statement. "They may even kill me in the process, for I am not strong, but they cannot take away my freedom of spirit or my determination to fight this good fight to the end."

Billinghurst in 1913 leading a procession of suffragists. She was arrested several times.

She would go on to join the Women's Freedom League, which encouraged resisting taxation and boycotting the national census, and the Suffragette Fellowship, which celebrated the accomplishments of suffragettes.

Victory for them came first in 1918, with the passage of the Representation of the People Act, which gave property-owning women age thirty and older the right to vote in England. Ten years later, women twenty-one and older were given the same voting rights as men.

Billinghurst died on July 29, 1953, at seventy-eight. She was survived by Beth Billinghurst, who said

Billinghurst had adopted her in 1933. She is the author of the memoir *Rosa May Billinghurst: Beth's Untold Story*, which was published in 2019.

———

**SARAH FIELDING** is an acclaimed journalist covering mental health, gender rights, and social issues. As someone living a hundred years after Billinghurst and still fighting for women's rights, she understands the urge to chain yourself to a palace gate in protest.

A portrait of Elizabeth Jennings published in the *American Woman's Journal* in 1895.

# Teacher Who Desegregated New York's Trolleys

# Elizabeth Jennings

## 1827–1901

BY SAM ROBERTS

BECAUSE SHE WAS RUNNING behind one Sunday morning, Elizabeth Jennings turned out to be a century ahead of her time.

She was a teacher in her twenties, on her way to the First Colored American Congregational Church in Lower Manhattan, where she was the regular organist, when a conductor ordered her off a horse-drawn Third Avenue trolley and told her to wait for a car reserved for Black passengers.

One immediately arrived, but it was full.

When Jennings flatly refused to leave the whites-only trolley that she had already boarded, she was bodily ejected.

She sued the company for damages and won in 1855—exactly one hundred years before Rosa Parks rejected a Montgomery, Alabama, bus driver's order to give up her seat in the colored section for a white passenger after the space reserved for whites was filled.

In the mid-1950s, Parks was elevated to a civil rights heroine. Jennings was finally immortalized—in 2007, to a degree—after third- and fourth-grade students at PS 361 in Manhattan successfully lobbied to name a street corner in her honor.

Even in his revealing portrait *Black Manhattan* (1930), James Weldon Johnson did not identify by name the "courageous colored woman, a teacher," as he described Jennings, whose efforts led to the legal annulment of racially segregated mass transit in New York.

On July 16, 1854, Jennings and a friend, Sarah Adams, boarded the trolley at Pearl Street and today's Park Row. They were late and rushing to get to the church, on East Sixth Street near the Bowery.

The reluctant conductor only agreed to let them ride—instead of waiting for a trolley that proclaimed "Colored People Allowed in This Car"—if no white passengers objected.

Jennings wrote, "I was a respectable person, born and raised in New York, did not know where he was born and that he was a good-for-nothing impudent fellow for insulting decent persons while on their way to church."

Whether or not any rider voiced a complaint was unclear, but the conductor and Jennings scuffled. She resisted, clinging to a window frame, then to his coat. He enlisted the driver's help, to no avail.

"I screamed, 'Murder,' with all my voice and my companion screamed out, 'You will kill her. Don't kill her,'" Jennings wrote.

"'You shall sweat for this,'" she quoted the conductor as saying. Farther on, near what is today Canal Street, he spotted a police officer, who boarded the car and ousted

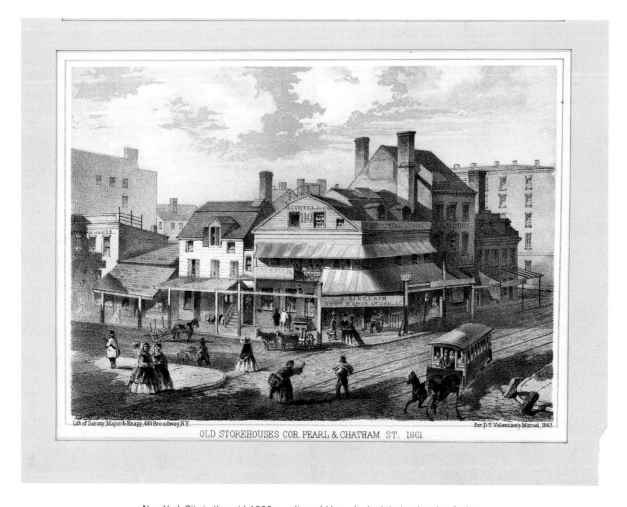

OLD STOREHOUSES COR. PEARL & CHATHAM ST. 1861.

New York City in the mid-1800s, as it would have looked during Jennings's time.

Jennings. He shoved her onto the sidewalk, dirtying her dress and crushing her bonnet.

Jennings's encounter with the conductor was seren-dipitous; she had been primed, by temperament and family ties, for a confrontation over racial equality and to seek retribution.

Elizabeth Jennings was born in Manhattan in March of 1827 (some records say 1830).

Her mother was Elizabeth (Cartwright) Jennings, whose own father had fought with the Continental Army. Young Elizabeth's father, Thomas L. Jennings, was a prosperous tailor on Church Street and is said to have been the first Black person to be awarded a patent in the United States, in 1821, for a method of dry-cleaning clothes.

When Elizabeth was only ten she delivered from memory a lecture titled "On the Improvement of the

Mind," according to a biography, *Streetcar to Justice* (2018) by Amy Hill Hearth.

When she finished public school, she wasn't allowed to participate in commencement, so, in a separate ceremony, she received her diploma, which qualified her to teach in public school.

Her father, who had helped found the New York African Society for Mutual Relief, a charitable group for free Black people, enlisted his fellow abolitionists to publicize his daughter's mistreatment and recruit a newly minted twenty-six-year-old lawyer and future president, Chester A. Arthur, and his partners to sue the Third Avenue Railroad System, based in Brooklyn, for discrimination.

(In 1852, Arthur's advocacy had helped liberate slaves who were being transported to Texas through New York.)

*Frederick Douglass' Paper,* published in Rochester, and the *New York Daily Tribune* were among those that printed sympathetic accounts, relying largely on Jennings's version of the altercation. (*The New York Times* apparently overlooked the case.)

On February 22, 1855, Judge William Rockwell advised a jury in the state supreme court that the company was required as a common carrier to convey all respectable passengers, including "colored persons, if sober, well-behaved, and free from disease," and that it was liable if they were excluded.

Jennings sought $500 in damages. The jury ruled in her favor but apparently decided that amount was too much for a Black person and instead awarded $225 (about equal to her annual salary teaching). The judge added 10 percent (for a total of about $7,000 in today's dollars) plus costs.

"Railroads, steamboats, omnibuses, and ferry-boats will be admonished from this, as to the rights of respectable colored people," the *Tribune* declared. "It is high time the rights of this class of citizens were ascertained, and that it should be known whether they are to be thrust from our public conveyances, while German or Irish women, with a quarter of mutton or a load of codfish, can be admitted."

Jennings taught for thirty-five years, mostly in Black schools.

In 1860, she married Charles Graham. They had a son, Thomas, who was sickly and died when he was one. His burial would take place during the Draft Riots by white people opposed to conscription during the Civil War, and since it was unsafe for Black people to be seen outdoors, Jennings and her husband had to sneak to their son's graveside service at Cypress Hills Cemetery in Brooklyn, where the Reverend Morgan Dix of Trinity Church presided.

After the riots, in which dozens of Black people were killed, the couple fled the city. They settled in Eatonville, New Jersey, near Long Branch. Graham died in 1867. Jennings returned to Manhattan in 1871.

Jennings later taught at the Colored Grammar School, where the principal, Charles L. Reason, was a pioneering Black educator who challenged school segregation.

In 1895, she founded what was described as the first kindergarten for Black children, at her home, 237 West Forty-First Street, in Manhattan, where she died on June 5, 1901.

———

**SAM ROBERTS** is a correspondent and obituary writer for *The New York Times*. A biography of Elizabeth Jennings is included in his latest book, *The New Yorkers.*

## Teenager Who Voluntarily Lived in an Incarceration Camp

# Ralph Lazo

## 1924–1992

BY VERONICA MAJEROL

WHEN RALPH LAZO saw his Japanese American friends being forced from their homes and into incarceration camps during World War II, he did something unexpected: he went with them.

In the spring of 1942, Lazo, a seventeen-year-old high school student in Los Angeles, boarded a train and headed to the Manzanar War Relocation Center, one of ten incarceration camps authorized to house Japanese Americans under President Franklin D. Roosevelt's executive order in the wake of Japan's attack on Pearl Harbor a few months earlier. The camps, tucked in barren regions of the United States, would incarcerate around 115,000 people living in the West from 1942 to 1946—two-thirds of them United States citizens.

Unlike the other inmates, Lazo did not have to be there. A Mexican American, he was the only known person to pretend to be Japanese so he could be willingly imprisoned.

What compelled Lazo to give up his freedom for two and a half years—sleeping in tar-paper-covered barracks, using open latrines and showers, and waiting in long lines for meals in mess halls, on grounds surrounded by barbed-wire fencing and watched by guards in towers?

He wanted to be with his friends.

"My Japanese American friends at high school were ordered to evacuate the West Coast, so I decided to go along with them," Lazo told the *Los Angeles Times* in 1944.

By the time Lazo left Manzanar, his social consciousness had deepened and his outrage over the indignities suffered by Japanese Americans had grown. It would define how he lived the rest of his life, as an activist who sought to improve education for underprivileged groups and push for reparations for Japanese Americans who had been detained.

Unlike Lazo, most Americans were swept up by anti-Japanese sentiment propagated by politicians and the media. After the attack on Pearl Harbor, the Los Angeles Police Department shut down businesses in the Little Tokyo area, and teachers barred Japanese American students from reciting the Pledge of Allegiance, Richard Reeves wrote in the book *Infamy: The Shocking Story of the Japanese American Internment in World War II* (2015).

By Christmas 1941, FBI agents were raiding the homes of Japanese Americans and arresting them without due process. Public officials, including California's governor and attorney general, endorsed the idea of detaining people of Japanese descent, even if they were born in America.

Ralph Lazo in 1944, the year he was drafted into the Army.

Lazo, far right in the middle row, who voluntarily was incarcerated with his Japanese friends.

Though the Munson Report, commissioned by the State Department, concluded that Japanese Americans did not pose a national security threat, President Roosevelt signed an executive order on February 19, 1942, that cleared the way for their relocation.

Amid the hysteria, expressions of solidarity were rare, said Eric Muller, a professor at the University of North Carolina School of Law in Chapel Hill and a scholar of Japanese incarceration.

"There were very small numbers of active allies," Muller, who created a podcast about life in the camps, said in a phone interview. "There were almost no groups nationally in 1942 that stood up for and alongside Japanese Americans."

Lazo was born on November 3, 1924, in Los Angeles, to John Houston Lazo and Rose Padilla. He and his family lived in the Temple Street neighborhood, near Little Tokyo. Lazo's mother died when he and his sister, Virginia, were young, and they were left in the care of their father, who worked as a housepainter and muralist.

At the ethnically diverse Belmont High School, Lazo counted Japanese Americans among his closest friends. "I fit in very well," he told the *Los Angeles Times* in 1981. "We developed this beautiful friendship."

And as many Americans were distancing themselves from their Japanese neighbors—or worse, attacking them verbally or physically—his identification with his friends grew deeper.

"Who can say I haven't got Japanese blood in me?" he said in 1944. "Who knows what kind of blood runs in my veins?"

Before he left, he told his father he was "going to camp," creating the impression that he was going to summer camp. His father did not press him, and neither did government officials whose system for entry into the camps relied largely on self-reporting, Muller, the UNC professor, said.

When Lazo's father found out where his son had really gone, he did not reprimand him. "My father was a very wise man," Lazo said in 1981. "He probably was very happy I was there."

The Manzanar Relocation Center, where Lazo gave up his freedom for more than two years.

About ten thousand people were imprisoned at Manzanar, in the Owens Valley in Eastern California. They lived in military-style barracks in punishing summer desert heat.

Despite their grim surroundings, the prisoners demonstrated resilience, re-creating the rhythms of normal life by running schools, newspapers, sports teams, gardens, and hiking clubs, all of which the government allowed, Muller said.

Many at Manzanar were aware of Lazo's ethnicity. One of his high school classmates, Rosie Kakuuchi, said that Lazo spent time amusing the orphaned children at the camp with games and jokes. He had a quirky way of telling stories, and one Christmas he rallied thirty friends to go caroling at the camp.

"We accepted him and loved him," Kakuuchi said in a phone interview. "He was just one of us."

It wasn't until August 1944, when Lazo was drafted into the army, that the government discovered his secret. But he didn't face any repercussions. In fact, the government issued a news release disclosing his unusual story, which led the *Los Angeles Times* to write about it. Lazo served in the Pacific until 1946, receiving a Bronze Star for bravery, among other honors.

After the war, Lazo earned a bachelor's degree in sociology at UCLA and a master's degree in education at California State University, Northridge. He married Isabella Natera, and they had two sons and a daughter; they divorced in 1977.

Lazo maintained ties to the Japanese American community throughout his life, attending Manzanar reunions and supporting efforts for government redress payments, which were eventually granted, along with an official apology, as part of the Civil Liberties Act of 1988.

In January 1945, shortly after a Supreme Court ruling that the government may not incarcerate "loyal" citizens, the War Department announced that prisoners were free to leave. Most of the ten camps closed in quick succession, with the last of Manzanar's prisoners released by November 21, 1945.

Lazo worked as a high school teacher and later as an academic counselor from 1970 to 1987 at Los Angeles Valley College, where he pushed for educational equity for Latinos and others.

"He was very committed, all his life, to what's fair and what's just and what's morally correct," Edward Moreno, a longtime high school principal who sat on committees with Lazo, said in a phone interview.

Lazo was sixty-seven when he died on January 1, 1992, of liver disease.

His experience as a voluntary prisoner resurfaced in 2004 as the subject of the short film *Stand Up for Justice: The Ralph Lazo Story.*

But in his lifetime, Lazo sought to deflect the spotlight. In 1981, he urged a *Los Angeles Times* reporter to turn the focus away from him and toward what he considered to be the more important story.

"Please write about the injustice of the evacuation," he said. "This is the real issue."

———

**VERONICA MAJEROL** is an editor on the Business desk at *The New York Times.* Three years after writing this obituary, she has still kept in touch with Rosie Kakuuchi, who was Ralph Lazo's friend at Manzanar.
DORIS BURKE contributed research.

# Beyond the Obit:
# A Singular Experience

———

## BY KRISTINA MCMORRIS

Karl Yoneda was already imprisoned in a Japanese incarceration camp during World War II when FBI agents went to his family's Los Angeles home. They were planning to forcibly take his child away from the boy's mother, Elaine Black Yoneda, as well. Elaine, who was white, refused to be separated from her child, and so she voluntarily boarded a bus packed with evacuees, identity tags dangling from each of their coats.

Once at Manzanar War Relocation Center in the California desert, she lived a life of endless queues, incessant dust, and frequent stomach ailments from food that had spoiled in the heat, all while surrounded by barbed wire and watchtowers from which guards pointed machine guns in their direction. Even more heartbreaking, the Children's Village held captive more than one hundred children of Japanese descent, taken from orphanages or from their non-Japanese adoptive families.

I learned about the Yoneda family in 2010 while doing research for my second novel, *Bridge of Scarlet Leaves,* which follows the story of a skilled violinist who secretly elopes with her Japanese American boyfriend the night before Pearl Harbor is bombed. As a US-born daughter of a Japanese immigrant, I was stunned to learn that of the approximately 2,100 interracial family members incarcerated during the war, at least 134 lacked Japanese ancestry, according to the historian Paul Spickard. As little as one-sixteenth Japanese blood labeled a person an enemy of the state.

I have written and spoken about this topic a great deal because there is so little known about it. Ralph Lazo stands out because he devoted his life to highlighting the sheer injustice of the incarceration.

Invisible Force for Black Suffrage

# Adella Hunt Logan

## 1863–1915

BY VERONICA CHAMBERS

IN 1897, Adella Hunt Logan drafted a letter to Susan B. Anthony, widely considered the mother of the suffrage movement, asking to speak at an upcoming National American Woman Suffrage Association meeting.

By then, Logan, who held a college degree and worked as a teacher and librarian at the Tuskegee Institute, had helped found the Tuskegee Women's Club and was part of the National Association of Colored Women's Clubs, in the company of such prominent African American women as Harriet Tubman, Ida Bell Wells-Barnett, Josephine St. Pierre Ruffin, and Mary Church Terrell. The motto of the NACWC was "Lifting as We Climb," and in this particular era, Logan was recruiting Black women to join the suffrage movement.

Having heard that Anthony was not always welcoming of Black activists, she wrote her letter with the support of two white suffragist friends, Emily and Isabel Howland.

Anthony denied the request, addressing Isabel Howland rather than Logan.

"I cannot have speak for us a woman who has even a ten-thousandth portion of African blood who would be an inferior orator in matter or manner, because it would so mitigate against our cause," she wrote, adding, "Let your Miss Logan wait till she is more cultivated, better educated, and better prepared and can do our mission and her own race the greatest credit."

Incidents such as these ultimately shrouded Logan's contribution to suffrage history. It would be about a hundred years before her full story came to light.

In the late 1970s, Logan's granddaughter Adele Logan Alexander received a call from a historian named Rosalyn Terborg-Penn.

"She called because she had heard that I might 'somehow' be related to Adella Hunt Logan. 'Somehow,' indeed!" (she was named for her) she later wrote in a *Ms.* magazine essay, adding, "But I had never imagined that she was a suffragist—nor had I even heard about Black women in the suffrage movement."

That conversation led to a reclaiming of Logan's life and legacy.

Adella Hunt Logan was born on February 10, 1863, in Sparta, Georgia, two years into the American Civil War, to Henry Hunt, a plantation owner, and Maria Hunt, a free Black and Creek Native American woman. Adella grew up in the complicated but privileged world of the Black Southern elite. She graduated from Atlanta University in 1881. (That year, only about fifty-five Black students received degrees from accredited colleges in the United States.)

*Hudson* — THE EDWARDS GALLERY — 58½ Whitehall St. ATLANTA, GA.

W. E. B. Du Bois served as her thesis adviser, and she received a master's degree in 1905. She was the second woman to join the staff of the Tuskegee Normal School for Colored Teachers (now Tuskegee University), where she taught English and social sciences, and was the college's first librarian.

Logan was a treasured leader and thought partner to great men of her age such as Booker T. Washington, Du Bois, and George Washington Carver. The range of her work set a template for Black women leaders for decades to come. She was, for a time, the only African American lifetime member of the National American Woman Suffrage Association (NAWSA), in part because of her ability to pass for white.

At the Tuskegee Women's Club, she worked on suffrage, but like many organizations run by women of color, the club also campaigned against lynching and for prison reform.

In 1888, she married Warren Logan, the first treasurer of Tuskegee.

Logan would bear nine children. But motherhood, with all of its demands, did not sideline her activism. She more than once risked her own safety to attend large-scale meetings of white Southern suffragists. There, she purchased reading materials on women's rights that she donated to the Tuskegee library. On one occasion, she took out her wedding dress and joined a cadre of white suffragists, all wearing white dresses and yellow satin sashes with the message "Votes for Women" printed on them.

Accompanied for safety by a friend who could also pass as white, Logan listened, angrily, as white suffragists spoke in thinly coded terms about the moral superiority of white women and the tacit approval of lynching as a means of protecting white women's virtue. She eventually succeeded in convincing more than a dozen members of NAWSA, including Susan B. Anthony and Carrie Chapman Catt, to visit the Tuskegee Institute and address the student body.

In 1905, Logan published an article called "Woman Suffrage" for *The Colored American Magazine*. In 1912, W. E. B. Du Bois published her essay "Colored Women

Logan in her wedding dress in 1888. Even as she became a mother of nine, her activism never wavered.

as Voters" as part of a special issue on women's suffrage in *The Crisis* magazine. For a 1912 campus march at Tuskegee, Logan wrote a poem called "Just as Well as He," which was set to the same melody as the Scottish poem "Comin' Thro' the Rye."

"We should heed President Lincoln's words: 'Government of the people, and for the people,' but those requisites are only partially realized if women have no vote," she wrote in the 1905 article.

"Some observers claim that their husbands represent women at the polls," she added, "but what of those who have no spouses, or have ones who oppress, abuse or abandon them? What about the woman whose callous husband patronizes saloons, gambling dens and brothels? She meanwhile stays at home to cry, to swear, or to suicide."

> If Black women were an invisible chapter to suffrage history for much of the twentieth century, Logan's shortened life and tragic death made her doubly so.

In 1915, suffrage was defeated in the Alabama Legislature under the guise that it was a Trojan horse for Black power. Logan was exhausted, suffering from kidney problems and, it is believed, worn down by her own marriage—her husband, who only grudgingly approved of her suffrage work, was said to be having an affair with a younger woman. The death of Tuskegee's founder, Booker T. Washington, left Logan and the entire community unmoored and in grief.

On December 10, 1915, Logan jumped out of the window of a top-floor classroom at Tuskegee. She died of her injuries later that night. She was fifty-two.

If Black women were an invisible chapter to suffrage history for much of the twentieth century, Logan's shortened life and tragic death made her doubly so. But an effort to rewrite the story of American suffrage to include women of color has shown that she was one of the suffrage movement's most powerful leaders and bridge builders.

Terborg-Penn, the historian, went on to write about Logan in her groundbreaking 1998 book *African American Woman in the Struggle for the Vote, 1850–1920.* Adele Logan Alexander went on to earn her PhD in history at Howard University and write her grandmother's story in *Princess of the Hither Isles: A Black Suffragist's Story from the Jim Crow South,* published in 2019.

And Logan's great-granddaughter, the noted poet Elizabeth Alexander, recited her poem "Praise Song for the Day" at the 2009 presidential inauguration of Barack Obama. In it, she offers an ode to her ancestors, writing, "Sing the names of the dead who brought us here / who laid the train tracks, raised the bridges."

"Both of my grandmothers were Black Southern suffragists in the early 1900s, and their beliefs and activities remained important family legacies through several generations," Adele Logan Alexander told *The New York Times* in 2020, but she added, "I would say it is not one person nor one event, but the scarcely recorded efforts of anonymous women of all races and educational and economic levels who, for decades, talked with neighbors, held meetings, challenged their fathers, sons, husbands, and employers—often putting themselves in physical and economic jeopardy to do so. They are the unknown heroes of the movement."

———

**VERONICA CHAMBERS** is a London-based award-winning author and the lead editor of Narrative Projects, a team dedicated to telling multiplatform stories at *The New York Times.* Her most recent book is *Shirley Chisholm Is a Verb.* Born in Panama and raised in Brooklyn, she writes often about her Afro-Latina heritage.

Stella Young in 2014 performing for the Melbourne International Comedy Festival.

# Stella Young

## 1982–2014

BY WENDY LU

STELLA YOUNG WAS A TYPICAL TEENAGER: she went to class, worked an after-school job, and watched television in her spare time.

So when a resident of her hometown in Stawell, Australia, wanted to nominate her for a community achievement award, her parents were befuddled. They couldn't figure out what, exactly, their daughter was supposed to have achieved.

"She's just such an inspiration," the resident said.

The Youngs then realized that the woman was referring to Stella's disability; she was born with osteogenesis imperfecta, a genetic condition that causes bones to break easily, and she used a wheelchair. But to Stella, having a disability was hardly a reason for an accolade.

The woman wasn't the only one to think she was heroic for simply doing the same things nondisabled people did. It was as though having a disability and enjoying life were inherently incompatible.

"Disability is not, and never has been, an antonym for ability," Young wrote in 2010 when she was the editor of Ramp Up, a website housed under the Australian Broadcasting Corporation that focuses on disability news and opinion. "Acknowledging my disability is not an admission of weakness. It's just recognition of fact."

Young went on to popularize the term *inspiration porn*, which she described in 2012 as an image, slogan, or story based on the assumption that people with disabilities "have terrible lives, and that it takes some extra kind of pluck or courage to live them."

For example, she presented a picture of a disabled man running alongside a disabled little girl, with the caption, "The only disability in life is a bad attitude." She argued that such images, which are intended to be motivational, ignore the real and significant challenges that people with disabilities face on a daily basis.

"I want to live in a world where we don't have such low expectations of disabled people that we are congratulated for getting out of bed and remembering our own names in the morning," she said in a 2014 TED Talk called "I'm Not Your Inspiration, Thank You Very Much."

Young continued to spread her message as a writer, comedian, and disability activist. Today, inspiration porn is widely taught in classes on disability studies and has become a regular subject of conversation on social media. The Center for Disability Rights and the National Center on Disability and Journalism share guidance for media professionals on how to avoid writing "charity" articles. The term has also been used to call out similar issues in other fields, including literature, sports, and Hollywood.

# "Disability is not, and never has been, an antonym for ability."

Stella Jane Young was born on February 24, 1982, in Stawell, some 150 miles northwest of Melbourne, the eldest of three girls. Her father, Greg Young, was a butcher and record shop owner. Her mother, Lynne Young, was a hairdresser who owned a salon where Stella Young worked as a receptionist during high school.

When Stella was little, doctors discouraged her parents from having more children out of fear they would also have osteogenesis imperfecta.

"My mom was shocked by that," Madison Thorne Young, Stella's sister, said in an interview with *The New York Times*. "She didn't think it was a burden the way doctors perceived it to be."

Stella grew up feisty and confident, often immersing herself in conversations with adults instead of doing "kid stuff," Madison said.

"Her opinion, to me, out of everyone in my family, was most important," she said. "She gave me so much guidance. She was my harshest critic and biggest supporter."

As a teenager, Stella would take the bus to Melbourne on weekends and go clubbing with a friend, Caroline Bowditch, who also has osteogenesis imperfecta.

"A big part of what I did was show her what life could be with disability pride," Bowditch said in an interview.

Stella studied journalism and public relations at Deakin University in Geelong, Australia. She became a proponent of the "social model of disability," which argues that people are limited not by their disabilities but by systemic barriers in society.

She also started reading memoirs by other disabled people and referring proudly to herself as a "crip."

"I was not wrong for the world I live in," she wrote in 2014 in an opinion article titled "Stella Young: A Letter to Her 80-Year-Old Self." "The world I live in was not yet right for me."

Young graduated in 2003 and moved to Melbourne with plans of becoming a schoolteacher and worked toward a graduate degree in education from the University of Melbourne. But she faced discrimination when looking for a job.

"During the interviews she got some very ableist questions thrown at her," George Taleporos, a disability rights advocate who was a friend of Young's for nearly fifteen years, said in an interview. "Things like, 'How do you write on the whiteboard?'"

It was nearly impossible to find schools with accessible toilets. During one three-week teaching round as part of her degree program, Young abstained from liquids all day to avoid having to visit the bathroom. In a high school legal studies class, a student believed Young was there to be a motivational speaker—not his teacher.

"'When people in wheelchairs come to school, they usually say, like, inspirational stuff,'" Young recalled the student's telling her. "That's when it dawned on me: this kid had only ever experienced disabled people as objects of inspiration."

A poster advertising Young's comedy show *Tales from the Crip*.

When people with disabilities are propped up as inspirations, she came to realize, more important issues, such as lack of accessibility, fall by the wayside.

"No amount of smiling at a flight of stairs has ever made it turn into a ramp," she said in her TED Talk. "Never."

Young left teaching to work at the disability organization Arts Access Victoria, and to put together educational programs for children at Museums Victoria.

She honed her public speaking skills as a host of *No Limits*, a community television program about disability culture.

Later, on the ABC show *Q+A*, Young appeared alongside Barnaby Joyce, Malcolm Turnbull, and other Australian public figures, debating social issues and national affairs.

In 2010, she created Ramp Up, which covered topics like welfare reform, genetic screening, and the 2012 Paralympic Games in London.

Young also started performing stand-up comedy, using humor to illustrate the appalling experiences she often endured as a disabled woman. In 2014, she received the award for "Best Newcomer" at the Melbourne International Comedy Festival for her show *Tales from the Crip*.

"I had a woman come up to me on the train once, and she said, very politely I might add, 'Excuse me, do you have a vagina?' Like . . . what, like, a spare one?" Young often quipped. She told the woman no, but pointed out that there was another type of hole—in the rear—standing right in front of her.

She was also a state finalist in RAW Comedy, an annual competition in Australia, two times.

Young dated both men and women and was once engaged but never got married.

Friends called her a fashionista, as she often sported bold patterns, bright lipstick, and a fiery red pixie cut. She loved dancing, going to concerts, and drinking wine. She was part of a knitting group, Stitch 'n Bitch, and enjoyed picnics at Moonlight Cinema.

Young died unexpectedly on December 6, 2014, at the height of her career. She was thirty-two. Reports suspected the cause was an aneurysm, but her family did not specify details. Nearly 1,500 people attended her memorial at Melbourne Town Hall, and the event was broadcast live on ABC, said Bryce Ives, a close friend who organized the event.

In March 2022, the local government announced that a statue honoring Young would be built in Stawell. Sarah Barton, a filmmaker and the creator of *No Limits*, created a short film about Young's life and is working to expand it into a feature-length documentary.

Two months before she died, Young wrote on Facebook: "I am not a snowflake. I am not a sweet, infantilizing symbol of the fragility of life. I am a strong, fierce, flawed adult woman. I plan to remain that way in life, and in death."

——

**WENDY LU** is a senior staff editor at *The New York Times*. She is also a disabled woman who, like Stella, prefers not to be called an inspiration.

Jovita Idár in the early 1900s. She fought for the rights of Mexican Americans and women.

## Activist Who Promoted Rights of Mexican Americans and Women

# Jovita Idár

## 1885–1946

BY JENNIFER MEDINA

WHEN THE TEXAS RANGERS showed up outside the office of the newspaper *El Progreso* in 1914 with the intent of shutting it down, Jovita Idár, a writer and editor, was waiting at the front door to block them from entering. And she was not about to back down.

The officers, who by then had gained a reputation for their violence against Mexicans, were furious over an editorial that criticized President Woodrow Wilson's order to send military troops to the Texas-Mexico border amid the Mexican Revolution. Idár argued that silencing the newspaper would violate its constitutional right to freedom of the press under the First Amendment.

The Rangers eventually turned back. But the next day, when Idár was gone, they returned to ransack the office, smashing and destroying the printing presses.

Their actions would not stop Idár from writing about her view of justice, one that she had formulated from childhood.

Jovita Idár was born on September 7, 1885, in Laredo, Texas, a city on the Mexican border. She was the second of eight children of Jovita and Nicasio Idár; her father, an activist, worked as an editor and publisher of a local Spanish newspaper, *La Crónica*.

Laws of the Jim Crow era enforcing racial segregation also limited the rights of Mexican Americans in South Texas (they are often referred to by scholars today as "Juan Crow" laws). Signs saying "No Negroes, Mexicans or dogs allowed" were common in restaurants and stores. Law enforcement officers frequently intimidated or abused Mexican American residents, and the schools they were sent to were underfunded and often inadequate. Speaking Spanish in public was discouraged.

As a daughter of relative privilege, Idár had access to the kind of education she dreamed of for others. Educated in Methodist schools, she received a teaching certificate from the Laredo Seminary and went on to teach young children in Los Ojuelos, a town in southeast Texas. She quickly became appalled by the school's conditions, including run-down buildings and a dearth of books.

She decided she could have more impact by focusing on activism and writing, joining her brothers and father at *La Crónica*. And after she learned of lynchings of Mexican American men, her commitment to the civil rights struggle only deepened.

Idár believed in a kind of cultural redemption of *la raza*, a term widely used to refer to Mexicans and other Latinos. She believed that the poor living on both sides of the border could be uplifted by education and empowerment.

Idár in 1914 with colleagues in the print shop of El Progreso in Laredo, Texas.

"She was ahead of her time, fighting against the erasure of their history" as well as "celebrating that nobody should feel threatened by the power of women," Gabriela González, an associate professor of history at the University of Texas at San Antonio, who is working on a biography of Idár, said.

*La Crónica* reported extensively on the borderlands and on the Mexican Revolution, with a particular focus on those Mexican Americans, known as Tejanos, who had been living in Texas before the modern border with the United States was established in the 1840s.

"Through their newspaper, the Idár family sounded off against separatist and inferior housing and schools, the abysmal conditions faced by Tejano workers that took on the visage of peonage and the gross violations of Tejano civil rights," the historian Zaragosa Vargas wrote in *Crucible of Struggle: A History of Mexican Americans from Colonial Times to the Present Era* (2011).

Frequently taking on pen names—among them Astraea, the name of the Greek goddess of justice, and Ave Negra, Spanish for "black bird"—Idár also wrote about equal rights for women and regularly urged women to educate themselves and seek independence from men.

She defined the modern woman as someone with "broad horizons."

"Science, industry, the workshop and even the home demand her best aptitudes, her perseverance and consistency in work, and her influence and assistance for all that is progress and advancement for humanity," she wrote, according to *Texas Women: Their Histories, Their Lives* (2015).

And she made the argument that educating women would improve society as a whole: "Educate a woman, and you educate a family," she would often insist.

In 1911, she joined the First Mexican Congress in Laredo to organize Mexican American activists. She then started Liga Femenil Mexicanista, or the League of Mexican Women.

That same year California granted women the right to vote, and Idár urged women in Texas to "proudly raise [their] chins and face the fight."

"Much has been said and written against the feminist movement," she wrote in *La Crónica*, "but despite the opposition, women in California can vote on a jury and hold public offices."

In addition to becoming the first president of the *liga*, she oversaw its effort to identify and educate poor children, urging schools to teach Spanish as well as English.

The language is "increasingly forgotten, and each day it suffers adulterations and changes that materially hurt the ear of any Mexican as little versed as he might be in the language of Cervantes," she wrote.

Idár also decried ignorance of Mexico's national heroes and Mexican American history as a whole. "If in the American school our children attend, they are taught the biography of Washington and not the one of Hidalgo, and if instead of the glorious deeds of Juárez they are referred to the exploits of Lincoln," she wrote, "as much as these are noble and just, that child will not know the glories of his nation, he will not love her, and he might even see his parents' countrymen with indifference."

By 1913, during the battle of Nuevo Laredo in the Mexican Revolution, Idár had left Laredo to cross the border. She worked with La Cruz Blanca, a medical aid group similar to the Red Cross, as a nurse for the army. She later returned to Laredo and began working for *El Progreso*.

After marrying Bartolo Juárez in 1917, she moved to San Antonio, where the couple established the local Democratic Club and she worked as a precinct judge for the party. She established a free kindergarten, worked at a hospital as an interpreter for Spanish-speaking patients, and taught infant care courses for women, all while editing *El Heraldo Cristiano*, a Methodist Church newspaper.

Idár never had children of her own, but she helped to raise the children of her sister Elvira, who died while giving birth.

Idár died of a pulmonary hemorrhage and advanced tuberculosis on June 15, 1946. She was sixty.

---

**JENNIFER MEDINA** is a national correspondent for *The New York Times*, focusing on politics and policy. She is a California native and, like Idár, maintains a lifelong fascination with the borderlands.

Musician Who Protested Segregation

# Jimmy Davis

## 1915–1997

---

BY JONATHAN ABRAMS

THE MUSICIAN JIMMY DAVIS was low-key and conscientious; he did not usually speak up unless he was confronted with a great social injustice.

He found that injustice during World War II. Davis wanted to join the fight and was prepared to pause what would become an influential music career, one that birthed one of jazz's most recorded songs. But he could not overlook the military's overt hypocrisy: they expected him to fight Hitler's fascism while segregating Black Americans like him into separate units.

"I feel it is my constitutional right to serve my country without being discriminated against because of my race," Davis told *PM,* a liberal New York newspaper, in 1942, adding, "I can't for the life of me see how I can honestly fight against Hitlerism in an army that itself practices racial discrimination."

Instead, he asked to serve in the Canadian Armed Forces and appealed to President Franklin D. Roosevelt. His request was denied, and the FBI threw Davis in jail for refusing to serve in the military.

While there, he was supported by notable novelists like Langston Hughes and Richard Wright, who rallied to his side and publicized his cause.

He joined the army after two weeks of imprisonment, sensing he had pushed his peaceful protest to its limit.

Davis experienced the racism he had anticipated: during his three and a half years of active duty, he was tested separately and had inferior eating and sleeping arrangements compared to his white counterparts.

Davis often sent letters to Hughes, who became his close friend, relaying his experience with Jim Crow. Once, Davis accompanied a group of fellow soldiers to dinner at a Maine hotel and was refused service. "Well, the fellows raised hell, but there was nothing to be done at the time about it," Davis wrote. In another letter, he described being hospitalized with depression while stationed at Virginia's Camp Pickett.

He told Hughes: "Something seemed to snap and I felt that I couldn't endure Jim Crow any longer; felt it strangling me; felt as if I'd lose my mind any moment. Lang, I don't know what the outcome of this will be but I don't think I'll be able to stomach any more of this; probably will wind up in a court martial or something, but it haunts me day and night."

In 1948, President Harry Truman signed an order desegregating the US military. By then, Davis was living in France, which he found more welcoming of Black people. He spent nearly all his adult life there as an expatriate, carving out a career as an actor, songwriter, composer, and musician.

Davis in 1942. He joined the Army after
two weeks of imprisonment.

Even before joining the army, Davis had written the hit ballad "Lover Man (Oh, Where Can You Be?)," with Roger Ramirez for the influential jazz singer Billie Holiday.

In her 1956 autobiography, *Lady Sings the Blues,* Holiday, perhaps not remembering the exact sequence, wrote, "Jimmy was in the Army when he wrote 'Lover Man' and brought it straight to me."

Holiday's poignant 1944 release, expressing heartbreak and agony, became one of her only major chart successes. The single was inducted into the Grammy Hall of Fame in 1989.

*The Jazz Discography* lists 1,278 different recordings of "Lover Man," making it one of the most recorded jazz songs of all time. It has been performed by the likes of Whitney Houston, Patti LaBelle, Charlie Parker, Diana Ross, and Barbra Streisand.

Much of Davis's contribution to jazz would have been overlooked without the work of François Grosjean, a former director of the Language and Speech Processing Laboratory at the University of Neuchâtel in Switzerland, who began researching him in 2011.

When François was twenty-one, his father, Roger Grosjean, introduced him to Davis at a dinner party. "This is Jimmy Davis," Roger said. "He's a jazz musician and you owe him a lot."

François did not think much of the interaction until nearly forty-five years later when he inherited some of his family's documents, including a short autobiography written by his mother, Sallie Shipway, and had a stunning revelation.

"One day [my husband] brought home to dinner an American soldier, Jimmy Davis, a musician," Shipway wrote. "He had just finished writing a song called 'Lover Man' which became a big success. He persuaded me that it was wrong to abort. With his help, I decided to keep the baby."

After reading the autobiography, François Grosjean embarked on a quest to learn everything he could about the American musician who had played an unlikely role in his life, digging through Davis's correspondence with Hughes, tracking down his friends, and discovering that Davis and Ramirez likely penned "Lover Man" years earlier than Holiday recalled in her autobiography.

"When I went in search of Jimmy, I discovered a talented songwriter, composer, pianist, singer, and actor," Grosjean wrote in an email. "His fame came with 'Lover Man,' but we should not forget his many other songs in English, in French, and even in Spanish."

James Edward Davis was born on April 15, 1915, in Madison, Georgia, to Emory Davis and Lessie Jackson.

The family—which included Davis's two younger sisters, Hazel and Iniz—moved to Gary, Indiana, when Davis was six and to Englewood, New Jersey, a couple of years later, according to a 1941 article in *The New York Amsterdam Star-News.*

Davis graduated from Englewood High School (now Dwight Morrow High School) in 1933 and worked with the pianist Marguerite Upshur, "who prepared him for three years of intensive study in piano and theory at the Juilliard Institute in New York," the *Star-News* wrote.

He was one of few Black Americans at the time to attend Juilliard, where he also studied composition, Grosjean discovered.

Davis first earned wide recognition in 1940 with "Why Is a Good Man So Hard to Find."

"Before you could say Jack Robinson, recordings of it were made by the Charioteers for Columbia and by Midge Williams for Decca," the *Star-News* wrote.

The military summoned Davis a few months later. Grosjean found that the selection committee wanted to declare Davis unfit for medical reasons, but he refused and insisted he be acknowledged as a conscientious objector. The NAACP represented Davis while he was jailed at the Federal House of Detention in New York.

By the time he landed in France, in March 1945, with an army musical unit, he was a warrant officer. He registered in a course for American soldiers to study French at the University of Paris.

"Paris is just what the doctor ordered," he wrote in a letter to Hughes.

Later that year, he was discharged from the army and moved to Hollywood, enrolling in acting classes at the Actors' Laboratory Theatre and appearing in a play.

He decided to return to Paris for good in 1947, taking the path forged by Josephine Baker and other Black American artists to Europe, where they sought, in Baker's words, "freedom."

In France, Davis found that "Lover Man" had become popular, along with songs like "Especially," "Blue Valley," and "When I'm in a Lovin' Mood." Davis joined the vibrant artistic community and composed, sang, and acted in France as well as Italy, the Netherlands, Spain, and Switzerland. In 1959, he released an album, *Jimmy "loverman" Davis par Jimmy "lover man" Davis.*

Though he found success, he struggled with financial security throughout his professional career. Hughes occasionally sent him money.

"Hope I can stick it out until I get some of these bills out of the way—and until one of my songs catches on," Davis wrote to Hughes shortly before the writer died in 1967. "But hell, that's life."

The cover of one of Davis's albums, *Jimmy "loverman" Davis par Jimmy "lover man" Davis.*

Davis died on October 21, 1997, in Paris. He was eighty-two.

During the years he spent in France, Davis returned to the United States only once. In 1981, he decided to seek royalties owed from "Lover Man" and met with ASCAP, the music licensing agency. Jacqueline Baraduc, his longtime friend, accompanied him to see that he carried through.

"The justice for himself is not enough," said Jay Gottlieb, an American pianist and friend of Davis's, in an interview.

"He's serving the all when he writes those beautiful protest letters," he added, referring to Davis's refusal to serve in a segregated army. "But it took his friend of fifty years to accompany him to the airport to make sure he got on the plane to defend his own rights."

---

**JONATHAN ABRAMS** is a reporter on the Sports desk at *The New York Times.* He once spent a long layover in Paris and can't wait to get back.
KITTY BENNETT contributed research.

# "So What's It Like to Write Obituaries?" and Other FAQs

You're at a dinner party, and the question inevitably comes up: "So, what do you do?" Usually, I just say I work at *The New York Times* and leave it at that, unless someone prods and asks which section. Then I tell them, "Obituaries." The reaction is something I relish—usually one of curiosity. A sequence of questions generally follows. Below is a sampling of them.

**Q: I hear that you prewrite obituaries for certain people. Is that true, and if so, how does a subject react when you call and say you are working on their obituary?**

A: It is true! We have nearly two thousand of what we call "advance" obituaries for people who are still alive. Long ago, these obits sat in a locked cabinet in the morgue. Today, they are floating around our system electronically. The breaking-news cycle is fast, and we have to be prepared to hit the publish button as soon as we can confirm a high-profile death. Some people merit a longer obit, which takes additional time to research and write. It would have been impossible to write a seven-thousand-word obituary for Queen Elizabeth in a few hours, for instance. (The *Times* wrote an early draft of her obit in 1940; needless to say, it needed a lot of updating over the years.)

We often reach out to subjects to interview them for their obit. Some find it uncomfortable and hang up the phone or slam the door. But most are honored. Some have even participated in our "Last Word" video series, in which we interview subjects with the understanding that the video won't be published until after they die.

One of my favorites is of Stan Lee, the creator of Marvel Comics. When asked, "What would you like people to be left with from your career?" he answered, "When I'm gone, I really don't care."

**Q: What is the difference between a death notice and a news obituary?**

A: A death notice is a paid advertisement in the classified section. Anyone can take out a death notice. A news obituary, however, is written by a reporter, often one with knowledge of the subject's area of expertise.

**Q: How do you decide who gets an obituary? Has your process changed with "Overlooked"?**

A: I won't lie; it isn't easy. Every morning, our team goes over a list of names and begins our research, asking, "Did this person make news in their lifetime?" If so, chances are their death is news as well. We look at other criteria, too. Did the person change a way of life for society or a large group of people? There is no hard and fast way to measure such impact, and so we rely on our news judgment. We have to be picky; we have only so much space in the newspaper.

As Bill McDonald, the head of the Obits desk, so eloquently said:

*Some might think our process presumptuous. Who, after all, anointed a handful of* Times *editors to stand by the roadside as a parade of humanity passes and single out this one, this one—but not that one—as worthy of being remembered?*

*The answer is that no one did, actually, because that is not precisely what we decide. We make no judgments, moral or otherwise, about human worth. What we do try to judge, however, is newsworthiness, and that's a whole other standard.*

It's a big responsibility. Since "Overlooked" began, we've given extra attention to researching people from marginalized communities who come across our desk. As "Overlooked" has proven, sometimes a person doesn't get the attention they deserve in their lifetime. So we lean on another criterion, determining whether the subject had an interesting life story that we think our readers would want to learn about.

Q: What makes a good obituary writer?

A: Another good question for Bill McDonald, who has answered this one probably more times than he can count:

*A good obit writer has to have the curiosity and doggedness of a sleuth. A big, and satisfying, part of the job is simply digging into lives, researching where people came from, how they lived, and what circumstances and influences made them into the people they became. Then the storyteller takes over, recognizing a narrative thread in all those facts and anecdotes and letting it unspool in a coherent and lively*

*way. In some ways, the best obits are ones that tell us about people we've never heard of and leave us sorry that we never got the chance to meet them.*

Q: How is writing an obituary for "Overlooked" different from writing an obit for someone who dies today?

A: It can be tricky. Often facts are lost to history, and we have to be resourceful to get to the truth. For instance, many Black lives were not recognized by mainstream newspapers, so we'll have to look in papers like the *Baltimore Afro-American* or visit the New York Public Library's Schomburg Center for Research in Black Culture.

At other times, we have to be creative in corroborating facts. When Nikita Stewart was researching her "Overlooked" obituary about Bessie Stringfield, known as the "motorcycle queen of Miami," she called me to say she had found some discrepancies between what Stringfield said of her life and what was listed in old government records. For example, rather than saying she was from a small town, Stringfield fabricated a story about having grown up in a big city in Jamaica. Nikita wondered if we should run an obituary at all. I asked, "Well, was she still the motorcycle queen of Miami?" "Without a doubt," Nikita replied. I found it interesting that Stringfield felt the need to adjust her story to be accepted by the society in which we live. I suggested we include that in the article, because it made her a more complex human being. All of us are nuanced in our own ways, and to me, that element made Bessie's situation even more relatable.

# ACKNOWLEDGMENTS

Special thanks to Bill McDonald and the Obituaries desk at *The New York Times*, as well as to the mentors, family members, and colleagues who helped conceptualize and offer support for this project, which would not have been possible without the many, many editors, writers, researchers, photo editors, and designers who brought these stories to life. Thank you, too, to *The New York Times*'s book development team, my agent, and the team at Ten Speed.

# IMAGE CREDITS

**FRONT COVER**
Clockwise, from top left: Carl Van Vechten and Van Vechten Trust; James Burke/The LIFE Picture Collection, via Shutterstock; Mark Twight; Dezo Hoffmann Collection/Shutterstock; Science History Images/Alamy; Randy Wicker & Marsha P. Johnson Papers at the NYC LGBT National History Archives.

**BACK COVER**
Clockwise, from top: Robert Walker/*The New York Times*; Courtesy of Joe Duran; Courtesy of the Ohio History Connection; Rider-Waite™ Tarot images used with permission of U.S. Games Systems, Inc., All rights reserved, Photo by Sonny Figueroa/ *The New York Times*; Schomburg Center for Research in Black Culture, Manuscripts, Archives and Rare Books Division, New York Public Library; Emre Grafson Müzik.

**PAGE 3**
Clockwise, from top left: Universal Images Group, via Getty Images; National Portrait Gallery, Smithsonian Institution; Photo by Robert Giard, © Estate of Robert Giard, Beinecke Rare Book and Manuscript Library; Lisa Ben Papers, ONE Archives at the University of Southern California Libraries; Dr. Ron Simmons; Library of Congress, via Getty Images; Steve Kagan; From "The Silent Enemy," 1930, via Everett Collection.

**CAPTURING OUR IMAGINATION**
Page 6 *Annie Edson Taylor*: Pictorial Press Ltd/Alamy
Page 8 Science History Images/Alamy; Newspaper clipping: *The New York Times*
Page 11 *Margaret Garner*: Library of Congress
Page 12 Courtesy of the Ohio History Connection
Page 15 *Rose Mackenberg*: Courtesy of the Special Collections Research Center, Temple University Libraries, Philadelphia, Pennsylvania
Page 16 Photographs by Acme, via Getty Images
Page 18 *Sanmao*: Huang Chen Tien Hsin, Chen Sheng and Chen Chieh, via Crown Publishing Company Ltd
Page 21 Huang Chen Tien Hsin, Chen Sheng and Chen Chieh, via Crown Publishing Company Ltd
Page 22 Huang Chen Tien Hsin, Chen Sheng and Chen Chieh, via Crown Publishing Company Ltd
Page 24 *Emma Gatewood*: Photo by Peter Brandt, Courtesy of Appalachian Mountain Club Library & Archives
Page 26 Appalachian Mountain Club Library & Archives
Page 29 *Bessie Stringfield*: Courtesy of Ann Ferrar, biographer of Bessie Stringfield
Page 30 Courtesy of Ann Ferrar, biographer of Bessie Stringfield
Page 33 *Raka Rasmi*: Carl Van Vechten and Van Vechten Trust
Page 35 Hulton Archive, via Getty Images
Page 36 *Rattlesnake Kate*: City of Greeley Museums, Hazel E. Johnson Collection
Page 38 City of Greeley Museums
Page 41 City of Greeley Museums, Hazel E. Johnson Collection
Page 42 *Omero Catan*: Courtesy of HistoryMiami Museum
Page 44 William C. Eckenberg/*The New York Times*
Page 47 *Alice Anderson*: University of Melbourne Archives
Page 48 Kew Historical Society, Estate of Kathleen Hall
Page 51 *Terri Rogers*: Dezo Hoffmann Collection/ Shutterstock
Page 52 ITV/Shutterstock
Page 54 *Margaret Gipsy Moth*: *Otago Daily Times*
Page 57 Lou Waters
Page 58: Courtesy of Joe Duran

**PADDLING THEIR OWN CANOES**
Page 62 *Major Taylor*: Science History Images/Alamy
Page 64 Bibliothèque Nationale de France
Page 67 *Bette Nesmith Graham*: Courtesy of University of North Texas, Special Collections

**CREATING ART THAT ENDURES**

# ABOUT THE AUTHOR

Photo credit: Eileen Costa

**AMISHA PADNANI** is an award-winning editor at *The New York Times* and a keynote speaker on topics such as diversity, where she often highlights people who are underrepresented in society. She has been interviewed on NPR, *Democracy Now!,* the CBC, CBS, and the BBC, among other organizations. In 2018, she was named Incredible Woman of the Year by *Porter* magazine.

Text copyright © 2023 by The New York Times Company
Photographs copyright © 2023 by The New York Times Company

Published in the United States by Ten Speed Press, an imprint of the Crown Publishing Group, a division of Penguin Random House LLC, New York.
TenSpeed.com

Many of the obituaries that appear in this volume were originally published in *The New York Times*. Inquiries concerning permission to reprint any obituary (or portion thereof) which originally appeared in *The New York Times* newspaper should be addressed to The New York Times Company c/o Pars International by phone at 212-221-9595 or by email at nytpermissions@parsintl.com or at NYTreprints.com.

Ten Speed Press and the Ten Speed Press colophon are registered trademarks of Penguin Random House LLC.

Library of Congress Cataloging-in-Publication Data
Names: Padnani, Amisha, 1984- author. | New York Times
    Company, author.
Title: Overlooked: a celebration of remarkable, underappreci-
    ated people who broke the rules and changed the world /
    Amisha Padnani and the Obituaries Desk at The New York
    Times.
Description: First edition. | Emeryville, California: Ten Speed
    Press, [2023]
Identifiers: LCCN 2022055162 (print) | LCCN 2022055163
    (ebook) | ISBN 9781984860422 (hardcover) | ISBN
    9781984860439 (ebook) Subjects: LCSH: Biogra-
    phy. | Obituaries—United States. | History, Modern—
    Miscellanea. | Civilization, Modern—Miscellanea. | Social
    change—History—Miscellanea. | Women—Biography.
    | African Americans—Biography. | People with disabilities—
    Biography. | Successful people—Biography. Classification:
    LCC CT105 .P236 2023 (print) | LCC CT105 (ebook) | DDC
    920.02—dc23/eng/20230110
LC record available at https://lccn.loc.gov/2022055162
LC ebook record available at https://lccn.loc.gov/2022055163

Hardcover ISBN: 978-1-9848-6042-2
eBook ISBN: 978-1-9848-6043-9

Printed in Malaysia

Acquiring editor: Matt Inman | Production editor: Bridget Sweet
    | Editorial assistant: Fariza Hawke
Designer: Isabelle Gioffredi | Co-designer: Simonetta Nieto,
    *The New York Times* | Art director: Kelly Booth
Production manager: Jane Chinn | Prepress color managers:
    Neil Spitkovsky and Nick Patton
Photo research and permissions: Amanda Boe, Cecilia Bohan,
    Anika Burgess, Karen Cetinkaya, Phyllis Collazo, and
    Sarah Eckinger, *The New York Times*
Copy editor: Aja Pollock | Proofreader: Sasha Tropp
Additional copy editing and proofreading: Sunhee Evans, Jaclyn
    Gallucci, Augusta Greenbaum, Alexis Loinaz, Lara McCoy,
    and Natasha Rodriguez of *The New York Times* Syndicate
Publicist: Felix Cruz | Marketer: Monica Stanton

10 9 8 7 6 5 4 3 2 1

First Edition

...ty's house to learn how to make this ??? site! / pics for the party afternoon at my house / Ewwyerweird at the Hole / Larry Man Show and other th...
...a TN / Greensboro NC demo folks / Bus Party! / Ewwyerweird Transylvania / Richmond VA / ... / ... Benny's Birthda...
...anhole! RB and Dave's Birthday! / The new Morrissey record at Sway / Miami Vacation / Beac...
...page... later'd / LA and then the Fish / fish fish fish... i have a problem / Ben's new situation and t...
...ight time to pull your bone out of it's socket / website suffers / Al Skazeera / The best night at ... / ...stat...
...10th / rain, movie, name drops / br'ohio / Back in NY / Leo's unhappy birthday / TF Report / ti... / ...rerc...
...vs / Half-Life Special! / 5boro to Enjoi / Epic demo in Madison / Action Now / Madison stuff / ... / ...rda...
...n Town / Ben Cho Pre Show / Benjamin's beautiful show! / Bro-curbs / Fan-outs left and right / Ewwyer Hole / ... Th...
...y / Hat Party! / Am I Still Ill? / Can you squeeze me into an empty page of your diary? / Worst Dude Ever, or Best / you're the bees knees... but so am...
...is only singing / wake up late, put on your clothes and take / your credit card to the camera store / Frank the Tank / I don't remember halloween / glue...
...sn't pay to try, all the smart boys know why / November Spawned A Monster / Dill's Midnight Birthday / as we go up, we go down / Who said I'd lie...
...n't I? / I'll be with you in the morning boys, 'cause you know that if we wait for our time we'll all be dead! / May this lovely letter reach its destination...
...sleep / it's christmastime in the mountains, everything is white tonight / yellow and green, a stumbling block / yet more air travel / back to the future...
...ir, the air in which I must live / one sweet day you will be good to yourself / an ending fitting for the start / all the looks of love were staged / but befor...
...e / son, observe the time and fly from evil / don't try to take my life away / you ain't a beauty but you're alright / this dawn raid soon put paid to all th...
...no love in them scan the world / I will see you in far-off places / and I cannot - or, I do not / they don't know you like you know who / It's not comfortin...
...athing / in the old town, when I last came around / the night is still and the frost it bites my face / I'll haunt you when you laugh / whoa, i just found...
...eet have got no rhythm / I saw a highway of diamonds with nobody on it / I'd make a deal with God and I'd get him to swap our places / if I had a ma...
...es / we can go for a walk where it's quiet and dry / if they dare touch a hair on your head / you look like someone who up and left me low / it registere...
...know my luck too well / when you know how I feel I feel better / you wrote a book about yourself / I thought I was someone else, someone good / thi...
...so square, baby I don't care / tell me where did you sleep last night / each household appliance is like a new science in my town / although she's dresse...
...hear our story or not? / I concede all the faith tests / cho long farewell / that's a pretty bro amount of water / a very old friend came by today / he's su...
...ven know I was using / two hundred troubled teenagers / is just silly slang between me and the boys in my gang / six months on, the winter's gone / I'...
...n / parallel lines on a slow decline / as obvious as snow (as if we didn't know) / it isn't an urge, it is more like a duty, to begin to explore again things...
...e ways / Well, guess what? Now this is happening / commitment trailblazer, your trail is quite a puzzle / me - with a preference for making things wors...
...erry sent me a note and pictures / I want to leave, you will not miss me / you'll never know the trap it's set / I've heard that you'll try anything twice /...
...face / she threw me outside, I stood in the dirt where everyone walked / P.S. bring me home and have me / I don't care what you think unless it is abo...
...nted sunset with the prettiest of skies / from a seat on a whirling waltzer / always has to be the queen bee / devious, truculent and unreliable / how t...
...all my dreams / the butcher, the baker, the candlestick maker / they cannot do what you want them to do / when you see me between Cole and Cahueng...
...it would not be new / the lies are so easy for you / would you, ouija board, would you help me? / you can tell by his shoes he was born to lose / drean...
...I know, but it goes on / Ninjas With Awesome / spirits say boo and the paper bursts into fire / from passenger view / looking out of the window, starin...
.../ all nonsense / Demassek with a K / all those people, all those lives, where are they now? / Tooting Bec Wreck / then you'll see the glass hidden in th...
...z heads our sleeping dreams were haunted / sentimental as a cat's grave / why do you come here? / I wish I could give a shit, just a little bit / honey-p...
...nd feeling is lying but it never succeeds / to prevent me from trying / Teachers are my lessons done? I cannot do another one. / I go out every night an...
...ve you, they will wake up, yawn and kill you / well this is true and yet, it's false / I got a catholic block / I will not change and I will not be nice / I li...
...something, touching nothing's all I ever do / say something warm, say something bright, I can't stand / to see you when you're cold / I want to lose, o...
...d / I left the North, I traveled South, I found a tiny house / and I can't help the way I feel / I wasn't born with enough middle fingers / we roll tonight,...
...jah days streak into blues and greys / throw your homework onto the fire / I've changed my plea to guilty / I don't need no bracelets clamped in front...
...loneliness / I could hang about and burn my fingers / hideous tricks on the brain / push your neck veins bulbous and make those wires ring / Just 'c...
...keleton's worth? / When my arms wrap you around / Cold loving prose.We stole each other's clothes. / these pants tickle / I will never say I told you /...
...ke a caravan / we passed upon the stair, we spoke of was and when / I don't owe you anything / that joke isn't funny anymore / Am I Evil / Witchfind...
...know / Be my bloody Valentine / I have a new pony, her name is Lucifer / while I marched balking at how I had been so rudely placed / Panic! / Ash...
...features / my mirrors are black / he invented later'd and introduced us to C.O.B. / Hater I have your diamonds / I've been there and back again / Stacke...
...all / like anyone could even know that / Driving your girlfriend home / Did that swift eclipse torture you? / Swerving situations / People say "bewar...
...omen all standing with shock on their faces. / I kept my promise, I kept my distance / Eww Years Eve / halfway to a threeway / sewn to the sky / a st...
...funny bear / please fulfill me otherwise, kill me / please take me (don't go) home / the crow made me suspicious of your witchness / sweetie-pie, I...
...y, on the other side from you / once I heard a serpent remark "if you try to evoke the spark you can fly through the dark" / tiny striped socks for the la...
...p lousy faggot / there'll be blood on the cleaver tonight / some of them fell into Heaven, some of them fell into Hell / last year I was 21, I didn't have...
...moved here, a long time ago / I'm standing on a ledge and your fine spider web is fastening my ankle to a stone / they don't vote and they don't smoke...
..., they want to kill you / the radio reminds me of my home far away / in the name of glory, filth and fame / the girls at school you didn't like much ha...
...aving learned my lesson, I never left an impression on anyone / people say believe half of what you see, son, and none of what you hear / I misses yo...
...cause truth has a way of beginning an end / lionised maverick design if you can, the way to just be a man / chapter one again, here I go again / hey kic...
...te in my mouth just like a burning tire / zoologies / Instead of seeing monkeys biting, I lay on the ground / when will you die? / you chose your journ...
...s your way / I asked a young policeman if he'd only lock me up for the night / hey little bird, thank you for not letting go of me when I let of go you...
...' back to nature boys - vasser girls too / when I die I want my ashes thrown in someone's face - magic and dreams, Satan records the first note / it's th...
...ions tolerable / exchanging lies and digs / must you be so loathsome / don't let our love grow dim in the blinding glare of the city's greedy sensualit...
...e, big deal I'm still alone / you know you should be home in bed / castles and cakes / momentary resorts / I was hoping you might change your min...
...a grin / looking at you aproching / there is something I wanted to tell you o / when they are they and only I am I / i'd trade all of my tomorrows for o...
...l collide / photo showcase / you make a happy man very old / i'm gonna take you 'round the world / moaned and groaned and rolled my bones / seas...
...ssed me / you think I never see you when you accidently fall / if you don't like me, don't look at me / anything crooked / breakfast with computer / she...
...o be mentioned / told my wife I was going out for a couple of beers, said I'll see you in a couple of years / we'll see the city's ripped backsides / I wan...
...ou / mourning in the aerodrome, the weather warmer, he is colder. / fings ain't what they used to be / bruise 'em, you'll never lose 'em / never turn yo...
...lay, we were walking / does it make you feel better?I hope it makes you feel better / everything you hated me for... honey there was so much more / a...
...ck fuck fuck all else to do / in the summer that you came there was something eating everyone / everything you touch becomes a crutch / my irritabil...
...or our time, we'll all be dead / paired-off, pawned till I can barely stand it / pirate love / kicking away from the mundane everyday / they slowdance...

...o, ... quiet ... pass, you can curl ... ... ... you have a knife , sh...ied his face from her chest with her hands and prayed on h...

itch desire / now I'm in a million pieces, picked up for deliberation by the people listening at home / all these vicious dogs / more pictures of Harol...

lthy children from six absent fathers / you can never quarantine the past / some days in the years that had gone by / always I do forgive you / Harold I...

put my guns in the ground / and drinking in this way / girl in the snow, where will you go / I was worse than a stranger / Magnani you'll never be / lo...

the camera, messing around and pulling faces / good looking man about town / all these streets can do is claim to know the real you / I haven't be...

w for so many years / how discouraging, thank you / here everybody's friendly, but nobody's friends / qualify me for a part in your dream / for the l...

e drugs my faith had been sleeping / I am a ghost and as far as I know I haven't even died / and I will give you my heart, that's if I had one / when wi...

here I should be? / there is no such thing in life as normal / why can't it just be cool and free us? / a world in white gets underway / forest time / your b...

raight, your hair is smooth / I'm not saying that I'll care if you love me / each song a bitter lesson / my gal just up and left last week, friday I got fired...

y backs against the ropes I can feel it / I came here to hear the music / well, love is forbidden outwardly but inside there is no denying / suffer little ch...

surely there is no substitute for company / Panda Bear- Comfy in Nautica / you must go back home and I can't come along / trip on this / a circum...

eyond our control, the phone, TV and the news of the world / bust a lock with a rock, don't need a key to have me / no fixed address / the tiny childre...

ll you that you smell / one day goodbye will be farewell / remember what I told you, if they hated me they will hate you / the dead baby / indiffere...

osom ally to despair / and when you try to they make you say 'please' / I got my teeth fixed / throwing my arms around Paris / now I'm calling it arr...

lling it cruel / world tour, media whore, please depressing Belgians / a hot day, the smell of hairspray / people like you find it easy / aloha from Haw...

atellite / on the off chance that you're listening / tryin to make a livin watchin everybody have fun / six mile and narwhale / and if you ever have to...

hool remember how they messed up this old fool / purple clover, Queen Anne lace, you could make me cry if you don't know / I've searched and fou...

ays you used to lure me in / Arabs on the beach, lovers on the floor / but you still hold the greedy grace as you tidy the place / it was noon before she...

to the yard and pressed her hair / the awful rowing toward god / kept his gun in quiet seclusion / but I laughed so hard I cried / I don't get alon...

yself and I'm not too keen on anyone else / buzzkill, chick salt, cop magnet / In the absence of your smiling face, I traveled all over the place / seven...

ys and a dozen towns ago / sycamore has to grown down to grow up / you're rather common and coarse anyway / and time will never wipe ou...

vimming in lakes / doe, a deer, a female deerv / that will bring us back to do / someone who does not exist / we was all endangered charms / oh John...

ever be a man / art suffer England hatred / abnormals anonymous / excavations of the heart / and behind you, I have warned you there are awful things...

he chance left in a nine live cat / at least you left your life in style / everyone she knew thought she was beautiful only slightly mental / lying in a bo...

rmaldehyde / but that's how people grow up / You hiss and groan and you constantly moan but you don't ever go away / Oh look at those clothes! Oh l...

at face, it's so old! / you don't like me but you love me, either way you're wrong / it's hot, let's go to bed, don't forget to turn on the light / It could be any...

ost likely could be any frontier, any hemisphere / sad eyes, crooked crosses / each morning I get up I die a little / tomb it may concern / Don't leav...

rch behind / the night of the vampire / I go out back to look up at her smiling unluckily / you're gonna miss me / my head spins and you knew it woul...

en away so long / from Swank Zine / I promise that I'll always remember your pretty eyes / with the grace of a corpse in a riptide I let go / now how...

and and laugh with the man who redefined your body / but now you only call me when you're feeling depressed / sick and thirty / Pogue Mahone / 5...

eens & Jean / Jury, you've heard every word, but before you decide, would you look into those mother-me eyes / you have asked me and I did not say an...

ne headline, why believe it? / while I'm out here in the cold cold cold with a coat that is so thin / Shane Cross + Ali Boulala / The whispering may hu...

t the printed word might kill you / I know, I know, youll probably scream and cry that your little world wont let you go / she was eating her fingers like t...

st another meal / walk me to the corner, our steps will always rhyme / goodbye dear old stepstone / It's just a spring clean for the May queen / benea...

orch light we've all been circling / I'd rather live in a trash can than see you happy with another man / there you go, standin with the look of avarice / it...

explain what I was doing or thinking before you / you can call it a spinoff, say it's a knockoff, title it 'part two' / there's an iron cross still hanging...

om around her neck / forgive me any pain I may have brung to you / you're tender, your name's a whisper / like the tide at its ebb, I'm at peace in the...

me things are for keeping, some things are too good and they go / and the year 2000 won't change anyone here / drawn to what scares me and scared o...

res me / there must be lights burning brighter somewhere / the streets turn for pillowcase / I just want four walls and adobe slabs for my girls / we a...

received / snowbird / you handsome bitch, you movie twitch / but obviously the past is what makes any person / the past is a strange place / there is n...

can do to make you mine / to the rescue nobody ever comes / notes for future lovers / in the book mobile / I'm no fool, I know you're cool / you sho...

en all the things my shadow did / The fields may be whitening, but I will be gone / you've not changed / I don't carry dead weight / the woods & the...

the word of farewell / torches burn into the sad eyes / shame is the name / born to quit / I like the places where the night does not mean an end / I know...

ack in these dirty sidewalks of Broadway / the rent became whiskey / beauty and the beast / drifting down into the abattoir, do you see what I see, /

mping last day / Just enough to make us know we don't miss you / Campeling / Mr. Max / he has no enemies; and none of his friends like him / Ging...

al home / we've got five years, my brain hurts a lot / placed in a place for the insensitive and the insane / meet Wolfie (adoptable dogs update) / Sunr...

nger at my house / you had to not be there / you'll get eaten too / blues run the game / life is nothing much to lose / you could have introduced me p...

awning emptiness demands ever more diminishing treats / do I write write about myself because I wont be this way very long / you can put it out, but...

t it out / I may go out tomorrow if I can borrow a coat to wear / a sonnet from a sociopath / hand in hand down a waterslide in Chattanooga / you jus...

say the word / who hears animals? / you say you don't love me / where we've come to call the new century in / brother warrior / the conductor he's...

's still stuck on the line / if I say I'm not loving you for what you are but for what you're not / pain works on a sliding scale, so does pleasure in a can...

o on back to see the gypsy / Apocalypse, No! / please, please, before you bend your ear / misty morning, clouds in the sky / oceans apart / I would ne...

u / strange victory, strange defeat / open field with the window / Jerry's chillaxing contribution / my sentimental heart hardens / kick the shit out o...

ghtened children - wake up without thinking you're the one that I desired / what was not but could have been was my obsession way back when / what...

t could be if / baby don't be looking in my mind / I could list the details of everything you ever wore or said, or how you stood / fate has just handed...

e / who've brain-washed the small shy boy inside? / I've got my mobile phone full of silicon chips / do you happen to know where I am from? / I do...

ich but I guess it will do / I'm sick to death of seeing things from tight-lipped, condescending, mama's little chauvinists / there's something i've got...

u / I never really realized death is what it meant to make it on my own / I can live fine without love / good friday, midnight birthday / still drinking...

rner, just don't say I didn't warn ya / under the bushes, under the stars / they laugh `cause they know they're untouchable, not because what I say is w...

u make me empty and lean for another page in a magazine / i've got absolutely no one, no one but myself to blame / because we must / I think of de...

ey never kill / everyone was dancing, I stood over in the corner, I was listening, they were saying this and saying that / I couldn't believe after all these...

u didn't know me better than that / the hearty spirit of America combined with the grit and grime of the city slime / why would you pay to see me in...

here is nothing I could tell you that will ever make a change about you - he is too good to be true, he is set to self-destruct / Ben's show, Growing...

eryl made the head / I'd rather play a different sort of game that the girls are just as good as boys at playing / will I snooze, snooze, snooze for eter...

od lets me, I will / there is no love in modern life / bailiffs with bad breath, I will slit their throats for you / she's a hypnotist collector, you are a v...

igue / when I am laid in earth, may my wrongs create no trouble in your breast / it's not your birthday anymore / you were in your time / the fleas...

Epicly Later'd

Epicly Later'd / Patrick O'Dell

Anthology Editions
New York

# When We Were Epic / Amy Kellner

Patrick asked me to write this intro because I'm the nerd who taught him how to make a photo blog in 2004, back when putting photos on the internet was new. It was new and it sucked. You'd smoke a whole pack of cigarettes in the time it took to get your comically low-res pictures off your clunky Canon PowerShot and onto the web. You'd forever be untangling wasp's nests of wires and putting tiny bits of plastic into slots and then taking those things out of slots and then putting them into other slots before you even got to see your photos. Then you had to upload all of it over a landline. A landline!

Patrick was already an accomplished photographer by 2004, published in *Vice*, *Thrasher*, and other publications now lost to time. But film was expensive, and suddenly there were these affordable digital point-and-shoots that fit in your pocket and made pictures for free. Yet there were drawbacks. The flash was situated right next to the lens, so there was no depth or shadow; everyone's forehead looked shiny; and everyone had redeye. Patrick still used film for professional jobs, but the blog wasn't about capital-P photography. It was the digital equivalent of a homemade cut-and-paste Xeroxed zine—but much, much faster.

I had been making a photo diary called teenageunicorn.com (scrubbed from the internet, don't bother looking) with a modest following, where I wrote little stories alongside pictures of my friends goofing around at home and at parties, just being grubby little downtown hipster kids, many of whom were creatively involved with *Vice* in one way or another. This was back when *Vice* was an obscene, little-known print magazine that had just moved to New York from Canada and was available for free at record stores and skate shops.

Now, I am not a photographer. But I had the adorable hubris of youth making me think that my friends were the coolest and that everyone needed to know that. You wouldn't believe how excited people were to see themselves on our blogs. They were stoked. It's so strange to think about, but this was the first time you could see your life documented with such immediacy. Seeing yourself on a screen—and knowing that other people could see you on a screen—almost made you feel famous. The iPhone didn't come out until 2007, and Instagram came out in 2010. So, I'm not saying we invented Instagram, but... didn't we? Kind of?

On the day that Patrick came over for his first lesson, I cranked up my Dell desktop computer that was the size and color of an air conditioner. I gently guided him through the primitive worlds of

antique apps like Netscape Composer (it had the sophistication of a blank Word doc) and Yahoo PageBuilder (they meant well). I showed him how to tediously place each photo one by one, to write silly captions under them, and then to wait for what seemed like an eternity for it all to magically appear online. And thus, *Epicly Later'd* was born.

At first, the majority of the fanbase was there for the skaters. This was an intimate look into skate culture that didn't exist before, with people like Jerry Hsu, Spanky, and Jason Dill just being dudes, hanging out at Max Fish, Lit, The Hole, or Sway, dancing mostly to the Smiths or to whatever records their friend was DJing that night. (We all DJed. Every night of the week, one of us was DJing somewhere. It's so easy.)

Patrick is an unpretentious, self-deprecating guy who describes himself as a "weird introvert," and he admits that he didn't realize how addictive documenting his life would become. These days, the kids might call it clout-chasing. But back then, he just wanted to show you what happened that night, because it was a fun night. These were his real friends, famous or not, and they weren't showing off or being assholes. They were just going about their business being cool kids partying in the city, and people loved that shit. They always have. It was thrilling to witness different social groups converging in downtown Manhattan in the aughts. Skaters, "it" girls, artists, musicians, writers, graffiti crews. Hot or weird looking, gay or straight, a little bit eccentric or full-on bananas. *Epicly Later'd* told the story of one moment in New York City's subculture. Our moment. Kids from all over the world were always telling Patrick how much it meant to them to see New York through his lens. It was fun, being young and crazy. We had our time, and now you can hold it in your hands.

YOUR ACCOUNT HAS

INSUFFICIENT
FUNDS

PLEASE CHECK WITH YOUR
FINANCIAL INSTITUTION

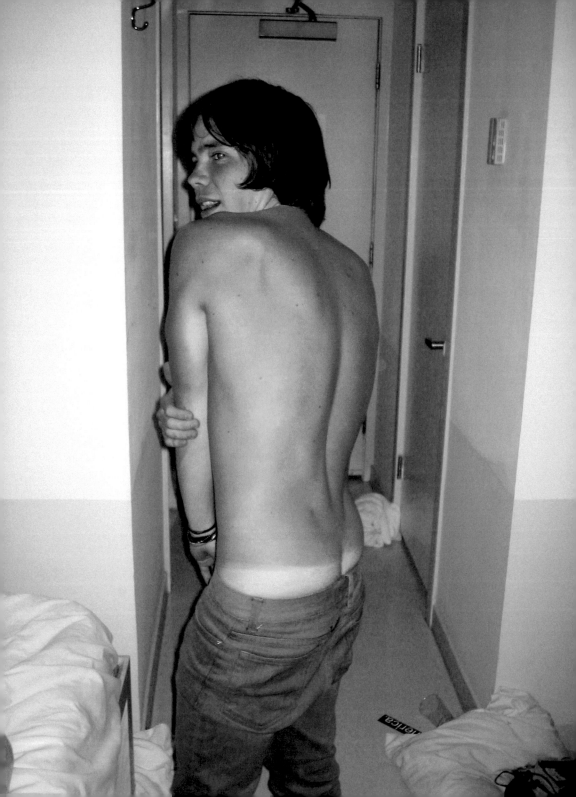

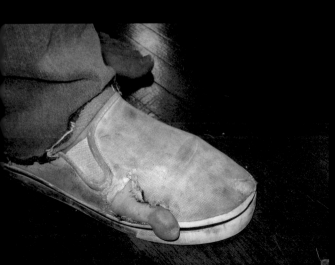

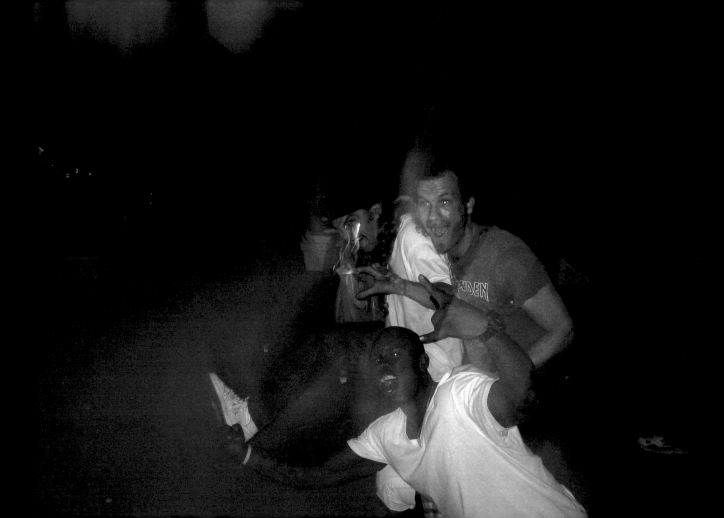

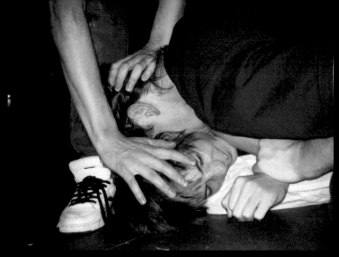

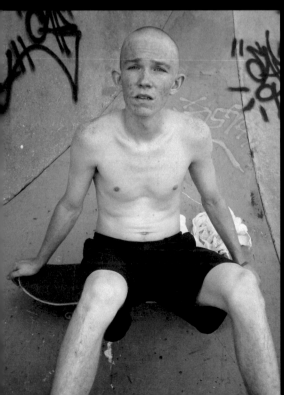

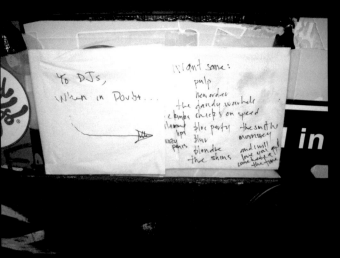

Meat is Murder
Remaining Time: 2:36

Search

| | Song Name | Time | Artist | Album | Genr |
|---|---|---|---|---|---|
| Library | | | | | |
| Party Shuffle | | | | | |
| Radio | | | | | |
| Music Store | | | | | |
| moz | | | | | |
| Acquisition | | | | | |
| beth | | | | | |
| smiths going | | | | | |
| smiths night | | | | | |

| # | Song Name | Time | Artist | Album | Genr |
|---|---|---|---|---|---|
| 42 | ☑ Sunlight Bathed The Golden Glow | 2:51 | Felt | | |
| 43 | ☑ The Boy With The Thorn In His Side | 3:16 | The Smiths | Best Of 2 | Rock |
| 44 | ☑ Head On | 4:11 | The Jesus & Mar... | Automatic | rock |
| 45 | ☑ Rusholme Ruffians | 4:20 | The Smiths | Meat is Murder | Alter |
| 46 | ☑ panic | 2:20 | The Smiths | | |
| 47 | ☑ Age Of Consent | 5:15 | New Order | Power, Corrupti... | Alter |
| 48 | ☑ you're the one for me fatty | 2:57 | Morrissey | your arsenal | Alter |
| 49 | ☑ some girls are bigger than others | 3:15 | The Smiths | best 1 | |
| 50 | ☑ Hang On To Yourself | 2:38 | David Bowie | The Rise And Fal... | Rock |
| 51 ◄)) | ☑ Barbarism Begins At Home | 6:57 | The Smiths | Meat is Murder | Alter |
| 52 | ☑ She's The One | 2:13 | Ramones | All The Stuff (An... | Alter |
| 53 | ☑ everyday is like sunday | 3:33 | morrissey | bona drag | |
| 54 | ☑ What Difference Does It Make? | 3:49 | The Smiths | The Smiths | Alter |
| 55 | ☑ Not Too Soon | 3:09 | Throwing Muses | The Real Ramona | Alter |
| 56 | ☑ Lipstick | 2:39 | The Buzzcocks | A Different Kind... | Alter |
| 57 | ☑ (Marie's The Name) His Latest | 2:08 | Elvis Presley | Elv1s 30 #1 Hits | Rock |
| 58 | ☑ Queen Bitch | 3:18 | David Bowie | Hunky Dory | Rock |
| 59 | ☑ Drive-In Saturday | 4:36 | David Bowie | Aladdin Sane | Rock |
| 60 | ☑ Fire In Cairo | 3:22 | The Cure | Boys Don't Cry | Rock |
| 61 | ☑ Break Up The Family | 3:55 | Morrissey | Viva Hate | Rock |
| 62 | ☑ That's Entertainment | 3:17 | The Jam | Compact Snap! | Rock |
| 63 | ☑ Wütendes Glas | 3:21 | Grauzone | Die Sunrise Tapes | Rock |
| 64 | ☑ Walking Down Madison | 6:37 | Kirsty MacColl | Electric Landlady | Pop |
| 65 | ☑ Haunted | 4:09 | Sinead O'Connor | | Ballad |
| 66 | ☑ Fire In Cairo | 3:22 | The Cure | Boys Don't Cry | Rock |
| 67 | ☑ Meinrad Jungblut / Sonnendeck | 3:06 | Meinrad Jungblut | Flieg Mit Ellen Al... | Electr |
| 68 | ☑ You Were On My Mind | 2:38 | Oldies | We Five | |
| 69 | ☑ Let Me Kiss You | 3:31 | Morrissey | You Are The Qu... | |
| 70 | ☑ our house | 3:15 | Madness | | |
| 71 | ☑ Hybrid Moments | 1:42 | Misfits | Static Age(Disc 4) | Alter |

Now Playing

71 songs, 4 hours, 283.3 MB

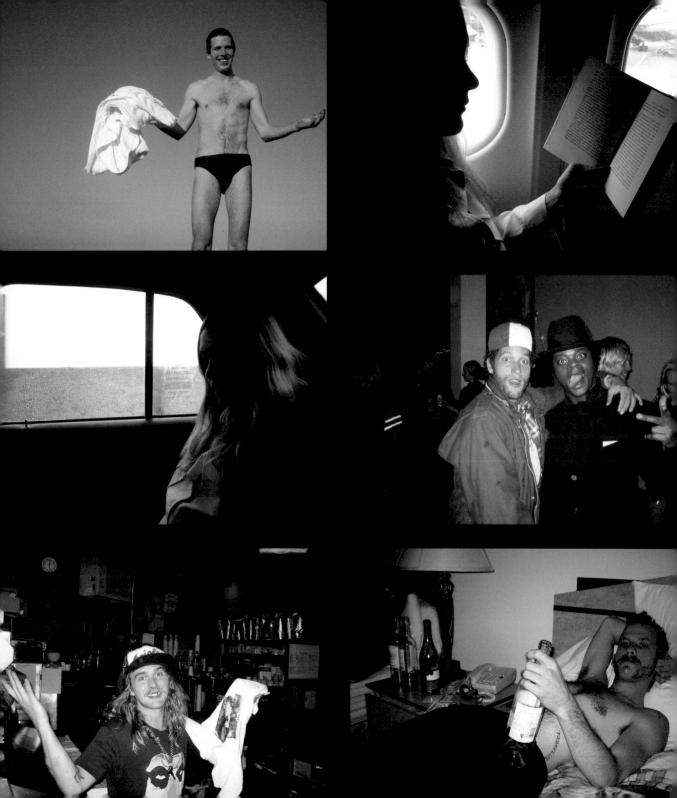

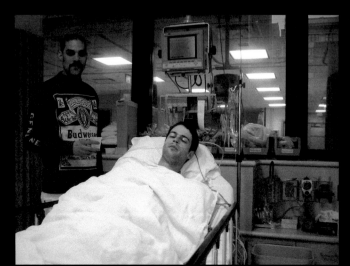

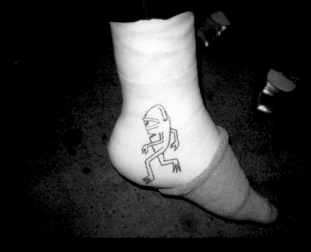

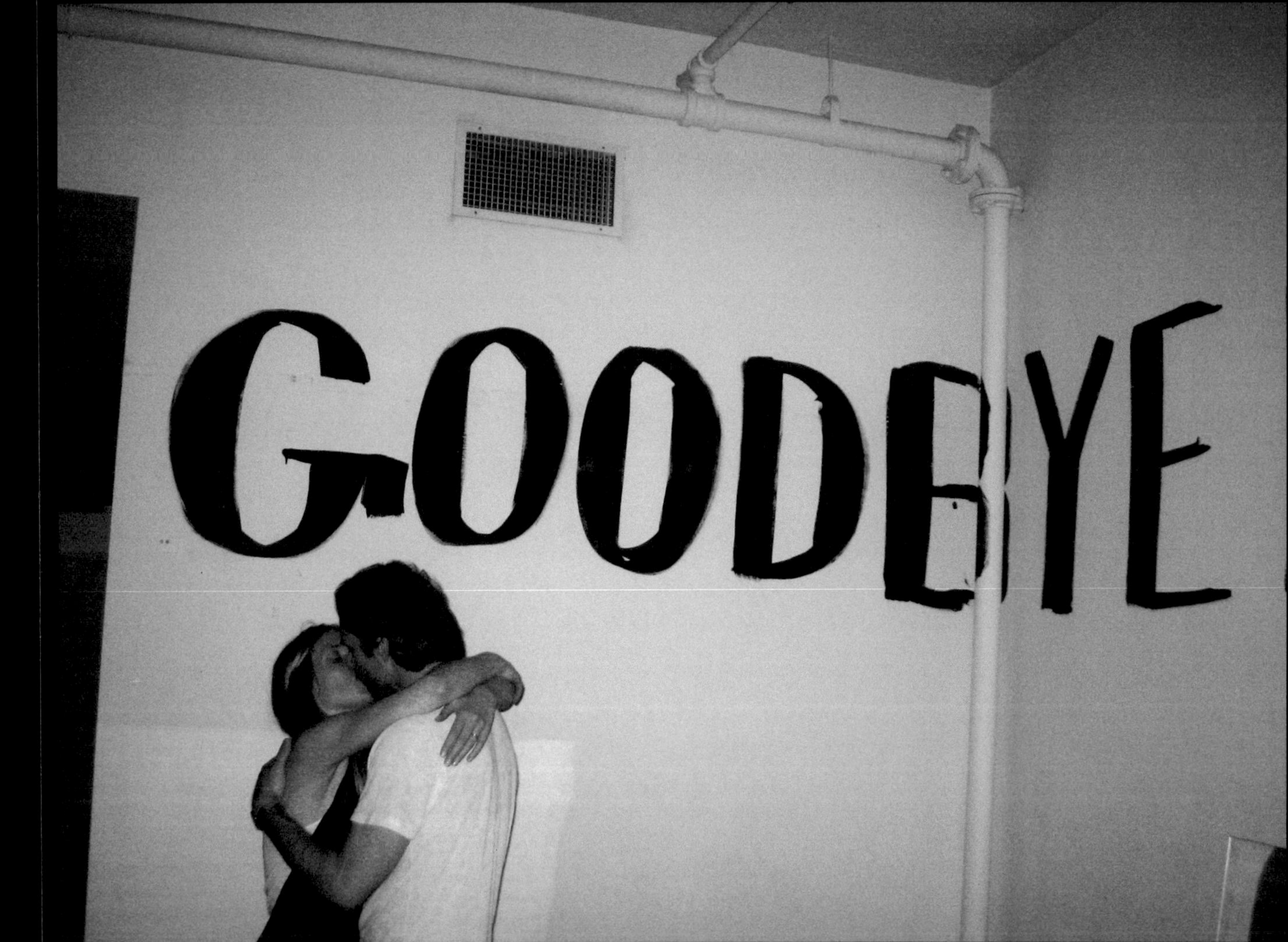
GOODBYE

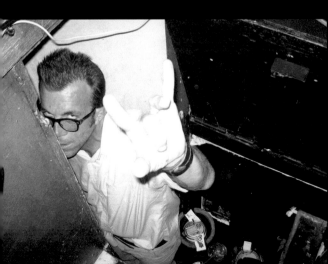

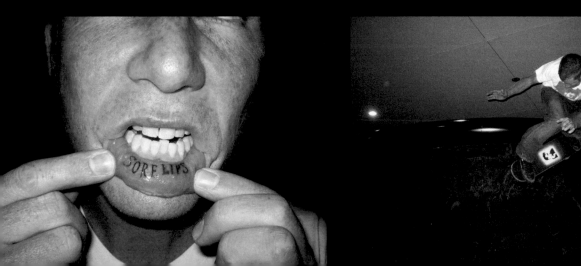

bag of suck

LIFE IS GOOD

Visitor

PATRICK
OOELI

Floor: 42
Date: 12/06/2006

V211265

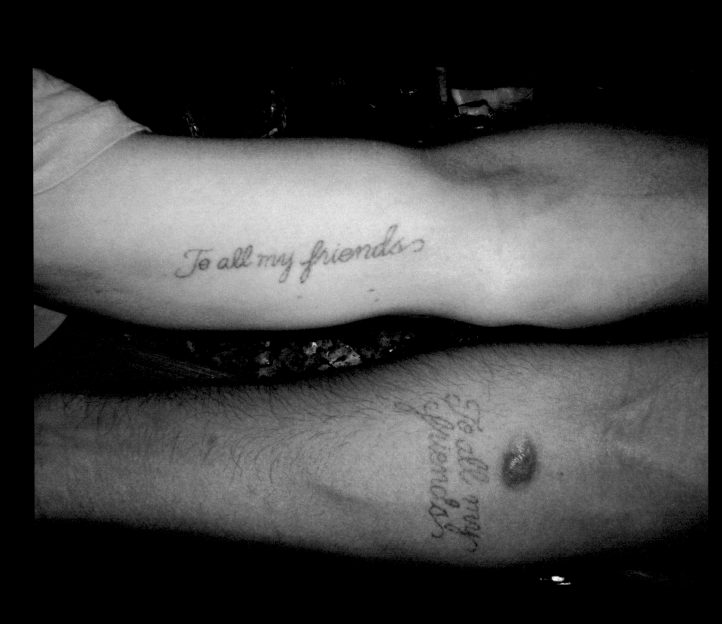

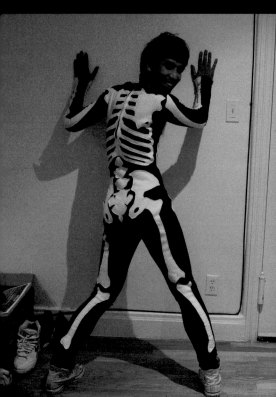

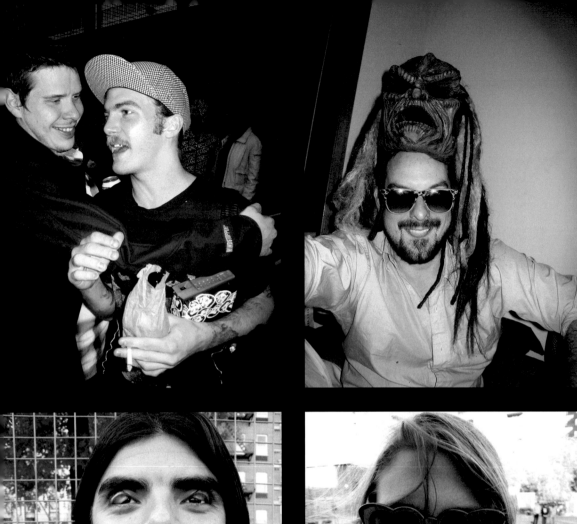

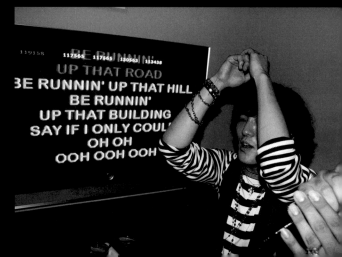

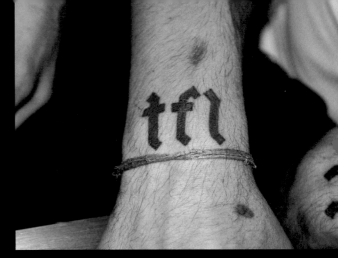

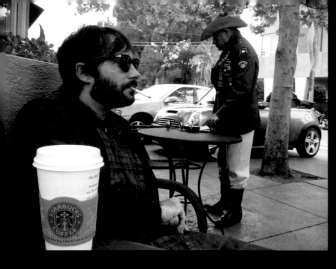

UP
4-ever

TINO
+
DESIREE
4EVS

PETIT
FROMAGE
♡

2006

AL IO

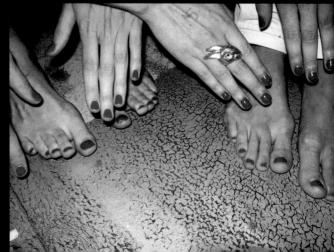

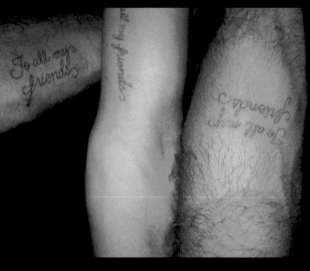

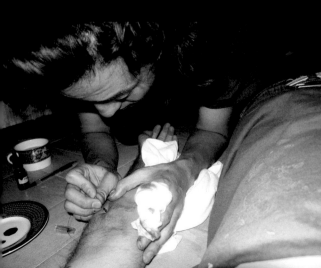
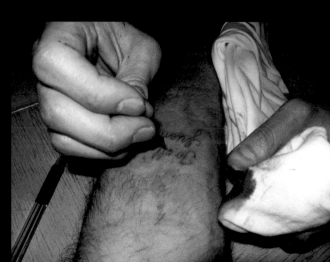

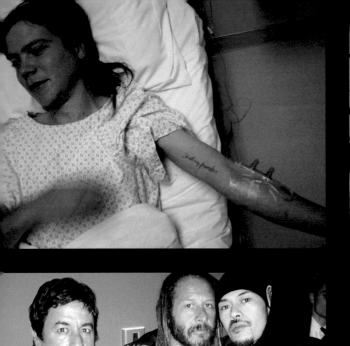

Neck

----Message----
The password is
dead baby tell the
guy at the door to

Reply        Options

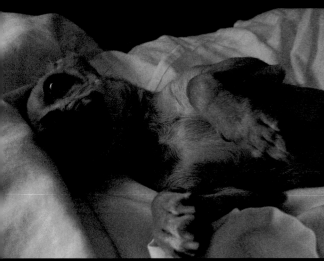

# Euphoric Recall / Patrick O'Dell in conversation with Jesse Pearson

As Patrick's frequent collaborator and longtime friend—not to mention a fan and occasional subject on his blog way back when—editing this book of photographs was a strange and wonderful task. Ruing times past, seeing friends who are long gone, reflecting on mistakes and triumphs alike; all this went down during the editing process. But it happened even more so, of course, for Patrick. Imagine digging through thousands of pictures you'd taken that tell the story, in minute detail, of a small patch of years during your youth. It's like Proust but with a Canon Elph. And while those of us who don't have such an archive possess the mixed blessing of being able to forget, Patrick can't help but remember.

"Epic," though it was just ironic slang back then, is also an apt word now for the accumulation of documentation that we see in this book. It is an epic being told here, of a very certain time in very certain places—mainly New York City and sometimes Los Angeles in the early-to-mid 2000s. It was a fraught and exciting time not just because we were living in the city in the post 9/11 haze of hedonism, but also because we were an extended family of artists, writers, photographers, actors, designers, and so on who were all informing and inspiring each other. If you missed a night out at Max Fish or The Hole back then, you risked missing events that could quite literally change the trajectory of your life and your creative work. It was heady, to say the least.

I'm grateful to Patrick for having had the drive to document all of it. While he, by his own admission, was thinking of EL as a journal back then—a very present-tense form—what he was also doing was carving into digital stone the story of our lives.

*Jesse: How did it feel, emotionally, to go through these old photos?*
Patrick: It was hard. I was going through thousands of photos, and it was all perfectly in order from every night. It was like entering some sort of virtual reality meditation chamber where I felt like I was going back in time, but also a movie where you and a guardian angel are watching your past.

*It's a Wonderful Life.*
Right, and it was like, here's where you fucked up, here's where you were doing alright.

*Did you find yourself having regrets?*
Not so much regrets. Well, maybe a little bit. I guess the biggest regrets were like, "Why was I acting like that?" Getting in beefs and stuff, seeing people I had problems with. Things where I was copping resentments, or taking things too seriously, or was just too caught up in a scene. But my biggest regret was if I'd had a little more money or a little more foresight, I would've shot film. If I'd had a film camera, I'd have been taking some legendary photos but, instead, some of these are a little bit shitty.

*Yeah, but that was just the nature of that moment. That's part of what makes this work special, that early digital quality. Photo blogs were getting huge, and these cameras were new and people embraced that aesthetic. It feels very nostalgic seeing a cheap digital camera photo now. But I'm curious to hear about what you felt you were doing with the blog. Did you feel like a documentarian? Did you feel like you were writing a diary?*
I think it was more of a diary, because I felt like there were a lot of my emotions in it.

*You put your personal life out there. You could always tell when you were dating somebody, for example.*
And back then I felt like I was going to keep doing it until I died and it was going to be a record of my life, like a journal. There was a little bit of documentation with skaters and stuff, but I wasn't so concerned with that.

*Something I noticed is that a lot of your regulars, like Meryl Smith, Tino Razo, or Ben Cho… they performed for you. They're posing and laying it on.*
Some of those people, they'd see me coming and they'd start doing something, like strike a funny pose or jump up in the air.

*When Epicly Later'd was at its peak, how did it feel to have so many strangers invested in and entertained by your personal life?*
I think I liked it. I don't know if I'm an actual narcissist, but at the time, I enjoyed sharing and knowing that people were looking at it and responding to it. When people came up to me and said they liked it, I enjoyed that. And I would check the views. It was funny. When I first started and I'd get 1,500 views, I would be like, "Wow, 1,500! Holy shit." Later it got into the millions. Like 20 million cumulative views, something like that.

*Jesus Christ. Really?*
Oh, for sure. I mean, that would be small potatoes compared to a major influencer now. But at the time, there wasn't even a word for that, and there wasn't the ecosystem for influencers that there is now. So I don't think I got to cash in on anything, but it had the feeling of a little bit of a dopamine hit, like, "Oh, shit, I'm famous." [laughs]

*I'll bet that feeling could become addictive.*
Yeah, it was an addiction, and I have addiction issues. I was going after that hit, or that flex, or that clout chase—which is weird, because I'm a recovered addict. All the negative things you could say about somebody that's on Instagram: they're the main character, they're there for attention, they're addicted to praise… that was me. I was chasing a high.

*Socializing a lot is also chasing a high.*
It was. I'd go out for, I don't know, romantic reasons, like to get a girlfriend or something, but it was also to get photos. It was like, "Oh, I'm hanging out with Ben Cho, the fashion designer. There's Dash Snow and there's Dan Colen. They're amazing artists." But I also had depression issues, so I was a little bit afraid of going home and listening to my inner voice talk. Instead, I went out and bullshitted and ate food and listened to music.

*What do you think about nostalgia for the mid-to-early 2000s? It's happening now.*
Well, it makes perfect sense. People always talk about this, but when I was in high school, we had '70s nostalgia. My friends and I would buy all these disco records. We would stay up and drink and listen to disco, and we were like, "This stuff is sick." And then, in college, we would go to '80s night in San Francisco. There was one that was called 1984. I fucking loved every '80s song and would get wasted and really celebrate the '80s.

*Nostalgia is a hell of a drug. There's not just a sense of nostalgia for the music of the 2000s now, but also for the art.*
There's the cult of Dash Snow or Ben Cho. But Ben was not big when he was alive.

*He was going to be. He was poised to be.*
We've kind of made him a folk hero. We do that to people who die young. Dash too.

*I think Dash is an even bigger star posthumously than Ben.*
Dash was like a light. You know what I mean? And now these people are like our ghosts. They were my friends, but also my muses. Ben was someone who changed my outlook on life by knowing him. He made my life better.

*You were pretty newly sober back then.*
I was, and I lived in a crappy apartment by Tompkins Square Park with a little bunk bed, and I would go up into my bed, and I was just afraid. I felt like I had demons talking to me. Now I'm not afraid to be by myself.

*So would you still want to go out now like you used to?*
If someone was like, "Come to The Hole," if The Hole still existed, maybe I would. If I was visiting New York and I was there for two weeks, I'd be like, "Fuck it. I'm going to all this shit." But now? Mostly it's a no.

*It must have been strange to see so much of not just your previous life but also your previous self while looking at all these photos.*
It was a mind-fuck. I would drop my son off at preschool, my wife would be upstairs doing stuff, and I would shut the office door and go into this mode where I was looking at ex-girlfriends, old friends, good times, and it was like euphoric recall. Seeing the photos and remembering: "We were going on a date. I remember that date. And then I remember her putting her hand on my leg." But then there were bad situations. I was remembering every little thing, and it was like doing 12-step work.

*What about good feelings when you were looking at the photos?*
There were a lot of good feelings, especially in seeing people that have passed. I like looking at pictures of Ben. That's a really good feeling, remembering the fun. It can be pure joy. But then sometimes I look at them and it's a

little hard. I'm like, "I'm old. I'm not cool anymore." So it's a mixed thing. Sometimes, when going through them, I would put the computer down and be like: "I want to go party," but, weirdly, in a reflective way. There's a Morrissey lyric, something about how at one time the future stretched out before me, but now it stretches behind. But that was more of a passing feeling, because now, having a kid, he's my priority. All the other stuff is just bullshit. Parenting is the thing I care about the most.

*And also, 20 years from now, you'll be able to look back at whatever you're making today. Keeping that in mind could cause you to approach what you're making now in a different way. How frequently do you take photographs these days?*
On my iPhone, I shoot probably every day, but it's mostly pictures of my son playing. But when I'm on a trip, I'll use a film camera to shoot portraits of people, or landscapes. I'm not going to do party photography probably ever again.

First published in the United States of America in 2024
by Anthology Editions
87 Guernsey Street, Brooklyn, NY 11222
anthologyeditions.com

Editors: Jesse Pearson and Su Barber
Editorial Assistant: Mark Iosifescu
Designer: Su Barber
Art Direction: Jesse Pollock
Retouching: Rachel Cabitt and Alex Tults
Sales and Marketing: Casey Whalen

First Edition
ARC 127

Printed in China
ISBN: 978-1-944860-61-5

...house to learn how to make this website! / piles for miles; early afternoon at my house / Ewwyerweird at the Hole / Early Man show and other hi-j...anes and airports (4/2/04) / I'm Bad I'm Nationwide / Demo Kids, Altlanta Georgia / If They Mated... / Atlanta Mob Action / Demo Kids Chattano...Greensboro NC demo folks / Bus Party! / Ewwyerweird Transylvania / Richmond VA / TF Report / Last Days of Tour! / Marc Razo's Birthday Par...port / KCDC skate demo / hotcrew shralp seshs in NYC / Lit / dinner, hole, barf / Gang Gang Dance / we are the roadcrew / broverload! / Early Manh...d Dave's Birthday! / The new Morrissey record at Sway / Miami Vacation / Beach / Gulf Shores / Vagabond / San Francisco / Spokane. Vegas. L...e on the scene! / Reno + Oregon / Luciana's Birthday Party / Los Angeles times and Beauty Bar / Vegas Again! / Lunch with Greco / boring text pag... / LA and then the Fish / fish fish fish... i have a problem / Ben's new situation and the Hole / everyday is like sundays / standing on corners / not to t...nventory... / Zered's video and early coolest man ever / Wild in the Streets! / Albany / Sway / Meryl's Birthday and stuff... / night time is the right t...your bone out of it's socket / website suffers / Al Skazeera / The best night at Hole ever / yall's mad at me / hicks and hickeys / Status Correction F...Man Down... Manute get well soon! / In search of Johnny Thunders girls / Club No Cards / ewwyork / the 4th of July day / post 4th / july 10th / ra...name drops / br'ohio / Back in NY / Leo's unhappy birthday / TF Report / tino's birthday; / Barcelona / "Donde estan los sombreros de los gangster...elona skate mob / mine mine mind / the last days of Barcelona / New York for a minute / 5boro Tour part one / 5boro Part Two / 365 days / Half-I...l! / 5boro to Enjoi / Epic demo in Madison / Action Now / Madison stuff / back in Burlington! / Up State / tour mutiny! / saturday night / do you li...ff? / The Cave! / New Jersey / Arival in Philly / 6:30AM wake up torture / BroBQ / that's what's up. enjoi demo in Bethlehem / Back in Town / Ben C...ow / Benjamin's beautiful show! / Bro-curbs / Fan-outs left and right / Ewwyer Hole / Fair Situations / The Last Night Of The Hole Ever / Hang ...arly / Isn't there more to life than being really really really ridiculously good looking? / Six Things / Lucy's Birthday / I'm not sorry / Hat Party! / ...Ill? / Can you squeeze me into an empty page of your diary? / Worst Dude Ever, or Best / you're the bees kness... but so am I / Children Of Bodom / ...part 1 / Pit Views part 2 / T.F.L. hats / Wipeout Cribs / the surf has swallowed him up he's a memory now / leave me alone I was only singing / w...e, put on your clothes and take / your credit card to the camera store / Frank the Tank / I don't remember halloween / glue-stick mousetrap and drink...eland. / If we can hurt them, well, we may as well... / Meeting with the tigas / Spawn / Los Angeles, you are too hot / It doesn't pay to try. all the sm...now why / November Spawned A Monster / Dill's Midnight Birthday / as we go up, we go down / Who said I'd lied because I never? I never! / ...aster ritual / love knife / Jamsday Lies / We are not so cold, are we? They are not so bold, are they? / and I am getting old, aren't I? / I'll be with y...rning boys, 'cause you know that if we wait for our time we'll all be dead! / May this lovely letter reach its destination... if only / Question one is w...pretend that you like me / who would you rather... what would you rather... / yesterday was tuesday, maybe thursday you can sleep / it's christmasti...mountains, everything is white tonight / yellow and green, a stumbling block / yet more air travel / back to the future / throw the switch, it's rock-n-r...while I'm blowing my change / Christmas at Bernie's / I don't want to fight tonight with you / you have vanished into the air, the air in which I must l...weet day you will be good to yourself / an ending fitting for the start / all the looks of love were staged / but before I go I gotta ask you dear about...e on your ring finger / I'm calling you from the foyer of this awful hotel / I try to catch my impressions before they fade / son, observe the time and...vil / don't try to take my life away / you ain't a beauty but you're alright / this dawn raid soon put paid to all the things I'd whispered to you / came h...erybody's staring at the strange clothes that you're wearing / dawn is mine, but I will share it / steely-blue eyes with no love in them scan the worl...e you in far-off places / and I cannot - or, I do not / they don't know you like you know who / It's not comforting, cheery or kind / still running 'rou...flesh rampage - At your age! / that november is a time which I must put out of my mind / everyone and I stopped breathing / in the old town, when I l...round / the night is still and the frost it bites my face / I'll haunt you when you laugh / whoa, i just found a website that saved an old version ofhere / ...uch more than you'll do / it was cold and it rained so I felt like an actor / if you have ghosts / because guilty feet have got no rhythm / I saw a highw...monds with nobody on it / I'd make a deal with God and I'd get him to swap our places / if I had a map, that is why I'm delaying / you slid right throu...gers, no not literally / its another year, will we meet? please say yes / our skin, and our blood and our bones / we can go for a walk where it's quiet a...they dare touch a hair on your head / you look like someone who up and left me low / it registered my name with the Catholic Hall of Fame / your ta..., my dear / could I write a requiem for you when you're dead? / up a discolored dark brown staircase / I know my luck too well / when you know ho...eel better / you wrote a book about yourself / I thought I was someone else, someone good / third finger, left hand / strange I know, but that's the wa...if he hadn't a saw'n it, i'd've had a lisp / their warm lips like a honeycomb dripped with honey / you're so square, baby I don't care / tell me where o...ep last night / each household appliance is like a new science in my town / although she's dressed up to the nines, that's sixes and sevens with you...k cat / glamorous glue / where I had revealed myself by crying and shouting / anyway do you want to hear our story or not? / I concede all the fa...cho long farewell / that's a pretty bro amount of water / a very old friend came by today / he's sure got a lotta gall to be so useless and all / in mexic...u please crawl out your window? / but nothin' seems to please me / I'm running out of things I didn't even know I was using / two hundred troubl...ers / is just silly slang between me and the boys in my gang / six months on, the winter's gone / I'm not like them but I can pretend / the year I was bo...ome rain-coated lovers' puny brothers / see the stars dropping out alright / an arrow through the bitch / parallel lines on a slow decline / as obvious...as if we didn't know) / it isn't an urge, it is more like a duty, to begin to explore again things of the world / anonymous call, a poison pen, a brick in t...of the back again / it says nothing to me about my life / I know you don't love me but let me count the ways / Well, guess what? Now this is happenin...tment trailblazer, your trail is quite a puzzle / me - with a preference for making things worse / roll your bones / I can't help quoting you, becau...hing that you said rings true / what do you see in her? / and I'm envying you never having to choose / Jerry sent me a note and pictures / I want to lea...ll not miss me / you'll never know the trap it's set / I've heard that you'll try anything twice / is it really so strange? / there will be no end soon, if I...ings right that have come / but just saying it could even make it happen / yes, the past is a strange place / she threw me outside, I stood in the dirt whe...ne walked / P.S. bring me home and have me / I don't care what you think unless it is about me / ease down the road / there's enough gloom in her wor...tain without my contribution / hovering silence from you is a giveaway / there's a black tinted sunset with the prettiest of skies / from a seat on a whirli...z / always has to be the queen bee / devious, truculent and unreliable / how the frustration renders me hateful / I know it's gonna happen someday to y...rtless hand on my shoulder, a push and it's over / when you cycled by, here began all my dreams / the butcher, the baker, the candlestick maker / th...do what you want them to do / when you see me between Cole and Cahuenga, I'm just plain desperate / your face is as mean as your life has bee...ing's got a hold on me and I don't know what / the day would surely have to break, but it would not be new / the lies are so easy for you / would yo...oard, would you help me? / you can tell by his shoes he was born to lose / dreams are aligning / I've entered the game of pricks with knives in the ba...you think you were my first love / my only mistake is I'm hoping / the story is old, I know, but it goes on / Ninjas With Awesome / spirits say boo a...er bursts into fire / from passenger view / looking out of the window, staring out at the sun / oh, I know you don't mean it / sullen kids / all roses / Jers...reissue, repackage, repackage / should I play ball with the dogs or walk away? / all nonsense / Demassek with a K / all those people, all those live...re they now? / Tooting Bec Wreck / then you'll see the glass hidden in the grass / They raised my stupid hand and said / "Ladies and Gentlemen, T...est Champion!" / they cannot taint you in my eyes / at night above our sleeping heads our sleeping dreams were haunted / sentimental as a cat's grav...you come here? / I wish I could give a shit, just a little bit / honey-pie you're not safe here / You lie to your friends and I'll lie to mine. L...

r other / let me tell you what I heard about a man to f... / ...hearing distorting and feeling... / ...lying but it never succeeds / to preter... / friend trying...

uzi suicide / the color of my dreams, if I had dreams / the teenagers who love you, they will wake up, yawn and kill you / well this is true and yet,
of what I say has been lifted off of men's room walls / I'm reaching out for something, touching nothing's all I ever do / say something warm, say s
attempt to seem dignified / the sound of strangers sending nothing to my mind / I left the North, I traveled South, I found a tiny house / and I can't he
...! / yes she's leading him on and she'll lay him right down / when my hallelujah days streak into blues and greys / throw your homework onto the fi
...ch sorrow dead as you did when you were alive / please help the cause against loneliness / I could hang about and burn my fingers / hideous tricks /
...ses and she hugs him are you the person i'm scheduled to meet to assess my skeleton's worth? / When my arms wrap you around / Cold loving prose
...nge for you who were such good friends / the girls have got a house that's like a caravan / we passed upon the stair, we spoke of was and when / I do
...stay / an illustrated book about birds / I take the cue from certain people I know / Be my bloody Valentine / I have a new pony, her name is Lucifer /
...nt on in the hall / older and wiser never applies to me / with jaded eyes and features / my mirrors are black / he invented later'd and introduced us to C
...rain, the basement of the Shelborne / the malady lingers on / hitting the wall / like anyone could even know that / Driving your girlfriend home / Di
...'e could see the sights in town / Down by the ocean it was so dismal, / women all standing with shock on their faces. / I kept my promise, I kept my
...uch me, squeeze me, hold me too tightly / yellow hair, you are such a funny bear / please fulfill me otherwise, kill me / please take me (don't go) hor
...once in my life let me have who I want / it gets dark, it gets lonely, on the other side from you / once I heard a serpent remark "if you try to evoke th
...i fell apart instead of them / you scumbag, you maggot, you cheap lousy faggot / there'll be blood on the cleaver tonight / some of them fell into Hea
...r was no match for the public image / I remember when I first moved here, a long time ago / I'm standing on a ledge and your fine spider web is fast
...m across the nation, you found yourself racing / good Christians, they want to kill you / the radio reminds me of my home far away / in the name of g
...nna do / so kiss me on the cheek and then go off to school / having learned my lesson, I never left an impression on anyone / people say believe half
...acquainted quite well / playboys short, right before court / because truth has a way of beginning an end / lionised maverick design if you can, the w
...babe, where'd you go, just left it sitting in the road / I got a taste in my mouth just like a burning tire / zoologies / Instead of seeing monkeys biting
...haunted? / that you would ruin me if I would not have you, this is your way / I asked a young policeman if he'd only lock me up for the night / hey
...nerican chemical waste / "do you want Zero to win?" / Orientation / back to nature boys - vasser girls too / when I die I want my ashes thrown in son
...talia / cursed love is never ending / reputations changeable, situations tolerable / exchanging lies and digs / must you be so loathsome / don't let our l
...o to Soho, go to waste in the wrong arms / and when I'm home, big deal I'm still alone / you know you should be home in bed / castles and cakes / m
...a drab day, you in a drab dress / taken in by a sun tan and a grin / looking at you aproching / there is something I wanted to tell you / when they are t
...co / and wait for the moment a million chances may all collide / photo showcase / you make a happy man very old / i'm gonna take you 'round the w
...y in 19 something and 5 / then the letting go / you discussed me / you think I never see you when you accidently fall / if you don't like me, don't look
...y in town / always looking for attention, always needs to be mentioned / told my wife I was going out for a couple of beers, said I'll see you in a
...friends you might not remember, fading away from you / mourning in the aerodrome, the weather warmer, he is colder. / fings ain't what they used
...nk you are the demon / on the streets I ran / Easter Sunday, we were walking / does it make you feel better?I hope it makes you feel better / everythir
...here were times, I'm sure you knew, when there was fuck fuck fuck all else to do / in the summer that you came there was something eating everyone
...it / I'd be safe and warm, if I was in L.A. / if we wait for our time, we'll all be dead / paired-off, pawned till I can barely stand it / pirate love / kicki
...' / football's still the roughest thing on campus / at the end of the storm is a golden sky / my life is an endless succession of people saying goodbye
...e from her chest with her hands and prayed on his last ditch desire / now I'm in a million pieces, picked up for deliberation by the people listening
...t had gone by / always I do forgive you / Harold Hunter / put my guns in the ground / and drinking in this way / girl in the snow, where will you go /
...n do is claim to know the real you / I haven't been sad now for so many years / how discouraging, thank you / here everybody's friendly, but nobody'
...ll give you my heart, that's ifI had one / when will I be where I should be? / there is no such thing in life as normal / why can't it just be cool and f
...son / my gal just up and left last week, friday I got fired / when my backs against the ropes I can feel it / I came here to hear the music / well, love is
...ck home and I can't come along / trip on this / a circumstance beyond our control, the phone, TV and the news of the world / bust a lock with a rock
...y hated me they will hate you / the dead baby / indifference, a bosom ally to despair / and when you try to they make you say 'please' / I got my teer
...hairspray / people like you find it easy / aloha from Hawaii via satellite / on the off chance that you're listening / tryin to make a livin watchin ever
...uld make me cry if you don't know / I've searched and found the ways you used to lure me in / Arabs on the beach, lovers on the floor / but you still
...elusion / but I laughed so hard I cried / I don't get along with myselfand I'm not too keen on anyone else / buzzkill, chick salt, cop magnet / In the abs
...d coarse anyway / and time will never wipe you out / swimming in lakes / doe, a deer, a female deery / that will bring us back to do / someone who
...hind you, I have warned you there are awful things / I got one chance left in a nine live cat / at least you left your life in style / everyone she knew th
...u don't ever go away / Oh look at those clothes! Oh look at that face, it's so old! / you don't like me but you love me, either way you're wrong / it's hot,
...et up I die a little / tomb it may concern / Don't leave your torch behind / the night of the vampire / I go out back to look up at her smiling unluckily
...ith the grace of a corpse in a riptide I let go / now how can I stand and laugh with the man who redefined your body / but now you only call me wh
...ose mother-me eyes / you have asked me and I did not say anything / one headline, why believe it? / while I'm out here in the cold cold cold with a co
...t your little world wont let you go / she was eating her fingers like they're just another meal / walk me to the corner, our steps will always rhyme /
...ppy with another man / there you go, standin with the look of avarice / it's hard to explain what I was doing or thinking before you / you can call it a
...der, your name's a whisper / like the tide at its ebb, I'm at peace in the web / some things are for keeping, some things are too good and they go / ar
...n for pillowcase / I just want four walls and adobe slabs for my girls / we all will be received / snowbird / you handsome bitch, you movie twitch / b
...r future lovers / in the book mobile / I'm no fool, I know you're cool / you should've seen all the things my shadow did / The fields may be whitening
...me / born to quit / I like the places where the night does not mean an end / I know every crack in these dirty sidewalks of Broadway / the rent beca
...u / Campeling / Mr. Max / he has no enemies; and none of his friends like him / Ginger in a real home / we've got five years, my brain hurts a lot / pl
...o / blues run the game / life is nothing much to lose / you could have introduced me proudly / yawning emptiness demands ever more diminishing tre
...ear / a sonnet from a sociopath / hand in hand down a waterslide in Chattanooga / you just have to say the word / who hears animals? / you say you d
...hat you are but for what you're not / pain works on a sliding scale, so does pleasure in a candy jail / go on back to see the gypsy / Apocalypse, No! /
...e window / Jerry's chillaxing contribution / my sentimental heart hardens / kick the shit out of very frightened children - wake up without thinking
...could list the details of everything you ever wore or said, or how you stood / fate has just handed you to me / who've brain-washed the small shy bo
...eing things from tight-lipped, condescending, mama's little chauvinists / there's something i've got to tell you / I never really realized death is what i
...shes, under the stars / they laugh `cause they know they're untouchable, not because what I say is wrong / you make me empty and lean for another
...er in the corner, I was listening, they were saying this and saying that / I couldn't believe after all these years, you didn't know me better than that /
...er make a change about you - he is too good to be true, he is set to self-destruct / Ben's show, Growing played, Meryl made the head / I'd rath